A Year in

Rock Creek Park

A Year in
Rock Creek Park

THE WILD, WOODED HEART OF WASHINGTON, DC

by Melanie Choukas-Bradley

with photographs by Susan Austin Roth

George F. Thompson Publishing

For the kingfishers and tulip trees
of Rock Creek Park

Contents

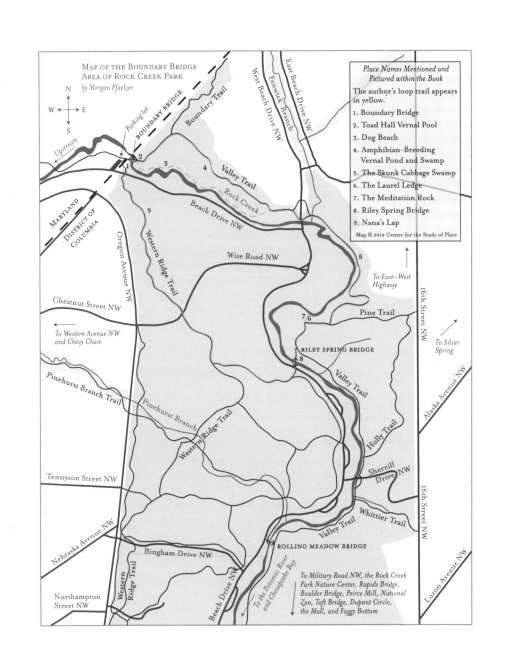

MAP OF THE BOUNDARY BRIDGE
AREA OF ROCK CREEK PARK
by Morgan Pfaelzer

N
W ✦ E
S

Parking lot
BOUNDARY BRIDGE
BOUNDARY BRIDGE
Boundary Trail
West Beach Drive NW
Fenwick Branch
East Beach Drive NW

Upstream

1
2
3
4
Valley Trail
Rock Creek

MARYLAND
DISTRICT OF COLUMBIA

Oregon Avenue NW

9
Western Ridge Trail
Beach Drive NW

Wise Road NW

5

Chestnut Street NW

← To Western Avenue NW
and Chevy Chase

Pinehurst Branch Trail

Pinehurst Branch

Western Ridge Trail

Tennyson Street NW

Nebraska Avenue NW

Western Ridge Trail

Northampton
Street NW

Bingham Drive NW

Beach Drive NW

ROLLING MEADOW BRIDGE

*To the Potomac River
and Chesapeake Bay*

To East—West
Highway

Pine Trail
7 6
RILEY SPRING BRIDGE
8
Valley Trail

Holly Trail

Sherrill
Drive NW

Valley Trail
Whittier Trail

16th Street NW

To Silver
Spring

Alaska Avenue NW

16th Street NW

Luzon Avenue NW

*To Military Road NW, the Rock Creek
Park Nature Center, Rapids Bridge,
Boulder Bridge, Peirce Mill, National
Zoo, Taft Bridge, Dupont Circle,
the Mall, and Foggy Bottom*

*Place Names Mentioned and
Pictured within the Book*

The author's loop trail appears
in yellow.

1. Boundary Bridge
2. Toad Hall Vernal Pool
3. Dog Beach
4. Amphibian-Breeding
   Vernal Pond and Swamp
5. The Skunk Cabbage Swamp
6. The Laurel Ledge
7. The Meditation Rock
8. Riley Spring Bridge
9. Nana's Lap

Map © 2014 Center for the Study of Place

MY FAVORITE PLACE

ROCK CREEK PARK—the wild, wooded heart of Washington, DC—has long been my refuge from a frantically paced, urbanized world. The park is my church, my school, my gym, and my therapist, the primary place where I seek to celebrate the restorative powers of Nature. When I walk through the bottomland forest and into the upland woods, I may be deep in solitary reverie, but I am never alone. In addition to familiar birds, trees, shrubs, and wildflowers, I encounter the park's visitors along the trails, and they are almost always smiling and happy to say "hello!" And it is easy to imagine that their dogs are smiling, too.

Rock Creek Park provides a welcoming sanctuary for millions of city-dwellers like me who feel a vital need to commune with Nature. Even more importantly, the park protects a vulnerable, wooded stream valley that is a major tributary of the Potomac River and a part of the Chesapeake Bay watershed. The park's legendary "wildness" has inspired not only American Presidents such as John Quincy Adams, who heralded Rock Creek as "this romantic glen," and Teddy Roosevelt, who led hikes and rock-scrambles there, but also other devotees such as Edward O. Wilson, the world-renowned scientist who, as a boy, fondly studied nature in the park's environs.

Within the pages of this book, I chronicle the natural events of a year in Rock Creek Park, concentrating upon the popular area near Boundary Bridge, a rustic footbridge that spans the creek at the District of Columbia/Maryland border. Like other nature writers, I describe a favorite wild place in reverential detail, yet, unlike naturalists' accounts of the past, my story contains a fearful new undercurrent—the looming threat of catastrophic climate change.

The book had its genesis on New Year's Day in 2007, the year of record, when I observed spring wildflowers beginning to blossom, alarmingly, many weeks ahead of their normal blooming time. And, as the year continued, I noticed other anomalies in the natural cycle at Rock Creek Park that gave me pause and stirred up concern. It was time for me to put down both my joys and fears onto paper.

As a long-time teacher, naturalist, and field trip leader for the Audubon Naturalist Society in Chevy Chase, MD, Casey Trees in DC, and other conservation organizations in the Washington area, I conduct and lead "nature forays" into the park and along its trails throughout the year, and I make frequent visits to the park either alone or with family and friends. I have grown to know this remarkable place and its trees, flowers, birds, animals, and flowing waters in intimate detail. Woven into my observations of Nature, which contain intertwining threads of pure delight and real worry, are glimpses of my life as a wife and mother, writer and friend. The defining message of the book is simple: Our relationship with Nature, especially as it evolves and thrives in our own backyards and nearby parks or "wild homes," can be every bit as compelling and essential as our relationships with family and friends.

The Rock Creek stream valley is rich not only in its natural attributes, but also its cultural history, reflecting more than 100 generations of human exploration and settlement. Native Indian people from various tribes, for thousands of years prior to the arrival of Europeans, traversed Rock Creek, gleaning blackberries, huckleberries, persimmons, acorns, and chestnuts from its wooded hillsides and harvesting the creek's plentiful fish and woodland game. They also quarried the rock outcrops straddling Rock Creek, crafting spear points and other tools.

Then everything changed when Europeans arrived in the area in successive waves of exploration and development. Captain John Smith, one of the leaders of the Jamestown settlement of 1607 in nearby Virginia, first sailed up the Potomac River in 1608, and soon the area and its waterways became known in Europe as one of America's first areas for settlement and economic investment. Following this initial European contact and despite ensuing decades of trade, the Indian tribes who lived in the region and who traveled through the Rock Creek Valley were tragically, and often violently, displaced. Many died from diseases for which they had no immunity.

Before long, new Euro-American settlers, many dependent on enslaved African-American laborers, arrived and quickly turned to growing tobacco as the primary cash crop in the greater Washington region, a practice which depleted the soil. As the area's farming switched from tobacco to wheat as a cash crop, water-powered grist mills for wheat and corn sprang up everywhere, including along Rock Creek. Peirce Mill in the park is a prime example. Built by Isaac Peirce during the 1820s at a key crossroads along the creek and operated commercially until 1897, in recent years Peirce Mill became operational again as an educational demonstration mill administered by the National Park Service.

Rock Creek's environmental history took a turn during the Civil War, when many acres of nearby trees were felled to construct Military Road and Fort DeRussy as part of the circle of forts created to defend the capital city against Confederate attack. Today, hikers in Rock Creek Park can still explore the ruins of Fort DeRussy, just north of Military Road not far from the Rock Creek Park Nature Center.

After numerous preservation attempts following the Civil War and spanning the latter part of the nineteenth century, Rock Creek Park became a federal park when Congress passed the Rock Creek Park legislation on September 27, 1890, the same year that Yosemite in California became a national park. In a symbolic act foreshadowing Supreme Court Justice William O. Douglass's famous C&O Canal trek of the 1950s, which resulted in the preservation of the Chesapeake and Ohio Canal National Historical Park, Charles Carroll Glover, who served as the president of both Riggs Bank and the Corcoran Gallery of Art and for whom Glover Park is named, led civic leaders on a scenic horseback ride through the Rock Creek stream valley on Thanksgiving Day in 1888. Inspired by the ride, the participants vowed to commit themselves to an ultimately successful attempt to pass legislation that established Rock Creek Park, making it among the oldest of America's national parks.

The main body of the park today, at 1,754 acres, is more than twice the size of New York City's famed Central Park and its 843 acres; and when you add in the other parkland administered under the jurisdiction of Rock Creek Park, the current acreage comes to 2,820.34 acres. Rock Creek Park has been administered by the National Park Service since 1933. During the

1930s, Montgomery County, Maryland, gave additional protection to the thirty-three-mile-long Rock Creek by creating a stream-valley park to shelter much of the creek's journey from its origins near Laytonsville, Maryland, to the DC border more than twenty miles downstream. The contiguous parkland in Maryland and DC serves as an oasis and natural retreat for more than 2,000,000 annual visitors who hike, jog, cycle, and walk, often with their dogs, along the scenic woodland roads and trails.

Even as the twentieth and twenty-first centuries have brought many environmental hazards and challenges to the health and stewardship of Rock Creek Park, challenges I explore in the book, the incomparable beauty of the stream valley in the heart of the nation's capital continues to inspire visitors today, much as it did the participants in Charles Glover's Thanksgiving Day ride more than 125 years ago. I think of Rock Creek as a mirror of who we are as a nation, as a people, for it reflects all aspects of our role as stewards of the place—and of our wisdom and foresight and too frequent lack of both.

Susan Austin Roth, my photographer-friend and fellow Nature enthusiast, contributed greatly to this project by walking the trails of Rock Creek Park with me and by herself, creating unforgettable photographs that convey a true sense of the place. Please join us for a year-long exploration of the wild beauty and often heart-breaking fragility of Rock Creek Park. As you walk with us, we invite you to look into the creek and reflect upon all that you see.

Part I

WINTER

January 1: UNTIMELY WILDFLOWERS

AS JIM, MY HUSBAND, and I drive along Beach Drive and into Rock Creek Park this morning, the sight of the winter trees stretching their limbs to the clouds works its familiar magic, replacing our worldly cares with hope and wonder. The ghostly pale sycamores lining the creek stand out against neighboring trees, whose darker trunks, branches, and twigs hold every shade of the infrequently celebrated palette of grays and browns. Wrapped in a light morning mist, the clustered, winged seeds of the tulip trees create graceful chalice-shaped silhouettes against the gray sky. For me, the papery fruit of the tulip tree high above in the canopy, whether softened to a warm tan by cloud-cover or awash in brilliant sunlit gold, is a signature aspect of Rock Creek Park in winter.

I begin the year with Jim in a place that both of us have come to love. Three years ago, at my family's insistence, we moved from our rural home near Sugarloaf Mountain in Comus, Maryland, to be nearer to work and schools in the city. How I hated leaving the farm country of Maryland's historic piedmont, where we had lived for many years. After the move, I felt exiled from Nature. Then I discovered the Boundary Bridge trail network in Washington's famed urban national park, one of the nation's oldest and twice the size of New York City's Central Park, only a few miles from our new home. It would soon become my refuge.

On this unseasonably mild New Year morning, Jim and I set out on the two-and-a-half-mile loop trail walking hand-in-hand along the wooded floodplain. After passing a small swamp filled with skunk cabbage and round-ing a bend in the creek, we switchback under low-hanging witch-hazel boughs and climb the trail into the upland forest. As we walk, we inspect every texture and color of the natural world around us. Each day of each season at the creek offers something new to quicken the heart, but an untimely sight soon interrupts our woodland reverie. "If it's this warm for a few more hours, these spring beauties will actually bloom," I say to Jim, as we gaze at a patch of narrow, green leaves that are springing up on the brown forest-floor next to an upland section of the trail. As I speak I realize with a sickening feeling that this is about to come true. There below us, rising an inch or two above the winter leaf-litter of Rock Creek Park, are several pale-pink flower buds, already beginning to open on New Year's Day.

Only yesterday did I see a clump of daffodils blooming in our neighborhood. As disturbed as I felt then, I am far more troubled today by the sight of a native wildflower, a "spring ephemeral" that usually blooms in March and April, displaying flower buds so early in winter. We and everyone else up and down the east coast of North America are having an eerily mild winter or, more like it, no winter at all. News of rapidly melting glaciers and polar ice caps, unusually destructive storms, and intransigent droughts is beginning to penetrate the collective consciousness. Suddenly, environmentalists aren't the only ones spooked by the specter of dramatic climate change.

As Jim and I thread our way back through the tall tulip trees and down the hill toward Boundary Bridge to complete our walk, I wonder, with an unsettled heart: What other untimely surprises might the unusually warm weather bring to the park?

January 20: A WALK IN THE WINTER WOODS

LAST WEEK I LED an Audubon Naturalist Society hike in Rock Creek Park, the first in a series of four seasonal forays into Nature. We met at Boundary Bridge, a legendary landmark. I felt a bit tongue-tied as I tried to communicate my love for this wild urban park to the expectant faces gamely gathered around me on a morning threatening a chilly rain. Unfolding a map of Rock Creek Park, I explained my plan to walk the Boundary Bridge loop trail, beginning on the flat floodplain of the richly wooded bottomlands, followed by a steep climb into the upland forest of beech, oak, and hickory. Our loop would traverse stretches of the Valley Trail along the eastern side of Rock Creek; a linking trail over the Riley Spring footbridge and across Beach Drive; and a still-higher section of Rock Creek Park's Western Ridge Trail, bringing us back to our starting point. The crowns of the tall tulip trees with their candelabras of winged seeds would accompany us overhead for much of the way, wherever the terrain allowed their sun-loving branches to reach high into the canopy.

On the map I pointed out the rocky ledge that I have dubbed "Laurel Ledge," both for the mountain laurel that grows there and for the geological Laurel Formation the ledge is a part of. The moss-covered Laurel Ledge rises from Rock Creek mid-way into our route and marks a natural spot for a picnic. The thought of picnicking on such a day, however, didn't spark much enthusiasm among my field-trip participants, even with the promise that we might spot the bobbing blue crest of a belted kingfisher cruising for fish from the ledge or hear its unmistakable scolding call.

Standing on the stone-and-concrete footbridge that straddles Rock Creek at the Maryland-Washington, DC line—the origin of the name Boundary Bridge—and leaning on its brown wooden railing, we looked up at the trees before beginning our walk. I tried to bring the bare limbs reaching over the water to life for the group, using imagery that would help them focus on identifying botanical characteristics.

"See how the American elm's twigs and buds form a tracery that looks like the rickrack on a girl's old-fashioned dress?" I asked. This seemed to resonate with the older women in the group, who remembered rickrack from their childhoods. I continued: "Notice the round, brown fruit balls hanging from the sycamores? The small, dry-clustered and feathered fruits (called achenes) will break up in the early spring winds, land in the creek, and float downstream to colonize the shoreline." I urged members of the group to scratch and sniff a spicebush twig to release its spicy-sharp fragrance.

Through their insightful questions, some difficult to answer, I learned that several of my field-trip participants had knowledge of the arcane subject of winter botany equaling or surpassing my own. In addition, a crackerjack geologist named Tony Fleming had come along for the walk (the very geologist largely responsible for the USGS map for the Boundary Bridge area), and his knowledge of the Kensington Tonalite and metamorphic Laurel Formation quickly threatened to overshadow my own familiarity with the hieroglyphics of winter bark and twig. What new could I offer this group?

We were moving downstream, and the birders were birding, and Tony was explaining the physics of the flowing creek. Then a streamside colony of pawpaw trees caught my eye, and they helped me reestablish my connection with the group. I pointed out their fuzzy, reddish-brown leaf buds—which, I noted, look like small, watercolor brushes and have been called "Audubon's paintbrushes." For a few moments everyone stood still next to Rock Creek. In the silent spaces between botanizing we listened to the water flow. We looked up at bare tree limbs against the sky. And we all quietly witnessed the wonder of the moment—the large trees of the sheltering forest, the chickadees flitting above us in the branches, the flowing creek. There we were, inside the diamond-shaped borders of the nation's capital, sharing a wilderness moment. How many cities can offer such an experience?

Later, during the field-trip, we would admire many more trees, learn more geology, find the first skunk cabbage flowers, and collectively wring our hands over the untimely spring beauty flowers, now fully open. But the reason I led the group through the woods was not to dazzle them with my botanical knowledge but rather to share something deeper, something I couldn't go a day without, something that has carried me through childhood, through young love, decades of marriage and motherhood, and now into middle age—a love of place, *wild* place, an intimacy as profound as any I've known.

February 13: A NOR'EASTER ARRIVES

TODAY I CAN'T GO to Boundary Bridge. Snow is falling, and a layer of ice is forming on the neighborhood's roads and walkways as a nor'easter cranks up over the Atlantic. But I can imagine Rock Creek as if I were standing on the bridge and looking into its tea-colored water. Large flakes are falling, too light to imprint the creek's surface. Sycamores lining the shore are gathering a layer of white on their cream-colored limbs, and wine- and gold-streaked skunk cabbage flowers in the nearby swamp are frosting up. The winter bird flock is restless, and a belted kingfisher is scolding its way down the creek. I know all of this with near certainty, because I walk across Boundary Bridge every chance I get, across the rustic footbridge and into the wild wooded heart of Washington, DC, Rock Creek Park.

Henry David Thoreau's words from *Walden* (1854) about living deliberately often haunt and challenge me: "I went to the woods because I wished to live deliberately, to front only the essential facts of life, and see if I could not learn what it had to teach, and not, when I came to die, discover that I had not lived." I, too, wish to go to the woods and live deliberately, but family and work keep me in the city. Yet I am able to live my life in communion with Nature, here in Rock Creek Park, where, on some level, I feel I have lived in the woods all along.

February 14: VALENTINE'S DAY

IT'S VALENTINE'S DAY, and the world is white. After the initial, freaky winter warmth it finally got cold in DC. The nor'easter—our first big storm of the season—passed through at dawn, leaving us not with a felicitous snowfall, as I'd hoped, or the layer of freezing rain that had been forecast but with something in-between: Sleet. Millions of tiny ice-balls pinged through the night and now comprise a layer of something that resembles snow. The evergreen magnolia leaves outside my home-office window are laden with white, and a red-bellied woodpecker is pecking at the suet cake hanging from the feeder pole in the backyard. His scarlet head and the cardinals gathered in the Leyland cypresses are true Valentine's gifts, since my family is away. I hope the roads will be passable later so I can get to Boundary Bridge—to see the white woods and maybe find some wild animal tracks before the many dogs, who happily ply Rock Creek Park's trails with their families, obliterate them with their own prints.

With Jim in Nebraska on a business trip, our daughter, Sophie, enjoying a college semester abroad in Spain, our son, Jesse, in San Francisco performing with his high-school choral group, the woods currently beyond reach, and it being Valentine's Day, I can't help but wonder about longing and how much it permeates our lives. As children we long to celebrate the next birthday and as teenagers to grow up as fast as possible; as adults we long for love and success. We all long for things big and small, self-centered and altruistic: Peace and social justice, health and happiness, wealth and well-being, bigger homes and better jobs, vacations and chocolate mousse. We long, long, long our lives away.

It's no accident that many of our favorite popular songs are about longing and that so much music—whether bluegrass or blues, jazz or classical—stirs it up in us. We live, we long. Non-human animals do it, too, at least the domestic ones I've known. Is this a failure to live fully in the moment? A failure to be grateful for what we have? Or is longing the ancient fuel that gets the job of living and eating and procreating done?

As one who has passed an unconscionable number of hours simply roaming the woods in search of nothing in particular, I have discovered layers of longing inside me. Some longings are clear and sharp, some are vague and shape-shifting. It is hard to define them—I only know that my intimacy with Nature inspires longings as I wander through forest and field. Longings for past and future, for spring in autumn and autumn in spring, for Vermont in Maryland and Maryland in Vermont, longings that sometimes have no recognizable shape or character at all. Like a favorite piece of music, Nature elicits them.

My family is flung across nine time zones, and I have to time carefully my Valentine's calls. Nine time zones linked by longing and love.

February 15: THE BRIDGE AFTER THE STORM

I PULL MY CAR into the parking lot near Boundary Bridge, miraculously cleared after the storm, where I am quietly stunned by winter's beauty, once again. The tall trees of the forest—each with its own grooved, checkered, mottled, or smooth bark—rise from the snow or from the sleet that looks like snow. The sycamores, in particular, show off against the sky, their creamy limbs oddly more pronounced in the whitened landscape.

Why have I never before noticed that Boundary Bridge looks like the famous Japanese-inspired bridge in Monet's garden at Giverny with its crescent-moon arc? It must be the snow. Snow is better than a new pair of glasses for seeing things fresh. As I look down from the bridge, the swiftly flowing water is the color of green tea today. Shelves of gray-white ice straddle the shore, and just downstream from the bridge they touch in the middle of the creek. The ice shelves have large scalloped edges and curious gold veins, veins that mimic the veins of leaves. It's been a long time since I've seen ice on Rock Creek.

I start down the trail and immediately regret not bringing my skis. I have track-envy when I see that someone on skis is smarter than I. The snow is the consistency of wet sugar, and plodding through it on foot is harder than walking on sand. Many dogs have already bounded down the trail, far more light-footed than I. I can use the workout, because I'm recovering from the flu and from the inertia associated with a mild "post-performance" depression. After spending more than a year revising my book, *City of Trees,* for its third edition, and recently delivering the manuscript to the publisher, there has been little activity. Waiting for word back after submitting a manuscript is one of my least-favorite parts of the publishing process. A friend says it's like sending your child off to camp for the first time and wondering, "How's it going?"

But walking, even in difficult wet sugar, brings me back to life. The wind picks up, and I follow the sound to the treetops, which are wildly dancing. The tulip trees wave sun-filled goblets of winged seeds against the sky. One of the trees holds a bird's nest on a flailing limb, 100 feet above the ground and still perfectly formed in mid-winter. The wind reaches down from the higher ridges and into the creek's valley. The sinewy ironwoods fill the lower canopy with their delicate dancing twigs and even the small spicebush jives. Poison ivy vines—dark, hairy-looking, and as thick as anacondas—rope their way skyward. The forest is in motion as gray-and-white clouds sail overhead, and I hike past a stretch of whitewater whose sounds bring to mind the Winter violin concerto of Vivaldi's *Four Seasons.*

I've always loved the dried remains of winter weeds poking through snow, and my heart goes out to the ones I see along the creek, even though many of them are, regrettably, non-native invasives. Who can begrudge the

Asian perilla in mid-winter with its fragrant brown and persistent calyxes wind-waltzing on tall stems? Even the infamous multiflora rose looks small and innocent against the whitened ground. Then there's the decidedly non-innocent (toxic) jimsonweed, of the deadly nightshade family, a potent hallucinogen with its bobbing, prickly, egg-shaped capsules.

Looking back to the bottomland trees along Rock Creek, I notice I've walked to where some of the upland trees, including the beech groves, begin. Is there any more striking woodland tree in winter than the American beech? Its smooth bark is the color of polished sterling against the snow, and its slender and pointed mahogany-toned buds are the embodiment of "twig-elegance." The persistent wheat-colored leaves of the beeches growing on the steep slopes above the creek remind me of a delicious word that I have just learned from Gail Griffin, the director of gardens and grounds at the historic Dumbarton Oaks estate in nearby Georgetown, who said she learned it while reading Vita Sackville-West, the English novelist, poet, and gardener. The word is "marcescent." It means "withering but not falling off" and refers to flowers or leaves that choose not to quit the plant after they have fulfilled their vital roles. My spell-check has flagged this Old World word, which is rife with metaphoric potential. Some people have "marcescent" personalities, while others are quick to let things go. The botanical term for this is "caducous" or "soon falling off." Romantics have marcescent tendencies while pragmatists practice caducousness, and who gets to use the more poetic word?

Reaching the West Beach Drive Bridge, I turn around and return to my car via the road. As much as I'd love to continue on the trail, I'm not up for two more miles of wet sugar, even on a trail rich with marcescence. Looking down from the bridge, I notice that dogs or, perhaps, coyotes have walked across the ice, and it appears they have reached the opposite shore. A few more cold days and one could skate away.

February 17: REAL WORK

SATURDAY MORNING, and I awake before dawn, but the song sparrows were up before me, juicing the air with their spring tunes, despite the frigid temperatures. Shivering, I load my camera equipment into the car. I remember that, two Saturdays previously, a full moon was setting in the west as the sun rose in the east, and I realize that this must be the day of the new moon.

I enter Rock Creek Park at Calvert Street and drive on the parkway that winds through the national park, following the creek to its mouth, where it bleeds itself into the Potomac River near the Watergate Hotel in Foggy Bottom. Driving along Rock Creek to the river, I pass steep hillsides with quilted patterns of snow, earth, and dark rock, a prominent Islamic mosque and cultural center perched high above the creek on Massachusetts Avenue with its tall, skyward-pointing minaret, and the historic gravestones of Oak Hill Cemetery, all casting shadows on the snow. The high arched stone bridges spanning the parkway are bathed in early-morning light. The confluence of Rock Creek and the Potomac River lies under a silver sheet of ice, and I picture the merging of the cold, hidden waters below.

Anything frozen serves as a balm for my worries about global warming, and I silently celebrate the ice-encased Potomac as I drive along it from the fall line at Theodore Roosevelt Island to the Tidal Basin, which is also silver-white and bejeweled with gulls resting and walking on top of the frozen surface. The memorials and monuments glow in the waxing morning sunlight.

My destination is a flower photography workshop that I am taking at the U.S. Botanic Garden on the Mall near Capitol Hill. As I turn toward the conservatory I notice a large group of tourists assembling near the foot of the Hill. They look like they are from a Norman Rockwell portrait or Grandma Moses painting with their pink and purple hats and mittens, festive scarves and expectant air against the snowy backdrop. How wonderful that so many families are lining up on a cold Saturday morning to visit their nation's capital! But with a sinking feeling I remember what is going on inside the Capitol on this particular morning. The Senate has called a rare Saturday session to debate *whether or not* to debate a resolution on the disastrous Iraq War. Talk, talk, and more talk, most likely leading nowhere but to more partisanship.

I take my tripod from the trunk and head for the warmth of the glass-domed conservatory filled with tropical plants, wondering: Where do the solutions to our many national and global problems lie? And I then realize where the real work is getting done. There at the foot of Capitol Hill, under a dome far less famous than the Capitol's, tropical trees are busy spinning the morning sun into sustenance and converting carbon dioxide to oxygen. Thanks to the plants, we humans can live to eat and breathe another day. So which photographers are filming the real action? Representatives of *The Washington Post* and CBS News, hoping to capture senators locked in an endless debate on the Hill or the small band of amateur nature photographers setting up their tripods and macro-lenses to catch the secret beauty of the underside of a leaf or the pistils and stamens of a flower?

February 18: SHINY WHITE

THE WET SUGAR congealed and hardened, forming a shining but treacherous surface. Schools were closed for three days, and people flocked to emergency rooms after falling on the ice or spinning out and crashing their cars. I was nearly one of them, because I landed on my back while waltzing home from Bethesda one recent night. "Bless the calcium, magnesium, and vitamin D I have remembered to take lately," I said to myself, as I lay on a slick sidewalk in the twenty-degree cold under a street lamp, bruised but all of my bones in place.

The shiny snow, or sleet, or whatever it has metamorphosed into, reminds me of the snow sculptures from my New England childhood. At the Vermont boys' boarding school where my father taught, the students built elaborate snow sculptures for the annual winter carnival, hosing them with water to freeze them in place. Then their dates came for a once-a-year weekend event. Wearing colorful hats and mittens, the couples engaged in much hand-holding and kissing under the sculptures. This had a huge effect on my child psyche, permanently linking romance with snow. When I don't get enough snow, I get cranky. And, as I discovered the other night after peeling myself off the sidewalk and entering our yard—where the snow was richly sheened—icy snow, because of its association with those sculptures, is an even stronger memory stimulant.

As soon as Jim returned from Nebraska we went to Rock Creek Park. He was delighted and fascinated by the ice forming under Boundary Bridge. A dark current still flowed in the center of the creek, but the ice-shelves on either shore had widened, and just beyond the bridge they were united into a silver-smooth sheet that begged the unwise to walk or skate across. Sensible fifty-somethings, we chose instead to slip and stumble down the trail, now a rutted frozen jumble of human and animal footprints.

The air was still and the woods infused with winter calm, so unlike the windy day after the storm. But the story of those winds could be read on the surface of the snow. Winged seeds from tulip trees had landed everywhere, in graceful curves, ready to root during the warmth of spring or, more likely, to be carried off by hungry mammals and birds. We startled a field mouse who was probably doing just that. It scurried off to the safety of a hollow log, leaving no tracks on the frozen ground.

It was even tougher walking than right after the storm, but we reached the little swamp just beyond the confluence of Fenwick Branch and Rock Creek, where a few hardy skunk cabbage blossoms were already using their legendary internal heat to break through the frozen snow. Surely, skunk cabbage is one of the wonders of the world. This member of the arum family is usually the first plant to bloom each year in northeastern North America. Its hooded red spathe, which shelters the flower cluster, is the color of red meat and cleverly gives off a faint odor not unlike rotting flesh, attracting carrion insects as pollinators. The stiff spathe can survive bitter cold. Skunk cabbage has a beauty that only the motherly can love. When our children were little, the first rite of earliest spring was to gather up their friends and go for a "skunk" hunting expedition near Sugarloaf Mountain. The skunks are well-camouflaged along streams and in swamps, but, once your eyes adjust, they are everywhere. As our children and their friends figured out how to read the cryptic patterns of the striped and speckled spathes, their delighted shrieks rang out through the forest: "Found one, found one!" More fun for kids than an Easter egg hunt.

My first memory of our daughter discovering skunk cabbage is as etched on my heart as is her first step. She was an infant, and we were living on Seneca Creek, a few stream valleys west of Rock Creek. One late winter day, I walked two or three miles to the nearest skunk cabbage swamp with her close to my chest in her snuggly. As the wind howled above us and I slogged through the muddy terrain, I questioned my sanity. Normal mothers were safely at home with their babies or pushing strollers through warm shopping malls, but, when we got to the patch of skunk cabbage, I no longer cared about my erstwhile sanity. I knelt down, and Sophie leaned out of her snuggly with a smile of pure joy, reaching one baby finger out to touch the skunk cabbage's smooth spathe. Ten months old, she instinctively grasped the magic of the moment, connecting herself with the essence of the oddly beautiful plant.

February 21: DEATH OF WINTER?

OUR WINTER has been crammed into a dramatic few short weeks of February, after a spring-like December and January. Though some tuned-out souls enjoyed the untimely warmth, most Washingtonians were worried about the weather, and I even heard one of my son's friends call it "creepy." Then frigid temps moved in with a vengeance, and two big winter storms and some lesser bouts of frozen precipitation hit our region during these last two weeks.

Winter is my favorite season. To me, snowy hillsides are the gold standard for beauty, whether under sunlight, moonlight, cloud cover, fog, or, best of all, falling snow. Now that climate shifts are occurring in the Mid-Atlantic and New England and our deep winters are up for grabs, I'm appreciating every snowflake and ice crystal with the poignancy of impending loss, almost the way one appreciates a loved one when death is near. But the death of winter here would be an unnatural death, and this poignancy is leashed to the will and drive to do something, now, yesterday, tomorrow, to reverse the warming—but do what?

February 25: THE EARTH IS MY CHURCH

I AM SITTING in a pew of All Souls Church Unitarian at Harvard and 16th streets Northwest at the crest of the city's escarpment, high above the White House and Washington Monument. I recently joined this large, growing, multi-racial, and multi-cultural congregation that was founded in 1821. I have never felt more at home in any church. My church has always been our

Earth, but I have finally found an indoor place of worship, a place where I believe any soul can walk in off the street and feel welcomed. The aura of divine love is so palpable here that the response of most new people, including me, is to cry.

The choir is singing "Dirait-on" from *Les Chansons des Roses* (1993). Rilke's lyrics—*abandon entoure abandon, tendresse touchant aux tendresses* ("abandon surrounding abandon, tenderness touching tenderness")—are joined to an ethereal melody written by the contemporary American choral composer Morten Lauridsen. Outside the high arched windows, against a backdrop of evergreens, snow falls in large swirling flakes.

When the service ends, I discover that I am sitting next to a scientist who left academia to work as a specialist on climate change for the Union of Concerned Scientists. Like me, she is being welcomed as a new congregant on this snowy Sunday. Like me, she feels that climate change is bearing down on us and that we can't act quickly enough. We exchange email addresses and talk about joining the church's committee on the environment.

Outside the steepled brick church the city takes on a clinging cloak of white. I walk to my car with my friend, Kathy Jones, and two of her four daughters. Kathy is smiling at the unexpected snowfall whitening her large purple umbrella—a gift from her youngest daughter, Phoebe. During the service, snow has blanketed my new silver hybrid car, and, as I clear it off with my sleeve, two young men walking down the street say to me, "Hello, beautiful, hello, queen. Can we help you clear off your car?" The affectionate greetings of strangers always lift my spirits.

I drive home on the parkway through Rock Creek Park, which has become the proverbial winter wonderland. Every twig on every tree is laced in snow. My new church and the whitened woodland at the center of the city seem to hold the same sacred glow.

February 28: THE CREEK ICE IS GONE

THIS MORNING I stand on Boundary Bridge and admire the snowy landscape and winter trees. All ice is gone, including the scalloped shelves and the odd vertical stacks of rectangular blocks that followed their breakup. Last week, when my sister, Ellie Choukas Anderson, was visiting from Vermont, we marveled over the blocks of ice. I realize that Rock Creek's ice evolution happened with dizzying speed. Freeze, melt, and breakup, all in a few weeks' time. I mentally compare it to Thoreau's dramatic chapter in *Walden* about the breakup of spring ice on Walden Pond, ice that was frozen in place for months. Of course, Walden Pond is in Massachusetts, but deep freezes weren't limited to New England in centuries past. On my fiftieth birthday, which I celebrated at the Philadelphia Figure Skating Club, I saw a mural depicting nineteenth-century ice skaters on one of Philadelphia's rivers. It's been many years since skaters gathered and put blade to ice on the Schuylkill or the Delaware in the city of brotherly love.

I start off down the frozen path. When I walk the Boundary Bridge loop, I usually travel downstream where the trail skirts the creek. I used to walk the loop in reverse, but I discovered that walking in synch with the creek's flow is more meditative. I soon run into a small, gray-brown French bulldog that Ellie and I met and fell in love with last week. I remember her name—Jubilee—when I see her bounding joyfully through the snow, ears at attention. Unfortunately, I can't remember her human companion's name, a lovely young woman from Maine. But dogs are such vivid presences, and I always seem to remember them best.

A kingfisher is chattering down the Rock Creek flyway, and it turns to fly up Fenwick Branch. This small tributary of Rock Creek flows through the less-than-sylvan suburb of Silver Spring, picking up all manner of pollutants from runoff along the way. Is the kingfisher broadcasting, with its journey up Fenwick Branch, that fish are still living in the compromised stream?

When I reach the little swamp beyond Fenwick, I'm heartened to see a whole new crop of skunk cabbage. Ellie and I stopped at the swamp on one of the coldest days after the big sleet storm and discovered that all the skunks I'd seen earlier in the month had shriveled up. But here are some dazzling newcomers, most notably a pair growing side by side. One is facing me, and I can look through the arched window under its curled spathe to the small, egg-shaped spadix partially hidden inside and bearing the tiny true flowers. Both young skunks are wine-red with gold streaks and speckles, and they huddle together. Embryonic green leaves surround them in spiky clumps. I try to get close enough to touch one, the way baby Sophie had, but the snow-shelf gives way to the warmer swampy depths, and I can't quite reach them. But I am close enough to admire the wet tapestry of fallen oak and maple leaves that surrounds them, a tapestry linking life on the branch with microbial action in the moist soil.

Today I can't walk with my usual abandon, can't quite surrender myself to the beauty of the winter day, and even feel a little guilty that I am walking free in Rock Creek Park while Jim is negotiating a complicated energy deal in Montgomery, Alabama. I also miss Ellie and Sophie and worry about Jesse's upcoming tennis tryouts. And then the curse of every modern woman takes hold in my brain: The To-Do List. There in Rock Creek Park, where I should be swept away by the cold creek waters and a chattering kingfisher, my busy brain is chattering, chattering. I can see the To-Do List sitting on my desk next to my laptop, with entries written in red ink. All the school, community, and board duties I'd neglected during Ellie's visit, the call to the chimney sweep about the fireplace's downdraft, the calls and emails to return about speaking engagements, field trips, potential writing assignments. My own birdsong of busyness—*To Do To Do To Do*—is the enemy of solitude and deep thought.

And then I wonder if our speed-dial winter and my To-Do List are somehow linked. What is winter if not the chance to rest in a state of semi-hibernation, the stillness and cold serving as antidote to the industry of all the other seasons? Winter: The drawing in and drawing down. A trail of pomegranate seeds to the underground, the dark pregnant earth, the sap-filled root—resting, resting before the ecstatic work of spring. The stillness that is not death but the incubating prelude to exuberant rebirth.

And here we are, cramming our months of hibernation into a two- or three-week window of true winter weather between the untimely blooming of daffodils in December and the incipient flowering of a proper spring. In our frenetic, electronically oriented lives, will we lose even this—the chance to come in from the cold, to sit by the fire, to dream of flowers in the impossibly far-off spring? Will we never rest but continue incessantly *to do to do to do* during a freeze that grows shorter and shallower each year?

I ARRANGE TO MEET a new friend today at Boundary Bridge: Cecily Nabors, a fellow writer and naturalist. When I want to get to know someone, in lieu of coffee or lunch, I ask, "Would you like to take a walk?" On a walk one can quickly find the common ground in conversation.

I am not alone at Boundary Bridge as I wait for Cecily. Rock Creek runs high and racy with meltwater. A woman stands on the bank near the bridge with her arms outstretched, facing upstream, as if she is inviting the energy of the creek into her body and soul. She holds this pose for a long time and then moves into a gracefully executed *tai chi* form. While she is in motion, two large and friendly dogs come bounding down the trail with two women behind them talking companionably. It warms my heart to see people enjoying the park.

Cecily arrives, and we begin our meander over the bridge and down the now-muddy Rock Creek trail. As we explore the creek's bottomland and then switch-back into the upland woods, we encounter several other women, young and old, with friends or alone, with dogs or not. All are clearly enjoying this wild, wooded park, the heart and soul of our city.

Before I became intimately acquainted with Rock Creek Park, I was afraid of it. When the remains of a twenty-four-year-old intern, Chandra Levy, were found in the park, not very far from Boundary Bridge, I became especially fearful. So, when I first moved near the park, I was surprised to learn that women neighbors happily walked and jogged there alone or with their dogs. When I asked if they felt safe, they responded with startled looks. Clearly, my imagination of lurking danger was overloaded, and, in retrospect, I can't imagine why.

When Clarissa Pinkola Estés's acclaimed book, *Women Who Run with the Wolves,* came out in the 1990s, I heard the buzz about it, bought it, but never finished it. Still, with self-amusement, I began to think of myself as a "woman who runs with the dogs." At the time, we had a golden retriever and a black lab-shepherd mix—Honeysuckle and Emily—and they were my exuberant companions near our country home at Sugarloaf Mountain, where they followed deer deep into the woods and would disappear for twenty and thirty minutes at a time. I loved the way they became as wild as their wolf ancestors. Emily, the older of the two, endured a lot of crap at home from Honeysuckle but put up with none of it on the trail. With a few choice bark-growls, she established dominance. On the occasional days when my spirits were low and I felt disconnected from life, I envied the way my dogs became wild, sniffing-chasing beings, always alive and connected with the living as they roamed the woods.

For the first time in my adult life I now have no pets. Emily died at thirteen at our Sugarloaf home, Honeysuckle at fifteen after a year of living in Chevy Chase. Jim and I have also said good-bye to a twelve-year-old pet pig and three cats during our marriage. Our children knew all but our first two cats. I think of our animals often and dream vividly about each one. These dreams feel like visitations. I am no longer a woman who runs with the dogs, or walks with the hog, or cuddles the cat, but I love the energy of wildly happy dogs at Rock Creek Park. I feel their connections with their human companions, especially the women who walk or run alone, with not a glimmer of fear in their hearts—with only the beauty of the flowing creek.

March 3: ECLIPSE OF THE SAP MOON

ONE OF TODAY'S front-page stories in *The New York Times* is about the effects of a warming climate on Vermont's maple sugar industry. Could the editors be so nature-savvy to have timed the story with today's total eclipse of the full sap, or sugar, moon, as the moon is called at this time of year? Newspapers may run graphs of waxing and waning moons on their back pages, but the pressing news of the day trumps the lowly orbits of Earth and its moon, and I suspect very few writers and editors are familiar with such folk names as "sap moon" and "sugar moon." The timing may be a coincidence—this front-page story of how Vermont's sugar maple sap run is faltering, appearing on the very day that a lunar eclipse of the sap moon is visible from all seven continents—but the placement of this story is heart-rending for me. As someone who grew up inhaling the sweet steam of the sugar shack, I grieve the incipient demise of Vermont's signature industry.

Jim and I have come to Rock Creek Park to watch the lunar eclipse, which is supposed to be visible at moonrise, around 6:00 p.m. We station ourselves in "Nana's Lap," a comfortable crook in the base of a giant forked tulip tree I call Nana. She looks like my Nana did, with a bountiful body. I have spent many happy hours in her "lap," and I have invited some of my favorite people to sit there with me, high above the creek with superlative views, especially when the trees are bare of leaves. Often I can hear the call of a kingfisher gliding below over its waters. I never thought about who else might be sharing Nana's lap until I saw a raccoon's footprint in the snow next to the massive tree. This evening, Jim notices a hollow in her trunk, which just might tell the rest of the story.

The woods are still, without wind, and Jim and I talk and sit in silence, as we await the eclipsed sap moon to show its dark, reddened face. Jim decides to walk the trail above, his eyes scanning the wooded horizon, searching for the moon. Snuggled next to "my" tree, alone but with my lover nearby, gives me a primal feeling of safety. But the cloud cover thickens so much that the fully eclipsed moon never shows. Even so, life has a way of revealing its mysteries to us when we allow ourselves to listen. At first it is just one little piping peep, but soon the evening quiet is sweetened by a small chorus of spring peepers, the little tree frogs that enliven swamps and streams up and down the East Coast with their sleigh-bell music on the first warm moist evenings of spring. While the peepers call sweetly under the eclipsed and hidden moon, we watch the ghostly forms of several deer follow each other through the darkening woods. I can hardly believe my ears when I hear the staccato *beent beent* of a male woodcock and then the whistling song of wings as he begins his spiral mating flight. A train then whistles and a siren wails, reminding us that we live in the big city, but the loudest sounds of all are the calls of two barred owls near the creek below us: *Who cooks for you? Who cooks for you, all?!*

Walking hand-in-hand back to Boundary Bridge, we feel steeped in the unexpected mystery we found after dark. We came to the woods to see the eclipse but discovered instead the rich nightlife of Rock Creek Park.

A LIGHT SNOW is falling, and it's cold enough to stick to the ground. This morning, I awake to a cardinal's lusty, full-throated mating song. Winter and spring, winter and spring—they will waltz together for a time. Maybe this dance should more aptly be called "birth contractions." Cold days like today are the birth pangs, holding the womb of winter tight. Then, in the warm spaces between contractions, winter relaxes and spring begins to emerge, each contraction and release bringing the new season closer to birth.

Last night, as I was flying home from a visit with family in New Hampshire, I saw a red moonrise like the one Jim and I expected to see in Rock Creek Park on the night of the eclipse. A waning moon hung over Boston Harbor and Cape Cod, the color and shape of a blood orange. It was a clear night above the jeweled cities, all the way from Boston and Providence to Baltimore. I could make out the skyscrapers of Manhattan, the bridges along the East and Hudson rivers, and Central Park—the dark heart of New York City. I couldn't take my eyes away from the plane's windows, so dazzling were the orange and green lights and scalloped shores below. Over Philadelphia and Wilmington the moon slipped behind a hazy cloud, where it glowed milky white.

As I gazed down on the familiar neon-lit Northeast, I thought of the futility of the energy-saving light bulbs we are using at home. Every visible patch of earth below seemed dedicated to the goal of burning bright. Are these and other coastal cities doomed to an untimely death by drowning? Will Manhattan sink because it never learns to switch off the lights? When the plane circled for landing in Baltimore, I reacted viscerally to the vehicles and their headlights below us on I-95, as if I could feel their parasitic nature. The city's lights looked like pretty poisons, the end-to-end vehicles like life-sapping uber-worms of Earth. And here I was, thinking these thoughts while aloft in an aircraft spewing its fumes into the night air.

I went to New Hampshire to visit Jim's parents at a senior living community in Concord and to see my family in Hanover. Jim's dad, Bill, has Alzheimer's disease, and he and Jim's mom recently moved from their home in the White Mountains to an apartment with much-needed access to extra care. Bill can no longer stand without the aid of a walker. Paula, Jim's mother, has valiantly tried to care for Bill at home.

Paula suggested that I take Bill for a walk around the neighborhood in his wheelchair. It was cold, and I wondered if his Boston Red Sox cap would provide adequate head-cover. Bill is one of the few Red Sox fans to have been alive during Boston's widely spaced World Series wins—in 1918, the year of his birth—and in 2004, when the Sox won the series during a lunar eclipse. Bill is a Ph.D. philosopher and theologian and a world traveler. Despite the disease that has robbed him of his ability to converse, he is fully and joyfully present, laughing easily, as if he gets the joke. You can see him formulating a thought that he wishes to share, but then the thought gets lost between genesis and expression. I pulled up Bill's jacket around his ears and pushed the wheelchair down the front-door ramp with Paula's help, marveling at how she manages to do this on her own.

Bill and I fell into a comfortable rapport as we navigated the sand-and-salt-strewn sidewalks between snow banks, and once or twice I landed us in the ditch. The wind made the sweet sound it makes in the white pines of New Hampshire, reminding me of a line I composed for a poem years ago when Jim and I lived in the White Mountains: "The muse of the North / is the wind spinning secrets / in the softwood trees."

When we were quite far from home, I asked Bill if he wanted to turn around, and, despite the cold, he answered with an emphatic "No." Jim's parents and I share a love of Nature, and this summer I became aware of how Bill seemed to enjoy natural beauty even more with the advancement of his disease. I remember a day last summer when he sat at the living-room window, looking out at a large white birch tree and the northern peaks of the Presidential Range. For long stretches of time he was totally lost in the movement of the clouds over the rocky summits of Mount Adams and Mount Madison. I think Jim first articulated the observation that, in spite of his dad's illness, Bill seemed deeply happy, in some ways more so than when he was a younger man with worldly concerns.

As I steered the wheelchair past a white pine, I asked Bill if he wanted to stop and touch the bark. He did, and we both patted the tree with gloved hands as the wind stirred the bundles of soft green needles above us. When we passed a cedar and then a spruce, I picked small handfuls of foliage, bruised them with my fingers, and held them under Bill's nose so he could smell their woodsy fragrances. Wheeling him under a red maple, I showed Bill how the red buds were swollen and soon to burst into flower. He said, "We'll have to come back."

The next day the temperature never rose from the single digits, a near-record New Hampshire cold. I heard on the radio that it was thirty-seven degrees below zero on the summit of Mount Washington, with 100-mile-per-hour winds. I had driven to Hanover through blinding snow squalls the night before to visit my parents, sister and brother, and their families. My adorable long-haired nephews, Nate, eleven, and Phin, seven, were still sweaty from hockey practice as I entered my mom's fragrant kitchen. She'd been cooking all day, with a bad back, despite her promise not to fuss. That's my mom!

Returning to Concord the next day, I lamented the fact that Bill and I probably wouldn't be able to walk outside due to the bitter cold. I told Jim that I'd like to bring a picture book to Bill, and Jim had found a spectacular one at the bookstore—a collection of National Geographic pictures from around the world. As we leafed through the pictures of each continent, Bill became energized. He told me, "I've been there," in response to many of the places depicted in the book. And indeed he had, and he remembered.

It was hard to leave, but I extricated my ball of yarn from the paws of Pursee, the cat, and said good-bye. I left Bill holding a stone that Jim and I had given him—a smooth gray stone from a river in India, with the word LOVE carved into its surface.

March 9: SPEARMINT MELTWATERS

I HAVE BUT A FEW moments to visit Boundary Bridge, but I need my Nature fix for the day despite my limited time. I get out of my car and cross the arc of the bridge under the sunlit samaras of the tulip trees and the tiny, gently waving catkins of a large river birch. Wild meltwaters flow below, the color of spearmint tea. The creek's woods are snow-kissed, and the air is cold. When summer comes and the creek grows dark and jungle-like, I will remember this winter afternoon and how the woods looked under a light layer of powdery snow.

Except for the flowing water, the woods are quiet. Where is my friend, the kingfisher? I realize how much I've come to anticipate the chattering sound that precedes the bird with the brilliant blue crest. It flies low and briskly over the creek's water, chattering-chattering all the while. It frequently alights on snags overhanging the water, no doubt scanning the creek for fish. I look forward to the day when I witness a catch! Even when I don't see a kingfisher, I always feel the bird's presence at Rock Creek.

After my short walk I drive through the park to Tilden Street, on my way to Jesse's school. The stream valley is flecked with snow, highlighting the rocky cliffs and evergreen mountain laurel growing from them. Water races through the white-frosted rocks below Military Road. A pair of runners in red and blue jackets traverse a snow-covered trail along the creekside. I wish I had time to follow those colorful jackets and explore the park, but I am glad for the chance to inhale the natural serenity, if only for a few moments.

Few of us experience true wilderness. Living—or even backpacking—in the wilderness requires skill, guts, and a taste for adventure most of us lack. We are connoisseurs of more accessible beauty, and, thankfully, some forward-looking individuals had the sense to preserve the wooded acres of Rock Creek Park in 1890, 101 years before Jesse was born. As I steal a quick drink of beauty on my way to his school, I reflect on the moments of natural solace that people throughout time have grabbed on the fly: Stopping to rest on the handle of the hoe and scan the land for glimpses of colorful cardinals and bluebirds in the hedge-row; looking up from the back-breaking work of harvesting cotton, chiles, or tobacco to watch a hawk soar overhead; and strolling with sleeping babies to the nearest urban park for conscious or subliminal communion with its trees and the birds building nests in their leafy crowns. People the world over, looking up and out, feeling connected to the natural world that surrounds them and then moving on with the business of their everyday lives.

March 12: A DREAM OF PALIMPSEST

WHENEVER I VISIT Gail Griffin, the director of gardens and grounds at Dumbarton Oaks, I come away with a new word. The last time I saw her it was "marcescent." Today it is "palimpsest." Its literal meaning: "Parchment or other writing material from which one or more previous writings have been scraped away or erased to make room for another." Gail tells me that Charles A. Birnbaum, the founder and president of the Cultural Landscape Foundation in DC whom she knows and admires, applies the word to the landscape itself. Thus, Earth is a palimpsest, and its people constantly scrape away the old to make way for the new. The land is a palimpsest even if people are removed from the scene. Forest succession involves pioneer species that give way to the overlapping progressive plant communities that, ultimately, will become the mature "climax" forest. Invasive plants, however, interfere with the process of succession in ways that seriously worry botanists and ecologists and landscape designers alike.

And, with global warming bearing down on us all, it's an unfolding tale with an uncertain plotline. It's imperative that, in this forever-changing earthly script, we do whatever we can to save the natural places of wonder left to us, to give our "landscape palimpsests" every opportunity to preserve their integrity as wild or semi-wild places. The health of our home planet depends on it, a truth people are finally beginning to recognize. We also owe it to ourselves to celebrate every moment of beauty we can beg, borrow, or steal from our busy lives. That's why relatively small wild urban places such as Rock Creek Park are just as essential to humanity as the far grander places of wildness such as Yosemite and Yellowstone, the Everglades and Adirondacks.

Last night I had a vivid dream. In the dream, Honeysuckle, our golden retriever who died two years ago, was an elderly dog, and I took her back to visit Strawberry Moon Farm, our former home near Sugarloaf Mountain. In the dream we had not yet sold the house. Honeysuckle climbed out of the car and immediately started eating succulent greens in the field, which were dusted with snow. I realized how starved she was for greens. Then Emily, our other dog, showed up in the field. I knew she was a ghost, but I patted her, and she felt very much alive.

I walked toward the house with the two dogs and opened the door. Someone made a startled sound, and I realized that people were living in the house. There were children inside and children's furniture—small tables and chairs and toy-strewn nooks. Then I saw Anabella, the grown daughter of my friend Gioconda Roman, who has cared for our home and children for twenty years. Anabella apologized and said she needed a home for herself and her two children, so she had moved into the empty house at Strawberry Moon Farm. I told her I was happy she was living there and hoped she would stay. It was a dream of *palimpsest*, the word I would learn from Gail a few hours later.

March 13: BURST OF SPRING AND MORE PRETTY POISONS

YEARS AGO I NOTICED that spring seems to come to Washington, DC, on or around an obscure arboreal holiday called Johnny Appleseed Day, March 11th. Usually but not always. On March 13th, 1993, a so-called "storm of the century" brought as much as three feet of snow to the area when it hammered the East Coast with cyclonic force. Our pet pig was shivering in his straw pile inside his little house when the thermometer plummeted to near zero the night after the storm.

No such storm arrived this year on Johnny Appleseed Day, though I'm hoping for a little more snow before spring is officially here. I never get enough snow to satisfy my cravings for snow here in Maryland. That March 13th blizzard made me ever hopeful for last-minute possibilities. Sometimes these secret wishes are rewarded near, or even after, the equinox. And there can be wet-snow events even in April. But spring seems to be here today. Is that why last night I dreamed I was pregnant?

The wood frogs in the swamp near Boundary Bridge are quacking up a storm as they engage in their spring mating frenzy. These small masked frogs, which sound very much like ducks, create a racket throughout the day during the first warmth of late winter/early spring, and the sweet-sounding spring peepers enhance the chorus at night.

Amphibians are particularly sensitive to pollutants and a changing climate. There have been massive and alarming die-offs of frogs the world over, so

I am always relieved to see and hear the wood frogs in the vernal pool near Boundary Bridge. Yesterday, as I climbed the steep slope above the pool and sat under a beech tree, the lusty sounds of wood frog calls filled the outdoor amphitheater, and I could see concentric circles on the water's surface marking activity in the water below. Interlocking circles of frog love!

Last year, in late February or early March, Jim and I stumbled on this mating ritual during a walk. But a month without rain followed, and the vernal pond where the wood frogs had laid their eggs dried up prematurely, depriving Boundary Bridge of a generation of young frogs. Then, in June, an unpredicted, strange, and record-busting deluge of ten inches of rain fell in a single day. On its heels a long summer drought ensued, suggesting to me that the weather extremes associated with climate change are already churning.

But, yesterday, I wasn't thinking about drought or floods. Just the intoxication of spring. A kingfisher was hanging out on one of its favorite snags, eyeing the creek's waters below for nourishment. Cardinals were singing, and I heard the musical *churr* of a red-bellied woodpecker and the high raucous cackle of a pileated. Runners in the park were wearing shorts and t-shirts. A young man wearing a baseball cap was trying to coax his Chesapeake Bay retriever puppy into the creek. When I later encountered them on the trail, I mentioned to the young man that his curly brown-haired dog was adorable. He smiled like a proud papa and said, "Five months old!" Even the procession of DC's rush-hour traffic inching across the West Beach Drive Bridge seemed festively spring-like. But all was not happy and settled in my heart, even in the fullness of emerging spring. Some pretty little yellow flowers were the source of my angst as I walked the Boundary Bridge trail.

Boundary Bridge is a legendary destination for enthusiasts of spring wildflowers. Traditionally, trout lily, spring beauty, bloodroot, Virginia bluebells, wild blue phlox, and other "spring ephemerals" paint the small floodplain next to the bridge with seasonal pastels, blooming usually in March and April. But their numbers have severely decreased in a not-so-happy instance of palimpsest. In recent years, a small yellow flower from Europe and Asia—lesser celandine or fig buttercup (*Ranunculus ficaria* or *Ficaria verna*), which was once planted in gardens—has enthusiastically escaped and taken over the Boundary Bridge floodplain. Its tuberous roots, succulent stalks, and dark-green heart-shaped leaves form a nearly impenetrable mat that serves as a stranglehold for the native wildflowers here and elsewhere in the Northeast.

Last night, at the meeting of the Maryland Native Plant Society's Board of Directors, we talked about the pervasiveness of invasive species and the "weed warrior" programs that board members have developed to combat the growing problem of invasive exotic plants crowding out native plants. This problem seems to be intensifying in the face of global warming. An atmospheric increase in CO_2 favors the non-native woody vines, which have invaded Rock Creek Park and other Washington-area woodlands: The infamous smothering kudzu has been joined by English ivy, porcelain berry, mile-a-minute, Japanese honeysuckle, winter creeper, Chinese yam, and Asiatic bittersweet. These introduced vines escaped from cultivation, and they are literally strangling and smothering the natural trees of the forest. And a little global warming may be having a salient effect on the innocent-looking, low-growing, yellow flower that now gives me such a troubled heart on my walks. So numerous are the alien, sweetly shining yellow blossoms growing thickly next to the creek and across the floodplain and even scattered in the upland woods that I am reminded of the lights I saw up and down the Northeast grid from the windows of the plane last week. Pretty poisons of a different sort.

Cris Fleming, the current president of the Maryland Native Plant Society and a long-time friend and resident of a Rock Creek Park neighborhood, tells me that visiting Boundary Bridge in spring has become almost too painful for her, because of the demise of the native wildflowers. So far all attempts at controlled removal of the lesser celandine have failed. I, too, am haunted by a memory not three years old—of walking with my teenaged daughter during the height of spring next to the creek and noticing the way she delicately picked her way through the wildflowers in her nearly bare feet, clad only in flip-flops. I still see her bare toes next to the abundant trout lilies and Virginia bluebells (being crowded out by today's lesser celandine), and the sweetness of the memory makes my heart ache.

My heart does its own flip-flop this morning when I read about the poetic herbal history of the little yellow flower that is causing North American botanists such grief. Maud Grieve, the early twentieth-century English herbalist, wrote in her classic book, *A Modern Herbal* (1931): "Wordsworth, whose favourite flower this was. . . fancifully suggests that the painter who first tried to picture the rising sun, must have taken the idea of the spreading pointed rays from Celandine's 'glittering countenance.' The burnishing of the golden petals gives a brilliant effect to the flowers, which burst into bloom about the middle of February, a few days only after their bright shining leaves." Hmmm . . . our nemesis, Wordsworth's rising sun?

As I read Grieve and other authors I learn that the little plant that inspired three poems by England's preeminent romantic poet has also been valued as a nutritious and medicinal herbal, high in vitamin C, and used to treat scurvy and—largely due to the medieval "Doctrine of Signatures"—piles or hemorrhoids, because of the hemorrhoid-like knobbiness of its tuberous roots. Maud Grieve also quotes the following recipe from *A Plain Plantain* (1922), edited by Russell George Alexander: "For a Sore Throat take a pinte of white-wine, A good handful of Sallendine [lesser celandine], and boile them well together; put to it A piece of the best Roach Allome, sweeten it with English honey, and use it." Perhaps we should tout the medicinal virtues of this pesky invader and encourage a foraging pilgrimage to Rock Creek!

After last night's board meeting the creek beckoned. I parked where one is forbidden to park after dark and got out of my car. The sweetness of the night air felt wholly unlike the sweetness of the winter afternoon following our most recent snow. It was soft and heavy with fecundity in spite of the night chill. I could just make out the ghostly remnants of a few patches of snow in the deep woods. The spring peepers were calling, their sleigh-bell chorus barely audible above the music of the flowing water, which seemed louder at night. I walked to Boundary Bridge, where a celestial surprise greeted me. There above the rushing water, framed by the rickrack traceries of the swelling buds on the American elm branchlets, hung the Big Dipper constellation. Its starry handle pointed down, and its bountiful trapezoidal bowl tilted toward Earth, as if pouring out a generous libation of spring upon Rock Creek Park and the northern hemisphere.

March 14: HOW WILD AM I?

BEFORE DAWN I AWAKE to a robin's song. I remember how startled I was as a little girl to learn from my father—a lifelong birder—that the common red-breasted bird pulling earthworms from the yard has a melodious song.

When robins search for worms, they are mum and business-like. We rarely see them open their throats and sing, but the sound they produce from their semi-hidden perches conjures up unfurling leaves, bursting flower buds, and nests holding sky-blue eggs. When I step outside to get the paper shortly after dawn, I notice the pink crescent remnant of the sugar moon hanging above our black oak tree in the southeastern sky.

My brother, Mike Choukas, is visiting us from New Hampshire. This morning, as I wave goodbye to Jesse, in his robin's-egg-blue polo shirt, and to Jim and Mike in their spiffy business suits, I call out that I am happy to send them into the fray while I stay home with my laptop. They laugh, but no married man or woman can avoid the weightiness of the outside-work-versus-stay-at-home negotiating that goes on in every relationship with children. In our arrangement, I am the consummate free-lancer, which supposedly provides me with a schedule flexible enough to run the household and taxi the children and do my professional work.

So here I sit in jeans and red garden clogs, a mug of cold coffee next to me, earning no certain income, with a to-do list in front of me that never ceases its refrain. I may get out this morning to start shooting new photographs for the third edition of *City of Trees*. I have a meeting downtown this afternoon to discuss the post-screening panel I'll be moderating at the DC Environmental Film Festival next week. During the course of the day I will receive and send numerous emails related to various nature projects, some paid, some volunteer: Talks, field trips, articles, another natural history book that will soon be published in paperback, board memberships, and committees. All the business of a nature lover who is following her bliss while living largely on her husband's income.

How authentic is this life? Does it have integrity? I think my friends and family members, readers of my books, and participants in my field trips would emphatically nod yes—at least most of the time—but how emphatically do *I* nod yes?

Perhaps Thoreau felt some sheepishness about living on Emerson's land and visiting the village of Concord as frequently as he did. Sure, he hoed his row of beans and lived in a tidy one-room cabin built with his own hands (recording every expenditure), but was his life the exemplary life, lived in harmony with Nature? He lived at Walden Pond for only a short while.

Marjorie Kinnan Rawlings grew oranges and wrote rapturously of the beauty around her on her farm in Florida, and other writers have described their beekeeping, blueberry farming, fly-fishing, backpacking and wilderness exploration, crafts and pursuits that have kept them close to our Earth, in communion with their surroundings.

As I look out my home-office window, I see my friend, Esther Schrader, clad in a brilliant pink shirt and black workout shorts, about to put her two-year-old son, Nathaniel, into his baby jogger for a run down the Capital Crescent Trail. Before Nathaniel's birth, Esther was the Pentagon correspondent for *The Los Angeles Times.* She and I walk together in Rock Creek Park when time permits, and Jesse waters her flowers when she travels with her family. Esther's husband is an editor at *The Washington Post,* and our next closest neighbor is an editor for *The New York Times.* The Chief Justice of the Supreme Court lives a few blocks away. Our neighborhood is pleasant and affluent, and I'm in the distinct minority with my meager bachelor's degree.

We have herbs and flowers growing in the yard, and I hire my artistic friend, Nancy Strahler, to help me care for them. We usually plant some chard, tomatoes, onions, and a few green beans behind the house. Prior to living in this upscale suburban neighborhood we lived in a rural setting, but Strawberry Moon Farm wasn't really a farm. Although we had an old-time smokehouse and a pig, the pig was a beloved pet whom we ultimately buried in a pet cemetery. Two modern houses sat within spitting distance of our farmhouse. We cultivated a large vegetable garden that thrived on neglect. We had an apple tree with wormy fruit, an ancient Concord grape vine, and wild strawberries, blackberries, and cherries. I spent a lot of time picking berries with Jim and the kids, and I occasionally made pies, grape juice, and jelly.

But how *wild* a life has this been so far? How wild can you be with so many rooftops in sight? And how does pecking out words on a laptop constitute communion with Nature? If I had a real garden, or an old-time craft, or some serious time spent living and surviving in wilderness, wouldn't that constitute a more *Nature-oriented* life? The truth is, there are times when I feel genuinely wild, when my body and spirit feel connected to a divine yet earthly source. These moments sweep over me unbidden, more often when I am alone than in the presence of others and usually when I am surrounded by natural beauty. Perhaps we don't have to *do* anything to honor or develop our wild selves: We just need to let them be.

This lament of *How wild am I?* is not new for me. I remember walking with my first love in Vermont when we were seventeen. I was doing the same sort of hand-wringing then about not living a wild enough life. We were walking over a moss-covered ledge when some bees flew past us, and I told him that I envied their wildness. Curly-haired and t-shirt clad Ted replied, "Melanie, we are just as wild as they are." I knew instinctively that he was probably right, but I still struggle with the question. Well, bees—maybe. Maybe I'm as wild as a bee living in a hive.

March 16: SPICEBUSH BUDS

YESTERDAY, I TOOK Laura Rounds, my Sugarloaf friend of many years, to Boundary Bridge. Tomorrow is St. Patrick's Day, and, when our children were young, red-haired Irish Laura celebrated the Old World holiday by hiding a "pot of gold"—a black pot filled with gold coins and candies—in the woods near her house. She gave each child a treasure box, and sent them out into the budding woods to see what the Leprechauns and Fairies had hidden—and to see if her children and mine could spot one of the magical beings. Those woodland hunts, along with the colored-egg hunts on Sugarloaf Mountain (which were part of our spring equinox celebrations) and their late winter "skunk hunting" expeditions, are some of Sophie's and Jesse's fondest childhood memories. The primal appeal of woodland treasure hunts must hearken back to our foraging ancestors.

Laura loved walking the Boundary Bridge trail with me. We sat on what I call the "Meditation Rock"—a large rounded rock that juts out into Rock Creek just below the Laurel Ledge—and then in Nana's Lap for so long that we had to scrap our lunch plans. The day had been warm, nearly eighty degrees, but today it's in the thirties with a cold rain that may turn to snow. Spring's "birth pangs."

Laura is a fellow snow enthusiast, and together we try to conjure storms. We are still patting ourselves on the back over the blizzard of '93, which occurred right after Laura's mother's funeral. We had been "skunk hunting" with the kids a few days earlier and had talked about how much we hoped for one more snow.

Laura and her husband, Scott, a landscape painter whose work hangs in our living room, have lived in the same house in the Sugarloaf woods ever since we've known them. Years ago, they dug a well where they hoped to build a bigger house, but they've always been too busy to construct it. Jim and I have this in common with them: Rural land with a well dug and waiting for us.

When I lead field trips at Boundary Bridge and Sugarloaf Mountain, I always urge participants to find their special place and then to return to it throughout the year and over time. Traveling and seeing new sights is exciting and enlightening, but, to my mind and heart, nothing can compare with the thrill of witnessing the turn of the seasons, year after year, in one beloved place.

As Laura and I walked over Boundary Bridge, a familiar shrub growing next to the bridge stopped me in my tracks. The small round buds of the spicebush were swollen and tipped with a dazzling dandelion-yellow. On my walk the day before they had not been yellow-tipped: In fact, not since a warm day of late winter or earliest spring a year ago had these buds looked precisely so—yellow-tipped and ready to bloom. Laura and I walked along the creek where another sight ignited thrilled surprise. There in the creek's water, just back from who-knows-where, were three wood ducks—two males and a female. Looking a little weak and bedraggled after their journey from points south, the threesome paddled over to a sandy beach and climbed ashore where they seemed to be sighing and saying "whew!" Later, as we admired the skunk cabbage in the swamp near Fenwick Branch, a phoebe called down from the cliffs. I wondered if the bird had come back to nest again under the West Beach Drive Bridge.

Marjorie Kinnan Rawlings wrote eloquently in her book, *Cross Creek* (1942), about the return of spring to the bald cypress wetlands surrounding her orange grove in Florida. She speculated that, without context, spring would be meaningless. Spring is a process that can only be understood and appreciated by those who experience the preceding winter. And the more closely one identifies with a particular place, the more poignant and meaningful small seasonal changes will be. Certainly, a small dot of yellow at the tip of a bud would draw little attention from a first-time or casual visitor to

Boundary Bridge. And if I saw a bursting spicebush bud in an unfamiliar wood, although I would take notice, it wouldn't thrill me the way the buds on these familiar branches thrill me. The wood ducks and phoebe's songs, while pleasing to see and hear, would not carry the import of the announcement: "I'm back at Rock Creek Park!"

Perhaps true wildness is really about intimacy. Animals and plants live in intimate contact with their food sources and pollinators and with the settings where they thrive and procreate. The robin migrates "home" to familiar territory to build a nest, and it senses the movement of worms with its sharp eyes. The skunk cabbage has evolved over countless generations, in the fertile muck of swamps and streamsides, to woo its pollinators. Plants and animals have finely tuned relationships with their habitats. Maybe this is the source of my angst about wildness. I'm not required to have an intimate relationship with the natural world, because of all the intermediaries who feed and clothe me, and yet I desire that intimacy to gain a sense of wholeness. As a woman who has experienced sexual passion, natural childbirth, and breastfeeding, I have known my own wildness and the essential wildness of my husband and our babies. But I long for that level of connection beyond the human skin—beyond both the actual skin and the skin of the house, beyond the car and the city.

March 17: PLANT YOUR PEAS

I SHOULD HAVE KNOWN that Laura and I could turn a heat wave on a dime. Yesterday's rain did change to snow, and, today, March's birth-contraction dance is at a fever pitch. (And, yes, it *feels* like a mixed up metaphor!) Icicles are wildly dripping, a quick percussion to the interweaving melodies of the cardinals, the song sparrows, and the March wind. Wind-blown daffodil buds are shaking off snow, and on my way to get the paper I notice a pink budding hyacinth with a sugar coating of ice crystals next to the front walk. I have no time today to visit Boundary Bridge, but I open my window and see, hear, and feel the wind blow across our neighbors' snow-covered roof, where it sings through the Virginia pine in their front yard and sets our wind chimes ringing. The fresh air rushing inside feels frigid, and I must shut the window or don a parka. Another nor'easter has its sights on New England, but it gave us a good dose of frozen precipitation last night, and the wind is still coming from the northeast.

There's a Maryland saying: "Plant your peas by St. Patty's Day." Would-be pea planters have their work cut out for them today. One can feel the earth rising to shake off winter, and winter is sassing back. This is something Vermonters understand. In Vermont winter is reluctant to relinquish the upper hand, and spring—sweet spring—happens in the blink of an eye. But, here in the Washington, DC, area, spring will reign for weeks and months, in one long unfolding spell, and this snow-white St. Patty's Day will soon be history.

March 18: WHAT WOULD WORDSWORTH THINK?

A CLOSE FRIEND OF MINE, Lisa Lindberg, has returned from the San Francisco Bay area to live, once again, in Maryland's Blue Ridge Mountains. Her chief complaint about the Bay area? Not enough winter. So this morning I get an exuberant email from Lisa about the twelve inches of snow that fell on her Maryland mountaintop during Friday's passing storm. With giddy enthusiasm, she describes the last few weeks back on her wintry mountain and how she and her husband, Duncan Work, had to park their car at the bottom of their driveway. "Instead of a car-way, we used our solid sheet-of-frozen-snow driveway as a bobsled/luge course—getting going so fast in that 1/8-mile run that it was positively scary." Good to have this very Norwegian friend of mine back!

And, speaking of returns, my warrior husband has returned from the South, charting an impromptu and roundabout course that took him through the upper Midwest. His flight out of Atlanta was canceled during the storm, so he drove to Birmingham, where he got on a plane to Louisville. When the Louisville flight was canceled, he caught a few hours of sleep (at my insistence) and then headed out via a rental car at first light for Indianapolis, where he finally managed to get a flight home. I call him a warrior, because I believe he could slay any dragon. He does so, routinely, as a "public side" energy attorney, saving his clients—publicly owned utilities throughout the South and Midwest—millions of dollars on their natural gas bills with innovative cooperative purchase deals. He is the best kind of warrior, because, as soon as he slays the dragons, he fights hell and high water to get home.

During the last hour of daylight on yesterday's frigid St. Patty's Day I managed to sneak in a visit to Boundary Bridge. I was more than glad that I did. The American elms at the bridge were in full sepia-toned blossom, and the creek brimmed nearly at flood stage. The bottomlands between Rock Creek and the wood frog "amphitheater" were filled with temporary storm-generated streams, and the vernal pond had more than doubled in size. I was happy to see that the National Park Service was putting up a "frog fence," a simple wood-slat-and-wire affair that keeps dogs out of the amphibian breeding area. Some of the reddish fence segments were erected next to the pond, and some were still in jelly rolls near the trail. A thin layer of ice coated the pond, and the wood frogs were silent.

I had never seen so many birds near Boundary Bridge. The chickadees, robins, and sparrows are always out and about, but I don't often see towhees or golden-crowned kinglets, which are tiny, active birds that tree-hop right along the creek. I wished that Cecily or another birding friend had been with me as I got a very good look at what I thought was a hermit thrush hopping ahead of me along the trail. Cardinals were singing, woodpeckers were hammering, and then, just as I passed Fenwick Branch, I caught my breath. In a grove of trees, where I often see and hear tufted titmice, I looked closely and saw something else: At first one and then several eastern bluebirds. Never had I seen a bluebird in Rock Creek Park! I followed their little band over a snow-covered knoll and through the swamp. Their brilliant back feathers flashed cerulean when the twilight hit them just right. Where were they going? Will I see them again?

And then I had a "What would Wordsworth think?" moment. With no other walkers about, I felt free to wander. I explored the swamp closer to the bridge, finding two large trees that had fallen side by side. Each had a giant upturned root ball. The trees had fallen some time ago, and the root balls had been colonized by—what else?—lesser celandine, the local botanist's scourge. The yellow, lesser celandine flowers looked a bit haggard after the storm, and they were still flecked with snow. But the trees' root balls formed giant semi-circles, like rising suns, and on a bright day with the flowers blooming, if Wordsworth were to stumble on the scene, would he not be delighted and amazed to see his small rising suns colonizing two larger rising suns? Might he be inspired to write a poem about it? Wordsworth is my new-found shield against the despair I feel over the take-over by lesser celandine.

The actual setting sun created a peach glow in the west, beyond the bridge, and the bare trees at the top of the amphitheater lit up and glowed pink. I kept expecting the sky to darken, but the power of the approaching equinox could be felt in the expanding evening light. With no one about, and all inhibitions (the few meager ones I've got) lifted, I found a new "lap." This interspecies perch was formed by the intertwining of green ash and sycamore roots at the water's edge. I tucked myself between the two trees, sitting on their supportive basket of roots, and faced upstream, where the water had changed to burnished gold under the setting sun. I sat there for a long time, letting the magic of the flowing creek fill me. With the approaching dark the birds grew silent but for some muted peeps. The evening was too cold for spring peepers and wood frogs, and I never heard the owls or woodcocks that I listened for. But the water sang to me. It filled my soul with its golden-peach flowing hues and hypnotic music. Silver water wings formed from snags in the creek, with the snag forming the apex of the wing and the liquid wing expanding downstream toward me. As I looked upstream I thought about how much I miss when I walk *with* the current, something I've routinely done since I deemed it more meditative. Facing this way I could see everything floating toward me: Small twigs and leaves, sycamore achenes, a duck, if it would appear.

After a while I spotted something big coming around the bend, perhaps 100 feet upstream. As it came toward me I realized it was a white plastic milk jug. The jug bobbed gracefully along, perfectly crafted to float down Rock Creek. I knew it would soon hit the impenetrable snag that waited for it downstream, a major blow-down from last June's deluge of rain. I also knew that the March 31st volunteer cleanup crew was likely to find it there and recycle it. There was no message in this bottle, but the jug itself was a sort of message, reminding me that the creek's integrity is at the mercy of the multitudes living along it.

Part II

SPRING

March 24: VERNAL EQUINOX

WHEN SPRING FINALLY HAPPENS, I can't imagine why I was holding back. How can anyone choose cold and hibernation over warmth and growth? Last evening I surrendered to spring, and now I want to be out of the cave and into the day and the night, especially the fertile night.

Jim, Jesse, and I are going to Spain tomorrow to visit Sophie, and I have been ransacking the house and town to find everything on her wish list: Music, movies, a certain peanut butter, herbal shampoo in the travel size, gold sandals, t-shirts, and books—both high-brow and low. A very explicit list made by a young woman who knows herself well. I have had fun, as only a mother can, fulfilling her requests. But, by the end of the day, I need my Boundary Bridge fix.

I park at the creek, where I hear a sound I haven't heard in months—a dog shaking off water after a swim. I walk my trail loop in reverse so I can come back along the creek and enter the swamp at dusk, when I hope the spring peepers will be calling. About the midpoint of my circular route, at the Meditation Rock, a great blue heron is stalking fish. Male cardinals are loudly and musically announcing their lustful intentions from the wooded slopes and rock ledges. Dads are out in force with their children, and I see and hear something one rarely witnesses these days: Children are playing in the woods near one of the 16th Street neighborhoods. Children today don't play in the woods like we did; they go to soccer or cheerleading practice, rather than explore the wilds. Runners in shorts are silently jogging up the switchback trail. Down in the creek a small black dog dives for a stick.

When I get to the swamp, it seems silent at first. But, as I come closer to the vernal pond where the wood frogs were recently calling and mating, I begin hearing the music of the little spring peepers. I bushwhack across the floodplain and sit on a log next to the pond. This is the moment of my surrender to spring.

Above my log perch, red maples reach for the twilit sky, their branchlets clad in tiny fuzzy red flowers. Their roots are *in* the water. Next to my log, the vertical twirls of unfurling skunk cabbage leaves are several inches tall, their green the ephemeral lime of early spring. Grasses probe through the mud and water, stone flies dance above me, and the music of the spring peepers shoots a charge straight through my winter-heart. I strain my eyes to try to find one of the little tree frogs with an "x" on its back and singing swelling bubble gum throat. But I can't find one of the tiny creatures, even though some are no more than a foot away. The mating calls of the peepers near me sound insistent and shrill, each individual call distinct. But, all around me, the sound collectively merges into that disembodied, softer sleigh-bell song that is spring's sweetest symphony.

As my heart fills with the pulse of the new season, a pair of wood ducks flies in and lands in the pond. Is this the threesome I saw last week pared down? If so, their bedraggled look is gone, and the drake's dark green crest and white neck "bridle" are dazzling in the evening light. The female is quite a looker too, in her gray-brown, low-key way, and the two of them quietly paddle around the pond, dining on succulent plants at the water's edge. As I watch them glide through the water, my heart shakes off its last vestige of winter longing as sure as a dog shakes off the creek's water. I can feel my wildest self dancing with the stone flies, blooming with the maples, unfurling with the skunk cabbage leaves, and singing with the frogs.

Washington, DC, is blessed with both wild and cultivated beauty. During the past few days, my focus has been on the latter. I am taking pictures of magnolias and flowering cherries for *City of Trees*, an endeavor that takes me to the National Arboretum, Dumbarton Oaks, and other garden spots throughout the city. Looking through my new macro-lens, I see the blossoms of spring magnified and sharper than the naked eye can see them.

On March 20, the vernal equinox, I moderated a panel discussion after the premiere of a film on the imperiled American elm as part of the DC Environmental Film Festival. The screening of the film was held at the Naval Memorial on Pennsylvania Avenue between the Capitol and the White House. On the morning of the screening, I visited the National Mall to soak up the beauty of that historic, elm-lined greenway. I parked near the Smithsonian Castle (resulting in a parking ticket) and walked under the vase-shaped trees, which represent several generations and various disease-resistant forms of *Ulmus americana*. The elms were blooming, their small sepia flowers accenting the graceful arboreal architecture of what was America's most beloved street tree before Dutch elm disease came calling during the twentieth century.

As I silently celebrated the spring equinox under the elms, I remembered a powerful procession close to the autumnal equinox of 2004, when tens of thousands of native Indian people from every nation walked down the Mall toward the Capitol from west to east on the opening day of the Museum of the American Indian. The walk symbolically reversed the east-to-west Trail of Tears. I thought about Sophie and how she and I said a blessing on the winter solstice in Central Park before she left for Spain. For years our family celebrated seasonal changes with big gatherings on Sugarloaf Mountain, but city centers seem to be the new celebration venues for me.

That night a packed theater viewed the film, and I moderated the discussion afterward. I talked about the beauty of the elm blossoms and how they lack the fame and cachet of the cherry blossoms but nevertheless are a cherished sign of spring. I expressed hope that our venue—the Naval Memorial Theater—would symbolize "clear sailing" for the American elm.

Just up the street, on Capitol Hill, visitors from Alaska and throughout the Lower 48 had gathered on the equinox and the first full day of spring that followed to lobby their representatives about the seriousness of global warming. I caught some of the rally, including presentations by three children who are devoting themselves to mitigating climate change. One fourteen-year-old girl has started an organization called "Pump 'Em Up!," devoted to getting people to pump up their tires to the proper pressure in order to save gas. She told the gathering at the foot of Capitol Hill that Connecticut has legislated that sellers of gas must provide free air pressure for motorists and that Florida and other states are considering similar legislation. My heart aches for this generation that will bear the burden of our excessive energy use. The young people gathered on the Hill sure seemed ready to embrace the challenge.

As much as I look forward to seeing Sophie and traveling to Spain, I almost hate to leave the magic of spring in Washington! Every patch of earth has its charm, starting with the pink hyacinth next to our front steps. Sugar-coated with ice and snow just a week ago, its small pink buds have bloomed from the base of the plant to the top of the stalk, perfuming our comings and goings. And all the daffodils in the yard that were snow-covered buds a mere week ago are now fully open. Robins, cardinals, and song sparrows are singing on this warm, wet, spring morning.

April 2: SPAIN TIME

WE ARRIVED HOME from Madrid last night, and I awake before dawn and drive to Boundary Bridge, where the robins are singing the planets and stars to sleep. As morning breaks, every budding tree along Rock Creek seems to hold a melodic robin. When I loop through the swamp trail, I hear spring peepers adding their background music to the arboreal tunefest. Pockets of early morning mist and fox musk cling to the creek's banks. Great blue herons rise from the shallows and flap their long gray wings through the gathering light.

As dawn breaks, I see a wild city park transformed. I have only been gone a week, but what a week it has been in Rock Creek Park. The ubiquitous spice-bush—not a favorite deer snack due to its strong flavor—is covered in a haze of fuzzy yellow flowers. The boxelders along the creek are blooming and leafing out, their golden flowers like dangling earrings, and their small emerging leaflets a pure lime-green. The skunk cabbage flowers have died back, but their unfurling upright leaves are nearly a foot tall and also the brightest color of lime. A happily surprising number of native ephemerals triumph amidst the Wordsworthian carpet of lesser celandine: The mottled leaves of the trout lily and an occasional yellow trout lily flower, nodding and not yet opened in the early light; spring beauties, still closed at dawn but blooming at a far more proper date than New Year's Day; Virginia bluebells, with their pink and purple buds, and a few fully open sky-blue bell-shaped flowers amidst the dangling bud clusters. The leaves of the mayapple are just starting to open, with their characteristic, curious umbrella-like action. These and other ephemeral wildflowers will exploit the spring sun of the budding woods before the canopy fills in above Rock Creek.

As I switchback into the upland woods, I find many white bloodroot flowers next to the winding trail ready to open, their lobed basal leaves wrapped around their short, upright flower-stalks. The bloodroot gets its name from the orange-red juice exuded by its root, juice which has been used by American Indian tribes for everything from a remedy for warts to a love charm. From the higher elevations, I can look down on the lime haze along the boxelder-lined creek. When I reach the Laurel Ledge, another chorus greets my ears: Toads! Lowly American toads making very untoadlike music—a high musical trill that rises from the water and fills the canopy. Rush hour on Beach Drive adds a distant backdrop to the music of the toads. As the toads sing and water droplets bead on the branchlets of the beech trees above the rocks, I start to unwind.

I am still on Spain's time and not in the best of moods. Jet-lagged, missing Sophie, and worried about my father-in-law, Bill, who—we discovered upon our return—is hospitalized with pneumonia. How I wish I could go back to a week ago, when our brown-eyed, dark-haired daughter emerged from the crowd at the Madrid airport and flew into our arms! We spent a wondrous week with Sophie, as she expertly translated for us while sharing her medieval stone city of Salamanca.

I did what every naturalist does when traveling with family: Became frustrated. Lacking the proper books and operating on borrowed time when holding up an outing while I tried to identify a tree or wildflower, I hastily noted what I could. Each morning I hurried down the cobblestone streets and across a 2,000-year-old Roman footbridge spanning the Rio Tormes. Wood storks flapped overhead with twigs gathered from the wetlands for their steepletop nests. In Salamanca, every historic steeple holds a stork's nest. Magpies flashed past. Willows were just showing green, and ash buds were breaking, much as they were doing back home along Rock Creek and the Potomac River. I noted similarities and differences in the spring vegetation and recognized many cultivated trees in Salamanca and Madrid because of my research for *City of Trees*. I was surprised to discover that the boxelder, or ash-leaf maple, a common tree in Rock Creek Park and often considered something of a weed at home, was planted on the streets of Salamanca and in botanical gardens in Madrid. I smiled when I saw a giant sequoia, one of California's two official state trees, planted next to a cathedral dating back to the twelfth century.

The trees of Salamanca weren't just for show and shade. There weren't many of them in that golden-stoned city that predates the Inquisition and still glimmers with a bit of the ancient Moorish influence. But those few trees were put to surprising utilitarian use: Laundry lines were strung between the plane trees.

The itinerary Sophie planned for us included a family hike and picnic along the Rio Tormes in a park well outside the city, where she read Lorca poetry to us in Spanish under a sprawling evergreen oak tree that I ached to identify. Sophie's Spanish host "mother," Charo, later identified the tree for me as *las encinas*, and a Google search led me to the Holm or holly oak—*Quercus ilex.*

When we landed at home last night, I noticed the spring explosion with a pit in my stomach. I have *one* season to get book-quality photos of the flowering trees of Washington, and all the early magnolias, cherries, and other *Prunus* species bloomed while we were away. This morning I tried to photograph Yoshino cherry blossoms in the Kenwood neighborhood, famed for its cherry-lined streets. No matter that I faithfully used my tripod and shaded the blossoms with an umbrella: The slightest trembling breeze messed up every shot. I discovered that no amount of pleading with the wind would yield the desired result.

I'm jetlagged and worried about Bill and miss Sophie (did I say that already?), and I'm suffering from reentry blues. I feel disconnected from friends and can't bring myself to make the calls that I owe and/or that would make me feel better. Jim is packing for Lincoln, Nebraska, and then he'll go straight to New Hampshire to be with his parents. I wish I could go, too, but school starts for Jesse tomorrow.

Seeing Sophie thriving in a foreign culture brought joy and pride to my heart. But I ached on the trip home every time I saw a baby or a little girl in the arms of her parents. Jim and Jesse miss Sophie, too. I know it will take time to get reoriented, to feel like myself again. Rock Creek will help. And maybe the winds will die down enough that I can get some usable pictures for my book.

The full "pink" moon—a folk name for the April moon referring to moss pink, a wildflower that blooms this month—will rise in a short while. Our neighbors are getting ready to celebrate the first Seder across the street. I will think of my Jewish ancestors on this Passover night and try not to feel so achy and tired and blue. I am saying prayers for Bill.

April 6: SNOW PETALS AND THE REAL THING

I CAME OUT of my reentry cocoon to meet my new friend, Cecily, at Boundary Bridge yesterday. She walked from the bridge toward my car in a white knitted hat, parka, and gloves. "I keep trying to tell myself these are cherry blossom petals," she said, as snow twirled around her. It flurried again this morning, and we may get a dusting tonight and tomorrow. Everyone is complaining except me. What could be more poetic than snowflakes flying with the cherry blossom petals at the Tidal Basin, Kenwood, and other neighborhoods throughout the Washington area?

Cecily was on my Audubon field trip to Boundary Bridge in January, and yesterday we noted the irony of the spring beauty flowers, which were tightly closed against the cold on this April morning, although they were strangely and disturbingly open on that much warmer January day. Cecily was as delighted as I with the native wildflowers triumphing amidst the smothering celandine. The nodding yellow bells of the trout lily were still tightly closed, but I bet they opened on one of the warmer days this week when I was away from Rock Creek Park and negotiating with the wind during my magnolia and cherry photo adventures. Like two doting mothers, Cecily and I bent down to admire the round clusters of pink and purple Virginia bluebell buds and the occasional open "little boy blue" flower.

The boxelders had advanced in their lime-green and gold explosion, and high up in the canopy the young leaves of the tulip trees glimmered a brilliant green. The ironwood leaf buds were just beginning to swell, with a few embryonic leaves unfurling. Two of the common names of this tree—ironwood and musclewood—could not be more expressive. Knocking on the trunk is like knocking on iron or steel. Beavers occasionally try to fell them, no doubt seeking their durability for home and dam construction. When we lived on Seneca Creek, I'd find partially chewed ironwood trunks. I could picture the poor beaver giving up and dragging himself or herself home at dawn with an aching jaw. The alternative name "musclewood" refers to the sinewy shape of the trunk, like a pumped-up young body with "cut" muscles. The tree is also known as hornbeam and blue beech.

Cecily leaned over a small ironwood by the creek, noting its smooth gray bark—not yet "muscled" up—and bursting leaf buds. The young tree was perfectly formed, and we sprang into maternal mode again. Why was this tree so pleasing to us? "I guess what it comes down to is that all babies are cute," Cecily concluded.

I asked Cecily, an accomplished birder, about the nesting habits of Rock Creek's birds. The kingfishers nest in the banks of the creek, she said; the wood ducks in tree cavities. Hmmm, that seemed counter-intuitive. She explained that the great blue herons are colonial nesters. Together we wondered where Rock Creek's herons nested as we watched one of the tall birds stand Zen-like in the shallows, the blue-gray neck feathers of its breeding plumes ruffled by the cold wind. When we spotted some male goldfinches just beginning to glimmer with the yellow of mating season, I asked if they weren't a little late and shouldn't they be yellower by now? "No," replied Cecily. "They don't nest until summer. They use thistle down for their nests, and they have to wait for the thistle to flower and fruit." How efficient! A bird that dines on thistle seeds and uses the down of the same plant as nesting material.

When I came home from Spain, I had an exuberant message on my answering machine from Neal Fitzpatrick, the executive director of the Audubon Naturalist Society. The brand-new fish ladder at Peirce Mill, downstream from Boundary Bridge, and ten years in the making, was working! "Our phone chain for herring observers has been activated," exclaimed Neal, "and the first wave of spawning herring—the alewives—have made it past P Street and through the fish ladder!" Even *The Washington Post* took note of the fish tale, with David A. Fahrenthold reporting on March 31st, the day before our return, in his story, "Rock Creek Fish Head Home Again—With Obstacles Removed, Herring Return to Spawning Area":

For centuries, this region's spring was punctuated by a series of massive migrations of fish—shad, herring, striped bass— that crowded the area's rivers and provided a bounty for local fishermen. Even in shallow Rock Creek, biologists say, hundreds of thousands of alewives and blueback herring, a nearly identical cousin, swam upstream in an attempt to return to their birthplaces.

But then, people blocked the way. They built fords, using rocks or concrete to make the creek bottom passable for vehicles. They laid sewer pipes from bank to bank. And they built the Peirce Mill dam, as the tale is told, to provide some scenery for customers at a tearoom in the old mill building.

The waterfall created by the dam is about twelve feet tall— beyond insurmountable for a foot-long alewife. After a journey from the ocean, through Chesapeake Bay, up the Potomac River and about 4.5 miles up the creek, the fish would leave their eggs next to the dam . . .

This week, when [Bill] Yeaman [of the National Park Service] spotted those fish on the other side of the dam—which can now be circumvented via a fish 'ladder'—it was a signal that one of Washington's oldest spring rituals was on its way back.

'I was witnessing something that hadn't happened for over 100 years,' Yeaman said yesterday, standing by the side of the creek. 'That's pretty amazing.'

Pretty amazing indeed. When Cecily and I reached the uplands of Rock Creek Park, where most of the trees were still bare above the layer of blooming creek-side boxelders, I made a discovery that was tangentially related to the good news about the fish. I saw a small tree displaying some white flowers with thin petals unfurling amidst copper-colored young leaves: The first native shadbush I had found near Boundary Bridge! I had been looking, but every early-blooming rose family tree I'd previously found had turned out to be a non-native cherry. I ran my hands up the smooth, lightly striated gray bark as my eyes drank in the subtle colorful relationship between creamy blossom and copper foliage in the branches of the small tree. The shadbush is the first native tree to bloom in the area's woodlands. Many springtimes ago, when naturalists first discovered the timely magic of email, my friend, Anne Sturm, another birder, sent me this message from her farm in Barnesville: "There's a brown thrasher in my shadbush." This was a thrill that Cecily instantly "got" when I shared the memory with her. The brown thrasher, related to the catbird and the mockingbird, is perfectly color-coordinated with the early spring leaves and flowers of the shadbush.

Shadbush or *Amelanchier*, usually more of a small tree in our woodlands, although some species are shrubby, got its name because it blooms during the running of the shad in eastern rivers and streams. Thanks to the new fish ladder, perhaps the shad will be running in significant numbers again in Rock Creek. The shadbush has another common name: Serviceberry. Traditionally, funeral services couldn't be held in snowed-in mountain hollows until the preacher could make it up the road in the early spring, the time when the tree bloomed. This year, the name serviceberry is taking on new meaning. I think everyone is ready to hold winter's funeral service under the flowering serviceberries and move into spring–even me. With a real snow now predicted for tonight, Cecily later emails me: "Listen, is that inner snow-child of yours going to be satisfied soon?"

April 16: WIND CHILD

FOR THE RECORD, I have no inner "wind-child." Not only do I want the wind to die down so I can get on with my close-up photography, but I just plain don't like wind very much, unless it's a tickling ocean zephyr or a bracing autumn breeze. Wind before storms can be exciting, but relentless semistrong wind, or really scary winds like we are having today in the wake of *yet another* nor'easter, are my second least favorite weather type, behind drought.

Yesterday, New York City endured the second wettest day of historical record, with seven and a half inches of rain that turned streets into rivers in New York and New Jersey. Parts of Rock Creek Park are also closed to traffic today, with trees down throughout the area and many schools closed. And we are under a high-wind warning for the rest of the day.

With the exception of a handful of warm days, this spring has been unusually cold. For the past ten days, temperatures have been way below normal, and they are expected to remain in the 50s and low 60s through the week. In Vermont, where winter came four to six weeks late this year (as it did throughout the Northeast), April snow is piled above the windows of my sister's farmhouse kitchen.

A rumbling sentiment is stirring throughout the world. The weather is changing in disturbing ways, bringing melting glaciers and drought to some, violent storms to others. Things are off-kilter and no longer predictable. People everywhere are worried. In temperate zones, the four seasons have always served as a metaphor for life. After the withering winter cold comes the promise of spring and then the ease of summer. We endure late autumn's stripping winds and winter's deep freeze, knowing they are the prelude to another cycle of birth and renewal.

Everyone living in the temperate zone depends on these cycles, from farmers and poets to butterflies such as zebra swallowtails, which time the laying of their eggs on pawpaw trees just prior to the emergence of their leaves. Just as the caterpillars hatch, tasty young leaves unfurl for their dining pleasure. Evolution—of human sentiment and thought and of biological life itself—depends on the steady progression of predictable seasons. But stray too far from the cyclical script, and all is up for grabs. During the last Ice Age, which ended some 10,000 to 12,000 years ago, Earth was only a few degrees cooler than it is these days. And a rise of just a few degrees Fahrenheit, which is predicted by even the most modest climate-change models to occur by the end of the century, will have a dramatic effect on life and its interdependent cycles of plant pollination and fruiting, animal birth and food foraging.

But, in its slightly off-kilter way, life in my world goes on. My parents were here for most of last week, and I put them on a plane to New Hampshire yesterday so they could get home ahead of the storm (which they did, barely). My mom has written a wonderful children's book based on a true-life story of a relationship between a quarter horse and a tabby cat who rode around on his back. Her visit included giving a talk to the primary grades of Jesse's school.

My dad, a lifelong birder, joined me for the second in my series of Audubon walks: "A Year at Boundary Bridge."

If my field-trip participants could see me prepare for these forays, their confidence in my authority might be lost. My last-minute panics about knowledge gaps—What is that non-indigenous *Aesculus*? Are those male or female flowers hanging from the boxelder? What exactly is an alewife?—send me flailing to my neighbor botanist's kitchen and to meet hastily with the Audubon Naturalist Society's director at the fish ladder. I paw through field guides and surf the Internet, scouring any source I can find for answers to my questions about everything from butterflies to local history. If a geologist passed in front of my door, I would not hesitate to run out and buttonhole him or her about the Laurel Formation, the Kensington Tonalite, and the Rock Creek Shear Zone.

But, after the scramble I take a few deep breaths and then I morph into a smiling and confident naturalist, eager to share my knowledge and love for Rock Creek Park. On Saturday my group and I (including many repeat participants and my dad) gathered for our spring field trip at Boundary Bridge on a morning about as cool and cloudy as January 13th, the date of our last trip. As I had done on that winter day, which also threatened rain, I asked everyone to look up into the branches so we could observe the changes in the trees.

"Remember the rickrack pattern of the American elm's winter twigs and buds?" I asked the group. I told them that those buds had burst into sepia-toned flowers in March and now the branchlets bear the small notched winged samaras typical of elms. Across the creek, a large American sycamore still held onto some of last year's round bundles of achenes, but were fewer, because many had broken up and been launched on the wind and down the creek, where the fuzzy brown hairs attached to the fruits help them to bob along on the water's surface. Directing our collective gaze to a tall tulip tree just north of the bridge, I pointed out a similar story in its high-up limbs. A few upright samaras still clung to the branchlets, but many had been carried off by the wind, replaced by the tiny tulip-shaped leaves. Nearly everything about this tree is tulip-shaped, I pointed out to my group: Its fruit, the outlines of its leaves, and the flowers that will appear in late April and early May.

The ironwoods next to the bridge were covered with spring catkins and infant tiny-toothed leaves. Only the peely-barked, cinnamon-colored river birch looked unchanged, its winter catkins holding tight, its leaves still curled in the bud.

For the next five hours we explored Rock Creek Park, stopping at every new wildflower, where I explained its botanical diagnostics, herbal history, and family characteristics. My dad, who is accustomed to the excitement of birders chasing down birds, said he had never seen people *run* to see plants, which—unlike birds—aren't going anywhere. This group was eager and appreciative, and the plants didn't disappoint. By morning's end the trout lilies and spring beauties, which nod during cool mornings, were fully open. The pink and purple bluebell buds seemed to be popping and maturing to blue before our eyes, a few mayapple buds were showing amidst the umbrella leaves, and the first Jack-in-the-pulpits unfurled, their tri-parted leaves still hugging their lengthening stalks. We saw yellow and purple violets and cut-leaved toothwort. Early saxifrage (its name means "rock breaker") and star chickweed were blooming in their precarious perches on blue-gray outcrops of the Laurel Formation. Pawpaw and bladdernut flower buds were beginning to open.

I showed them a trick I learned the previous week from my botanist friend, Cris Fleming. "How do you tell a male spicebush from a female at this point in time?" (The spicebush is a "dioecious" plant, with male and female flowers on separate plants.) If you lightly touch the small yellow flowers between thumb and forefinger, the male flowers will instantly fall off, while the females won't. The males were done with their reproductive work, but the females had just begun. Their ovaries will swell and become green, single-seeded berry-like drupes that turn scarlet in autumn, serving as food for mammals and birds. I shared something else I first learned from Cris years ago. The Jack-in-the-pulpit can perform a neat sex-change trick. As Cris explained it (with an enigmatic smile), the Jack-in-the-pulpit bears female flowers and produces red-berried fruit when it's feeling strong and full of energy, but then it needs to take a break from the work of fruiting, so it reverts to male flowers for a restful season or two. The "girls" in the group seemed to enjoy this gender lore more than the guys, and I heard them laughing over the Jack-in-the-pulpits and saw them testing spicebush flowers as we wound down our trail.

The group was getting to know each other and good energy and shared information abounded. Someone explained that the pink stripes inside a spring beauty flower serve as "runways" for pollinators. Kneeling over a candy-striped blossom with my hand-lens in front of her eye, a young grandmother named Nancy discovered the wonder of a flower up close for the first time and her rapture was contagious. "*That's* what Georgia O'Keeffe saw," I said to her as she got off her knees with a flushed smiling face. Later I heard this same instant hand-lens convert exclaim over the inside of a wild ginger blossom as she was lying on the ground in front of the small brown-and-white flower: "It looks like a cathedral ceiling!"

Some rare yellow trilliums were growing next to the trail, a southern Appalachian species that was probably planted in, or next to, the park where it has spread, although not all botanists are certain of this. I scoured the trail-side for a flower that was fully open so the group could experience its lemon fragrance. When I found one, a young woman said, "It doesn't smell like lemons; it smells like Lemon Pledge." She was absolutely right! Some lucky pollinator has undoubtedly circled or wandered in, guided by the alluring fragrance of furniture polish.

The birding was less than stellar that day, but we heard the *keeyer keeyer* of a red-shouldered hawk above us as the large predator wheeled into view above the wood frog/spring peeper pond. We didn't see a rumored black-crowned night heron (news passed on by a dog walker), but we did see and hear the belted kingfisher and, most exciting of all, a Louisiana waterthrush—a large warbler that did a weaving dance up the creek bed and then landed on a low-hanging branch.

Marney Bruce, a friend and a wildflower enthusiast who still sees the world through the sharp eyes of a child, discovered a sassafras blooming in the woods, a favorite tree of mine that I may never have spotted on my own. I showed the group one rue anemone or windflower, a delicate, white buttercup-family wildflower that grows on a wiry thin stalk and trembles in the slightest breeze. Then they showed *me* more than a dozen. One of my participants solved a frustrating botanical mystery for me when she identified a non-native shrub I've puzzled over for two years as jetbead, a member of the rose family with uncharacteristic four-parted flowers and opposite leaves (most rose family members have five-parted flowers and alternate leaves). Just as two heads are better than one, many eyes in the woods see many more wonders.

We stopped next to what I call the Skunk Cabbage Swamp and marveled over the knee-high green leaves that replaced the wine red spathes of winter. Just beyond the Skunk Cabbage Swamp grew clumps of daffodils. This is the story of Rock Creek Park: Skunk cabbage and daffodils, the wild and the cultivated growing side by side in one of the nation's oldest and largest wooded urban national parks.

A highlight of the trip occurred as we had lunch on the Laurel Ledge. As my dad ate his sandwich, I asked him to tell his Marine Corps sandwich story, prefacing the query with the observation that, perhaps, you need to be five years old to find it amusing. He told the story, and apparently you don't. He was a young marine stationed at Camp LeJeune, North Carolina, where I was born. My mom had made him a BLT sandwich, and he had carried it into the field during maneuvers. It was scorching hot. After several hours in the field, he was starving. He opened the sandwich container and discovered that the sandwich was covered with ants. He opened the bread and peered inside, where he saw dozens of ants crawling over the bacon, tomato, and lettuce. He was hungry and there was nothing to do but close it up and take the first bite!

The group loved it. Not every naturalist brings along her father to tell ant sandwich stories. It was a good day.

April 18: A GRIMMER RECORD AND A HEALING EVENING

WHILE NEW YORK CITY was recovering from the second wettest day on record, a grimmer record was being set in Blacksburg, Virginia. A disturbed young student opened fire on the Virginia Tech campus, killing thirty-two students and professors and ultimately himself, the deadliest shooting of its kind in American history. One of the dark sides of American culture is the way a person can move through life here in a state of alienation. Occasionally, something snaps, and those around the person pay, in this case with their lives.

I feel worried about how Sophie will take the news, and I am concerned about Jim's father's ongoing health problems. Despite these worldly troubles, as soon as rush hour calms down a bit, I must head over to the National Arboretum to negotiate with my camera and the wind. There was no talking to the gusts in the wake of the nor'easter, but today we're back to a pattern I recognize—*flutterflutterflutter-withatinybreaktosnapapicture-flutterflutterflutter.* I do my best.

In the wake of a seemingly senseless tragedy, I meditated yesterday on how much we create our own realities *when and if* we are able to. We are blessed when we are able to do that.

Late in the day, I roused myself to go to the Adams Morgan neighborhood to serve dinner at Christ House, the health clinic and shelter with which my new church, All Souls Unitarian, is associated. I found a place to park a few blocks from the shelter. While walking steeply uphill to it, I marveled over the topography of this part of town, high up on the escarpment above Rock Creek.

Serving the evening meal was meditative and rewarding. I was the only volunteer in the kitchen, and a wizard named Chris was already painting bread with garlic and parsley butter when I arrived. I took over and tried to do my graceful best with the paintbrush. Chris was a man of few words but he got his message across. After I finished slicing and painting the garlic bread and sprinkling it with cheese, he handed me a bag of apples and several bunches of grapes and asked what I might do with them. When I offered to make fruit salad, he filled a large bowl with orange juice and told me to go for it.

It was all business in the kitchen, preparing the evening meal for forty people, but I peeked over the serving counter to the dining room beyond, where men and a few women were trickling in. The tables were set with plaid tablecloths, plates, and napkins. Easter lilies were massed along one wall with a wooden cross in the middle, which was draped with a white Easter banner. I felt the presence of divine love in the place.

I remembered the many elaborate crucifixes I'd seen in Spain just prior to Holy Week and how repelled I'd felt by the pervasive images of a crucified Christ on the cross and the violent history associated with the spread of Christianity. Our Easter sermon at All Souls, delivered by a visiting minister from Oregon, focused on how Unitarians don't really know what to do with Easter, since it's not the part of the Jesus story that most resonates with them.

And yet, as I stood in the shelter's kitchen, separating grapes from their stems and quartering apples, I had a very different sense of the crucifixion emanating from the simple wooden cross in this healing atmosphere. I could intuit the value of having a personal relationship with Jesus and how his suffering would comfort someone who is severely suffering in the here and now. Then I recalled an ex-nun and religious teacher whom I heard interviewed on NPR a few years ago. She was asked if she worshiped a god or goddess and if it mattered. She said the important thing was to develop a personal relationship to the divine, in any way that works for the individual. I thought about the divine feminine presence with whom I commune every day, and for the first time in my life—despite being christened in a Greek Orthodox Church and raised in a Protestant Congregational one—I really "got" the importance of Jesus and what a *personal* embodiment of divine love he is in people's lives. I wonder if that meditation made it into the fruit salad, which I scooped into small bowls that were then delivered to the tables by volunteers working in the dining room.

Tall, with dreadlocks and an inscrutable face, Chris was a strong, steady presence beside me. After the meal, I asked him what I could do to help with the clean-up. He glanced around, waved a wet dishrag, and said, "Just get in where you fit in." For the next half hour, I did just that, washing the serving dishes, cleaning counters, putting food back in the fridge. I contemplated the brilliance of the phrase and its philosophy: *Just get in where you fit in.* If only the disturbed shooter at Virginia Tech had found a way to fit in.

When I left Christ House, several of the men sitting in the courtyard out front smiled and thanked me. As I walked back down the hill, I reflected on the evening meal and how it was like any evening meal: The preparation, the serving, the eating, the clean-up. I picked the stems from the grapes as carefully as I do when making a fruit salad for my family, and I made a mental note to add parsley to my garlic bread for future family meals. I thought about how it felt more familial and communal to be in a setting larger than the small family one, where Jesse and I often dine in front of Seinfeld reruns. When my kids were little, I often wished for a communal dining room and shared labor, thinking about how exhausting it is for every mother or father to prepare every meal, start to finish, for her or his small family.

And yet my meditations had nothing to do with the lives of the men and the few women I served dinner to. I know nothing of their lives and health issues or why they were eating dinner at the clinic shelter. I only knew that I'd prepared some food, and they'd eaten it. Perhaps, when I do it again and again, I will get to know some of them a little, if any remain at Christ House long-term.

Walking back down the steep Adams Morgan street, I wondered about how many refugees there will be, like those unfortunate people at Christ House, if we don't stem the tide of global poverty, global warming, and our human catastrophes. Last night's dinner might become an even more familiar scene throughout the world. Kitchens serving meals to the displaced and homeless. The simple ritual of sharing food, a universal symbol of our humanity.

I drove home through Rock Creek Park, stopping at the fish ladder near the historic Peirce Mill. Yesterday I received an email from the executive director of the Audubon Naturalist Society with the header: "No fish." Apparently, the herring run has stalled—he saw no fish on his Saturday field trip—and I gather no one knows why. I, too, saw nothing moving in the muddy creek flow.

As I drove north from Tilden Street over the quaint, century-old Boulder Bridge and along the rockiest stretch of Rock Creek, I fell into a reverie. Shadbush, sassafras, dogwood, and redbud bloomed along the rocky hillsides. The pastel flowers of these small trees glowed in the evening light, offset by the wintry backdrop of the taller and still bare and barely leafing canopy trees. I could see mayapple leaves along the stream and—unfortunately—the leafing shoots of Japanese knotweed, an aggressive invasive.

When I got to Boundary Bridge, I stepped out of the car, where I heard the music of the creek flow and the sweet calls of a few spring peepers. I walked over the arcing bridge to see the Virginia bluebells, now almost fully open. I had just driven through the heart of the city, almost all the way from Christ House to my house, and I could have been driving through the wilds of Vermont. I probably missed some great urban drama when I followed the woodland route, but it is my preferred way.

I chose this route home. When we are able, for good or for ill, we choose our own routes. It is a privilege to be able to do so. May those of us who are able to choose our direction reach out to those whose options are cut off, for whatever reason, as ours may one day be. And may we all *just get in where we fit in.*

YESTERDAY, EARTH DAY, I witnessed an ordinary event that I had never before witnessed in more than half a century on this planet. Perhaps the author of the *Wind in the Willows* put more natural history into the character of Toad than most of us can appreciate, for last evening I saw something that clearly resembled the fictional character's manic behavior.

Jim and I had just meandered around the Boundary Bridge creek-swamp loop, through the knee-high bottomland bluebells, beneath tall trees surrounded with fairy rings of spring beauty and trout lily. We passed acres of brilliant skunk cabbage leaves under flowering crabapple boughs. Canines of all sizes filled the Rock Creek woods with the sounds of their diving and splashing and bounding through the water. Jim and I wandered off-trail and into the swamp, where we discovered hundreds of yellow trillium, their lemon scent infusing the air. As dusk approached, we watched seven spiffily plumed wood ducks eating plants in the vernal pond. We found vast patches of wild ginger and celandine poppies (not related to lesser celandine), their yellow-orange flowers closed for the evening. Jack-in-the-pulpits, still a tender green, were unfurling their triparted leaves, and the umbrellas of mayapple leaves adorned the rich, alluvial forest floor. A few wild blue phlox were mixed in with the bluebells. The tree canopy was seriously leafing out after a warm spring day. Everywhere we walked we could hear toads singing, their music rising above the sounds of the lower-pitched creek flow, interspersed with the calls of a few spring peepers.

Jim, looking handsome and celebratory in a pink polo shirt, felt compelled to return to his office to finish up some work before today's trip to Nebraska, but I couldn't tear myself away from the twilit magic of the swamp. The new leaves, high up in the canopy, were gathering a peach glow from the setting sun, much as bare twigs and branches had glowed peach on a cold Saint Patty's Day eve.

As I walked with Jim back toward Boundary Bridge and his car, we passed a smaller vernal pool filled with the sounds of toads. I said good-bye to him there so I could station myself near the action.

Well! All was quiet for a few moments, and then the racket restarted. I soon sighted several warty male toads, sitting in gorilla poses on logs and sticks, from which they broadcast their genetic attributes. Some were reddish, some mud-brown, and their sizes varied. But all had huge, gray-white bubblegum throats, swelled with toad-song. The collective musical trill one hears from a distance bore little relation to the sound up close. As with the spring peepers, the up-close-and-personal call is far shriller than the distant, disembodied collective sound. And toads, which I had only seen calmly hopping or sitting in my innocent former life, turned out to be far from calm. I witnessed several "king of the mount" dramas as one male toad knocked another off the high ground. A particular midstream log perch seemed especially desirable, and no toad held it for long.

There was much thrashing about in the water, and I couldn't tell if it represented combat, mating activity, or both. But these toads were fast, swiftly back-kicking to sneak up on a potential mate (or rival?) from the rear. And, as it grew darker, their gold eye-rims brightened, accentuating the mania of the amphibious frenzy. I was stunned. I'd never seen toads in the *water* before, let alone in full, flailing mating ritual. Later I learned that the mating behavior of frogs and toads is called "amplexus": The male squeezes the female from behind so that she will release her eggs into the water, where he fertilizes them.

The toad song grew louder and louder, and so did the peepers in a nearby pool and throughout the swamp. The last few human and wet canine visitors straggled back to their cars, and I was the only representative of the indoor species left at Boundary Bridge.

And then I heard something that trumped even the screaming toads. Barred owls, two of them, with their loud, deep, barking hoots: *Who cooks for you? Who cooks for you, all?!*

I followed the owls' sounds into the swamp. The evening was becoming cool and dark, and it felt like a country night. The lacey new leaves and flowers above me still held a touch of peach-green, and they framed a high, waxing crescent moon. Bright planets and stars switched on. The sky was perfectly clear, and a few bats energetically circled among the trees. I did what I often do at Boundary Bridge—pinch myself as I try to wrap my head around the reality that I'm actually standing, sitting, lying, or walking in the wooded heart of a large city and the nation's capital.

I was walking on a continuous carpet of lesser celandine, and the scene was one of such wild beauty that I embraced the celandine not just in my forced *What would Wordsworth think?* way, but truly. I reached a place where I was circled by trees, with the moon at the top of the sky. There was nothing to do but dance. I danced and twirled and thanked every divine presence that might have had a hand in the perfect wonder of the moment. I will forever think of that flat, tree-ringed ground between the swamp and Rock Creek as a dance hall.

The owls, which had been silent since their initial calling, sang again, full and deep, and then I saw one flap its large wings through the canopy and into the screaming toad night. Soon the second one flew through the canopy. I bushwhacked back to the creek trail, where toads were doing what toads usually do. *Hop hop hop, sit, hop hop hop, sit.* I had to step carefully to avoid the toads in the trail. As I returned to a more familiar world, I wondered if the frenzied gold-eyed mania I'd witnessed had been nothing but an Earth Day dream.

April 26: BECOMING

YESTERDAY, DURING ANOTHER evening visit to Boundary Bridge, I became intrigued by the word *becoming*. We usually use it as an adjective as in: "That scarf is *becoming* on you." But, as a noun, my dictionary defines it under the heading "Philosophy": "1. A coming into existence. 2. A change from one state to another."

At Rock Creek right now, everything is in a state of becoming. The deciduous trees are becoming leafy. This is something I don't want to miss. Last Saturday my friend, Terrie Daniels, and I lay on the Meditation Rock side-by-side for more than an hour, watching walkers and runners drift through the upland woods like apparitions on the trail. Our close, fifteen-year friendship was born and has been nurtured in a shared love of nature. The trees above us were swollen in bud, the buds whitened or goldened by the afternoon sun and cerulean sky. The kingfisher did a down-the-creek fly-by, and a great blue heron touched down in the shallows near the opposite shore. As we climbed back up the trail from the Meditation Rock, Terrie and I admired the swelling pink buds of the wild azalea called pinxter flower that crowns the Laurel Ledge.

Yesterday, after two hot days, the canopy had become so filled out that the Boundary Bridge woods were almost unrecognizable. The pinxter was leafing and flowering, in time-lapse trickery. And all the tree buds that had been merely swollen four days earlier were *becoming* leaves.

This process of becoming is something you don't want to miss. Each species leafs out in its own way. The new leaves of the tulip tree resemble babies' hands reaching for the sky. The beech buds unfurl so artfully that every creative person should study them: The pointed reddish bud births a twirled leaf that is downy-white as it spirals out of its bud scales. Unlike the stiff, uplifted new leaves of the tulip tree, the fuzzy beech leaves hang gracefully downward like dancers' skirts. They will eventually hold themselves on a horizontal plane, as will the tulip tree's leaves, each becoming level from its opposite, initial direction.

All the oaks are in the process of becoming, both in leaf and flower, each individual red, white, black, chestnut or scarlet oak leaf perfectly formed in miniature and the male flowers hanging in graceful aments, loose dangling clusters that ripple with the wind. The willow oaks, a species with unlobed leaves, bear slender blades resembling spruce needles when they first emerge.

Perhaps nothing is as poignant in its *becoming* as a fern. Last year's Christmas fern fronds now lie flat to the ground, changed from a shiny evergreen to a faded greenish-brown. But, in their midst, the new Christmas fern fiddleheads are beginning to unfurl, a burst of curly newness in the center of the fading and dying elder fronds. The delicate, deciduous New York ferns are unfolding near Riley Spring south of Boundary Bridge, their leaves a light spring-green. As I pass the unfurling fronds, I think of the mnemonics that help me remember them. Each little Christmas fern pinna or leaflet is "shaped like a Christmas stocking." The New York fern frond tapers not only to the apex, but also to the base. "New Yorkers burn their candles at both ends."

Several small tree and shrub species are now blossoming in Rock Creek Park. A few flowering dogwoods are blooming—wedding-white against the greening woods—survivors of the anthracnose blight that has killed and sickened many native dogwoods. And purplish-brown flowers dangle like tropical jewels from the sparse branchlets of the pawpaw trees along the creek. When I was a young girl, I envied my sister, Ellie, because she seemed to have a song written about her with the lines: "Where oh where is pretty little Ellie? Where oh where is pretty little Ellie? Down in the pawpaw patch." Pawpaw flowers and emerging leaves look tropical for a reason; the tree is a temperate zone representative of the largely tropical custard apple family. The savory fruit—a cross between a banana and a mango in texture, appearance, and taste—is soon snatched up by wildlife in the early fall. Or by pretty little Ellie "pickin' up pawpaws and puttin' em in a basket."

One of Boundary Bridge's pawpaw patches is bordered by a grove of bladdernuts, a small tree or large shrub named for its papery bladder-shaped fruit. Stephanie Mason, the senior naturalist at the Audubon Naturalist Society, calls these fruits "nature's maracas." Give them a good shake, and the dry seeds inside rattle musically. A few of the inflated brown fall fruits still remain on the bladdernut trees, which are now flowering. The clustered dangling flowers are small, greenish-white, and charmingly bell-shaped. The trifoliate leaves are emerging with the flowers.

Viburnums are blooming, too. Some, such as doublefile viburnum are not native. But my favorite native viburnum—blackhaw—is just coming into bloom, its roundish white flower clusters borne above its cherry-like leaves. The bark of this smallish tree or tall shrub is broken into little blocks ("alligator bark"), and its trunk is almost as sculpted-looking as musclewood. The summer-fall fruits, which ripen from green to blue-black, are popular with birds and mammals, including me.

As the canopy reaches toward full leafiness, waves of warblers flock through the park. I'm trying to learn their songs, but it's a steep learning curve for someone who "will always think of birds as visitors to my plants," as my friend, Tina Thieme Brown, likes to say. But I know the song of one bird intimately, and I eagerly anticipate it each spring. This bird returns to Rock Creek just before May Day, its song resembling an emanation from Pan's flute. When the wood thrush is back, early spring is over and high spring is *becoming*. Yesterday I heard a wood thrush singing in the park.

SPRING RAIN IS FALLING, the sort of rain that Maryland farmers call "poor man's rain." A gentle soaking rain that's good for the soil, the crops, the trees, and even the creek. I say "even the creek," because one of the most painful things about our over-developed part of the world is the way rain affects our waterways. Heavy rains rush over impervious surfaces such as roads, roofs, and parking lots, pouring toxic stormwater run-off and heavy sediment loads into Rock Creek, the Potomac River, and Chesapeake Bay. Several years ago we had an extremely wet spring and early summer. At the time, unlike most people, I rejoiced in a world that grew lusher each day. But later I learned that those rains, which should have been healing and replenishing, brought further damage to an already imperiled Chesapeake Bay. I would like to think of rain as healing, and today I will, although hail and damaging winds are threatened for later in the day.

For the first time in recent memory I have a clear calendar. I know I am nearly alone in Washington in the way I am able to celebrate this day of rain. I have a few windows open to the spring chill, and I can hear the sounds of song sparrows, white-throated sparrows, and cardinals above the steady rainfall. I'm sitting in our sunroom near the bird feeder, listening to the rain dance on the skylights. Mozart is playing, and I've filled the crockpot with split peas, onions, carrots, and celery. As a freelance writer, working alone in my home office, I've found that one of the best ways to keep myself company on rainy or snowy days is to make soup, letting the aromas simmer through the house all day. No photography today. Not anything but communion with the greening world. The pansies my friend, Nancy Strahler, planted in our garden on Sunday look cheerful, as only pansies can, and all the perennials are fully leafed and reaching toward flowering. When you open the front door, a Japanese flowering cherry rains pink petals that land in graceful patterns on the walkway.

A visiting rabbi delivered the Earth Day sermon at All Souls last Sunday. He urged the congregation to do something occasionally that is very difficult for us to do. Try doing nothing, he said. It will be good for you and good for our Earth. Today the rain is gently falling, and I am quietly doing nothing but rejoicing in the rainfall.

I just opened an email from pretty little Ellie, far from the pawpaw patch, in her Vermont farmhouse's kitchen. She writes: "It is one of those cool, rainy spring days but the Earth is unwinding like a surprise ball with all of her delights; sound of stream, robin in the mounting light, green lawns, forsythia, daffodils and hyacinths." Our gentle "poor man's rain" has reached Vermont and my eloquent sister's rooftop as surely as a nor'easter.

April 28: MOONSHADOW

I WENT BACK to Boundary Bridge last evening with Jim, and we experienced immediate drama in the singing peepers, hooting owls, and flute-like song of the wood thrush. Jim was quite taken with the increased leafiness of the woods since his visit on the Night of the Toads. (No toads call at all near Boundary Bridge now, so perhaps that party's over, although I continue to hear toads in our neighborhood.) The trout lilies have withered, the lesser celandine is winding down, but the forest floor is still adorned with Virginia bluebells and pink spring beauties, which close at the end of the day. The lemon-scented trilliums continue to exude their citric scents, and more and more Jack-in-the-pulpits are breaking through the lesser celandine. One flower that shines as its more glamorous neighbors fade is the star chickweed. This sprawling plant, thriving in Rock Creek's upland woods just above the floodplain, has bright white flowers with five petals that are so deeply cleft they look like ten. Star chickweed seems to spring from the rocks.

Jim and I breathed in the moseying freedom of nighttime at the creek. The dark clouds of the rainy day broke up, and a waxing flower moon, two thirds full, beamed through the canopy. I brought my binoculars and through their lenses watched a wood thrush singing in a small tree. As the sky darkened the creek flow sounds grew louder. We could also hear cars along Beach Drive, which, in this area, is closed to motorized traffic from Saturday morning through Sunday night.

There is a heartbreaking reality at the creek that I never seem to recount, perhaps because it's so painful. Last year, I wrote an article for *The Washington Post*, about the loss of trees, which ran in a more extended form in this year's Audubon *Naturalist News* as the cover story for its annual arts and literature issue. Following last June's ten-inch deluge, many trees were ripped from the creek's banks by the swift and sudden floodwaters. Most painful for me was the destruction of one of the beech trees across the creek from the Meditation Rock. As I wrote in the story, this rock and its special setting kept me sane after moving from my beloved country home near Sugarloaf Mountain to suburban Chevy Chase. Two beech trees reached out from either side of the creek, their limbs touching in the middle. When the morning sun bounced off the water, it created a light show on the leafy undersides of these far-reaching beech limbs. I would sit on the rock most mornings and absorb the reflecting light. Afterward, I could face anything the day had to offer.

When the beech toppled, the atmosphere at the Meditation Rock drastically changed, and here I am, nearly a year later, still trying to adapt to the loss. The felled tree lies lifeless in the water along the opposite shore and its across-the-creek companion growing next to the Meditation Rock is sparse with lost limbs. So, even when the wounded tree is fully leafed in a few more days, there will be little of the former light show's glory to comfort and inspire me. Sadly, this is just one of many tree losses I've witnessed during this past year.

On our January Audubon walk, the participants admired a tall, cinnamon-colored river birch near the Skunk Cabbage Swamp, the largest of the species that many of them had seen. This tree came down during one of the February nor'easters and became a chopped-up pile of logs by the time of April's field trip, much to the distress of those who witnessed the before and after. During our spring nor'easter, a young willow oak was uprooted next to the West Beach Drive Bridge, blocking the trail. When I saw its needle-like baby leaves unfurling, my heart broke. There is something so poignant about a fallen tree continuing to leaf. The willow oak was removed from the trail this week.

Most visually disturbing of all, perhaps, is the huge fallen sycamore that came crashing down during winter. It fell on the western shore of the creek and now lies completely across the water, extending onto part of the trail on the eastern side where we walk. My Audubon group spent a long time communing with this fallen tree. One never gets the chance to touch the upper branches of a mature sycamore, however much one may admire its mottled creaminess from the ground below. To me, the tree lying across the creek resembles a fallen animal. For some reason an elephant comes to mind.

Where its wood is split and exposed, it's the purest color of light wood. Anyone who comes close feels compelled to touch the limbs, to feel their olive and cream puzzle-pattern bark as smooth as silk. I have touched those fallen limbs many times on my walks these past few months.

Last evening, as Jim and I passed by the sycamore tree in the near dark, we noticed that some of the branchlets lying near the ground were leafing and flowering. The female flowers were enchanting—like the round fruiting balls in miniature, a felty green with tiny red stigmas and styles. Their short stout stalks were also felt-green. And the leaves, the baby leaves! Perfectly formed sycamore leaves no more than three-quarters of an inch across, thick and resembling small pieces of cut felt. Who knew? Who knew until the tree came down?

As Jim and I wound our way through the swamp and back to Boundary Bridge, I thought about the vulnerability of all the trees at Rock Creek Park. The seasonal floods that have sustained and replenished their life-giving soils over the ages are now far more unpredictable. Even an ordinary rain can become threatening in a hurry, as all the rivulets rushing over pavement and channeled into narrow culverts flow swiftly into the creek and can quickly overwhelm its fragile banks. And, as global warming intensifies, record rains increasingly bracket periods of drought. The droughts—we had two last year—weaken the trees, and then floods and high winds rip them from the ground. Of course, there is also the constant threat of pests and pathogens, just waiting to exploit weakened and stressed trees. As we walked in the dark under the tall leafing trees with the high-pitched music of spring peepers in our ears, my heart filled with a familiar mix of beauty and worry. I said prayers for the future as I followed my moon-shadow over Boundary Bridge.

May 1: MAY DAY

HOW STRANGE that I wrote about fallen trees the day before my father-in-law died. This May Day is a sad day for all of us, but it is also tinged with relief, because Bill is finally free. We are gathering in the White Mountains tomorrow to celebrate his life. Last evening, as I wrote a note to some of my friends asking for healing energy for my family, I told them about Bill's offbeat sense of humor, his love of Nature and Frank Sinatra, and the fact that he was our pet pig's favorite person. Porky, all 700 pounds of him, would stand on his hind legs and squeal when he saw Bill. My friend, Ellen Gordon, shared an image that is carrying me through my grief. "Bill is free now," she said, "and no doubt, Porky gave him a heck of a greeting."

After I heard the news about Bill from Jim, who was in New Hampshire, I felt the need to visit the Bishop's Garden of the National Cathedral. In the garden stands a stone sculpture of the Biblical prodigal son, wrapped in the loving arms of his father. Bill, at seventeen, was the sculptor's model for the son, and his grandfather—Dan Freeman Bradley, born in Bangkok, the son of a missionary—was the model for the father. The sculptor, Heinz Warneke, lived in a farmhouse across the dirt road from them in rural Connecticut, and his stepdaughter told me that he considered Bill and his grandfather ideal models. As I walked toward the statue through the budding rose garden, all the cathedral bells were ringing. I touched the sculpted young boy modeled after a young Bill, whose face was hidden by the father's arms, and I felt overcome by a radiant sense of peace.

When the news reached Sophie in Galicia, a Spanish pilgrimage destination for centuries, where she was traveling during her semester abroad, she also heard cathedral bells. Sobbing on the street, from where she was talking to me on her cell phone, I heard her answer the concerned questions of passersby in Spanish, through her tears. Within a few hours, she was taking a nine-hour bus ride to Madrid and then flying across the Atlantic to JFK, traveling with not so much as a toothbrush. Her pilgrimage in honor of her grandfather.

There's no time to wash my face in the May Day morning dew or visit my beloved Rock Creek. I'm scrambling to get the work and schedule reshuffling done that I must do before Jesse and I can travel north for Bill's service, where we will join Sophie and Jim. But, as I look out over our verdant yard to our leafy neighborhood canopy and watch the shadows playing across my desk, I'm thankful for May blessings through my grief.

As JESSE AND I drove through a dark and cold Franconia Notch, New Hampshire, on May 1st on our way to the gathering for Bill, it didn't feel like May Day or Beltane, as it was called in the Old World. When the full moon peeked out from the clouds, it shone on the snow-covered peaks of Mount Washington and the Presidential Range, a decidedly wintry image. We arrived at the Town and Country motel in Gorham, and Sophie and Jim flew out the door of their room to greet us. The spring peepers were calling loudly, no doubt thrilled to have a break from the death grip of this year's serial nor'easters. White birches, ghostly in the moonlight, surrounded us.

It was wonderful to have the family gathered in Bill's honor, telling stories and soaking up the early spring in the North Country. Sophie spoke at Bill's service, with Jesse standing by her side in the pulpit. She related a story of how her grandfather once told her to pay attention to where she was walking in the woods and how then, looking down, she saw a turtle's shell. After the service, she gave her grandmother a small sculpture of a turtle that she brought back from Santiago, in Galicia. Sophie purchased the turtle for her grandmother after hearing of her grandfather's death.

I took a walk alone to Mascot Pond in the Mahoosuc Mountains the next day. The familiar pond was ringed with spruce, fir, and hemlock, with the snow cones of Mount Washington and Mount Madison rising beyond the trees. The white birches lining the trail to the pond bore green leaf-buds a few days shy of popping open, and the red maples were blooming. Spring—when it finally comes—happens quickly in the north. I picked a wintergreen leaf and chewed on it, as I've done a thousand times on my New England walks, but never at Sugarloaf Mountain where wintergreen is rare. The northern viburnum called hobble-bush bore opposite pairs of naked gray-brown leaf buds, also ready to pop, and I found a pair of painted trilliums, a high-altitude species not yet blooming, near a small stream.

Jim and I lived in the White Mountains when we were first married, and we always fall into its familiar embrace. I became a serious reader when I discovered the Bradley family's book collection on the shelves of their summer house: Graham Greene, John Fowles, Vladimir Nabokov. Bill and I also shared a love of the budding feminist fiction genre of the 1970s and 80s. While living in New Hampshire and working for a radio station in Berlin, I covered the 1976 presidential primary and interviewed Jimmy Carter a week before he won the primary, with his national press entourage filming and taping the interview. I have a picture of me at twenty-four, holding a microphone in front of a rather long-haired Carter, whose elbow is casually leaning on our station's turntable. A year later, we were living in Washington, where I began writing *City of Trees*. Until this moment I never realized the irony!

I found it hard to say good-bye to Jim's mother, Paula, and his brother, Paul, which we did during an outing to Gordon Falls on Mount Madison. The rest of the family, including Jim's brother, Dwight, and his wife, Lauren, my mom, dad, and brother, had already departed. The creeks and rivers of the North Country were brimming with meltwater, and the little falls at the base of Madison was roaring. Grandma gave us the sweetest good-bye gift—fat, crunchy carrots from the garden, grown during Bill's last summer and protected in the ground until spring. Eating them as we headed home felt sacramental.

Sophie came home with us for a few days but flew back to Spain yesterday, two days shy of her twenty-first birthday. I put nearly everything on hold to spend precious time with her. We went to Boundary Bridge, where we inhaled the fragrant fully flowered pinxters, and to Sugarloaf, where we discovered a picture-perfect group of six pink lady's slippers growing from a bed of moss above Bear Branch. We visited our land in Comus where we both napped in the car, needing replenishment after the exhausting whirlwind of grief-filled days and international travel. Sophie then came with me on a photo shoot to the National Arboretum, where she held the branches of a dove tree, fringe-tree, and cucumber magnolia for me. For once I wasn't cursing the spring breeze.

Now I face a daunting work jag, with many photos still to take for the third edition of *City of Trees* plus revisions to the manuscript recommended by an independent reviewer. Plus three field trips in the next two weeks *and* at least fifteen family members coming for a reunion at our house next week. Whether to pop the tripod in the car trunk, begin tinkering with the manuscript, or clean up my piles of stuff is the decision I will agonize over every minute of every one of the next few days. It's all good stuff, every bit of it, just too much, too much. The familiar "To Do list." My number one motto is "keep it simple." May I do so during these verdant days of May. Keep it simple, keep it light, keep it sane. And drink every ounce of beauty. Yesterday, Nancy planted four o'clock, stock, and many other old-fashioned flowers in our garden, and today it looks like an English cottage garden. When I went out to thank her, she looked up from where she was kneeling with her trowel and said, "I'm having so much fun that I feel guilty taking this pleasure away from you."

Yes, part of me would like to be digging in the dirt, but my botanist-poet self always seems to have other projects and plans. Projects that can never be more rewarding than putting a trowel in the ground but call to me so insistently and sweetly that I dutifully wander off and follow.

May 8: PHOTOGRAPHER TO THE RESCUE

WHILE SCRAMBLING to get some flowering tree photographs today at the National Arboretum, I take a break to wander through Fern Valley, a woodland similar to the woods at Rock Creek Park but one that is planted throughout with wildflowers native to eastern North America. As I walk along a streamside path, I pass a woman about my age who stands quietly near a patch of foam flowers, her camera poised on a low tripod to capture a close-up. I smile at her as I walk past, lugging my own camera and tripod, and we exchange "hellos." A while later, as I try to photograph some bigleaf magnolia blossoms in the wind and imperfect light, she appears, greets me again, tells me her name—Susan Roth—and says that she is a professional photographer specializing in gardens and plants and the author of several gardening books. Best-selling books, I later learn. I introduce myself and tell her about my book. She looks surprised and then says: "This is really weird. I just got an email from a friend in Vermont, and she asked if it was okay to give someone in DC my contact info, because she needs photos of trees for a book she is writing. That must be you!"

I quickly realize what a fortuitous woodland meeting this is. Within minutes, Susan is helping me set up my shot and giving me photography pointers. I ask if she would like to submit pictures for *City of Trees* and she says yes! When I return to my home office, I discover an email from my friend in

Vermont, Polly Alexander, the illustrator for *City of Trees*, who—in response to my rather desperate plea for photography help—had asked some friends in the graphics business if they could recommend a photographer to help out. Polly reports that one of her friends says I should contact an excellent photographer of plants and gardens named Susan Roth, "who has just moved to DC."

This kind of serendipity seems uncanny, almost providential, making life all the more worth living. And Nature was the conduit to our "chance" meeting.

May 11: BUTTERCUPS AND LIFE'S MYSTERIES

THIS PART OF THE WORLD is awash in buttercups, flower of my first-born. Twenty-one years ago this week, I became a mother, and on this date I celebrated my first Mother's Day when Sophie was three days old. When Jim and I—nervous, ecstatic, and green-horn parents—drove home to Seneca Creek in Maryland with our five-hour-old newborn, the fields were filled with buttercups.

This week, as I drove through Rock Creek Park on my way home from photographing trees at the National Arboretum, the grassy edges of Rock Creek Park were speckled with buttercups. The park's interior was in full spring leaf, with dogwood and fringe-tree blooming along the edges of the canopy and the rocky creek waters brimming. Waxy white mayapple flowers nodded under umbrella-like leaves, and wild black cherry blossoms hung overhead in narrow clusters along Beach Drive. As I drove over Boulder Bridge and around the bend, pinxter flowers bloomed against a dark rock ledge. At that moment, I believed that I could bring any depressed person to this place and he or she would instantly and miraculously recover enthusiasm for life.

I always miss Boundary Bridge when I am away. My work is far-flung, almost all of it outdoors but away from my wild home at Rock Creek Park. Since Sugarloaf Mountain is no longer my primary place of refuge and renewal, the area around Boundary Bridge is. All week I've been in exile from the place where I want to be but everywhere I look, in country pastures and along the city's sidewalks, I see buttercups and think of newborn Sophie and her birth.

My children's birthdays are always joyous days. This birthday was challenging for all of us, with Bill's passing and Sophie back in Spain studying for an exam. But we celebrated before she left, and we'll celebrate again when she returns. In the meantime, her Spanish and American friends are picking up the slack across the pond.

As I celebrate my children on their birthdays, I have a secret internal celebration of their creation. The love and passion between Jim and me remains an intense mystery that has endured since we married more than thirty years ago. And then there were the wonders of discovering I was pregnant and all the prenatal milestones along the way—the first kick, the swelling belly, and the conversations with the unseen child.

And then giving birth, life's high point. Two days of labor with both Sophie and Jesse but beauty shining through pain. Jim gave me images of flowers during contractions: Imagine a water lily unfurling, a spring beauty, a black-eyed Susan, and—toward the end of Sophie's labor—a fiddlehead fern and a baby's hand. These unfurling portraits of Nature's gifts got me through my midwife-assisted births without drugs. It was my body's job to open, as a flower opens. During Jesse's labor, the peonies were blooming, and they provided the perfect visual display—a tight cervix-size bud opening to a blossom as big as a baby's head. When Jim tried to remind me of other flowering images during Jesse's contractions, I'd plead, "No, no—give me the peony, the peony!"

As a mother, I jumped over the moon, finding the deepest happiness I'd ever imagined. My babies were my world. I was a vulnerable mess of mother love, a turtle without a shell, living on the edge of ecstasy and pain. The week Sophie was born the world was reeling with the news of the nuclear disaster at Chernobyl. I was pained by empathy for the mothers of the Ukraine and those downwind. How were they giving birth? Were they feeding their babies tainted milk? And would the radiation reach our continent? I felt empathy for mothers of all species. How were the animal-mothers of the Ukraine coping? And would the baby robins in our own backyard successfully fledge?

I love and celebrate my children. But, secretly, in our still male-dominant culture, I also celebrate the miracle of feminine power, and wonder why I rarely see a woman openly breastfeeding today. True feminine power remains an underground aspect of American culture, but I know and appreciate my sexual-spiritual power, which is a unified thing. It is not mine, but it is there for me when I am open to it. It is part of Mother Earth—both living and divine—although feminine sexuality is still considered by many to be the root of evil. Evil Eve, the temptress and seducer, and original sin, I believe, are concepts that are deeply rooted in the male envy of the womb. Will more men and women become brave enough to recognize and embrace masculine and feminine power? I happen to believe that our survival depends on it. Will we continue to live on a fertile, mysterious planet? Or will we turn away from our own creation, fouling our water and air and soil, as we chase after material wealth antithetical to life itself?

I hope it is not too late to integrate feminine and masculine power in a deep and meaningful way in order that we might live in harmony with the gift of creation. I am mindful that, when I write about the reproductive aspects of toads and trees, I'm on terra firma, but, when I write honestly about my own fertility and passion, I stray into dangerous waters, knowing I may lose readers who wish to see me only as an ardent visitor to Boundary Bridge and Rock Creek Park.

May 14: NOTHING GOLD CAN STAY

EVERY YEAR IN MID-MAY, I'm haunted by the first lines of Robert Frost's poem, "Nothing Gold Can Stay": "Nature's first green is gold, Her hardest hue to hold." Jim and I went to Boundary Bridge on Saturday evening, after more than a week away, and I hardly knew the place. It was hot and humid with storm clouds gathering. The canopy felt oppressive in its leafiness, and all the golds and tender greens of early flower and leaf had become one uniform, albeit fresh, palette of green. I always grieve when the myriad springtime hues settle into the same green and obscure the architecture of the trees. I now envy Ellie not for her storied pawpaw patch but because, in her northerly habitat, she is still enjoying Vermont's early spring magic, about which she rapturously writes.

As is its yearly habit, the lesser celandine is now yellowing and dying back on the forest floor, its dark green foliage fading as the canopy fills in. Gold to green in the canopy, green to gold on the forest's floor. Jim and I saw a single Virginia bluebell, a few fading flowers of wild blue phlox and an occasional Jack-in-the-pulpit as we walked along the creek. But most of the spring ephemerals, which die back to dormancy with the approach of summer, are only a memory as summer begins to kick in. This requires a seasonal heart-shift in me, but I am still able to cherish the late-spring wildflowers that emerge along the park's trails, for both their beauty and relative scarcity. Small, yellow-green flower buds dangle from the Solomon's seal, soon to open. The false (or "plumed") Solomon's seal is blooming, with its cluster of frothy white terminal flowers. A few pink geraniums congregate along the upland's switchback. The maple-leaved viburnum is flowering, the wild hydrangea is budding, and a favorite, the Indian cucumber root, a delicate-looking member of the lily family, bears its small, nodding green flowers with their dramatic red pistils. The pinxter flowers also remain in bloom, with mountain laurel soon to follow on the Laurel Ledge.

I led a field trip to Sugarloaf Mountain last week, where the pinxter is also blooming, and my group made quite a discovery. We looked at the flowers with a hand-held lens and focused on the pistil of this fragrant, spectacular pink flower with its round, purple, shining-wet stigma. After viewing it with the lens and then looking at the flowering shrub with the naked eye, we could see each purple stigma sparkling in the morning sun, as if it had been cinematically tapped by Tinker Bell's wand. The wonders of magnification and the way it changes one's ability to see! The group fought over the lenses as we examined blossoms of wild black cherries, violets, mayapples, and lady's slippers. They fell in love with the centers of the flowers and their embarrassing riches of seduction, and, well, sex. Seduction of pollinators and sexual reproduction. That's what showy flowers are all about.

Jim and I witnessed some wondrous animal behaviors during our *three* weekend visits to Boundary Bridge. On Saturday, we climbed down a steep bank about 100 feet upstream from the Meditation Rock and Laurel Ledge. As we walked out onto a gravel beach, we stirred up dozens of yellow-and-black-striped tiger swallowtail butterflies who were "puddling" on the gravel-bar. They flew into the lower part of the canopy where they gathered nectar from the bittersweet flowers. The creek waters ran as clear as weak tea before Saturday's storm, when I sat by the water watching Jim skip stones, but on Sunday they carried a heavy sediment load and looked as murky as Turkish coffee. The tadpoles in the wood frog pond darted about in an eating frenzy. As they surfaced from the dark depths to dine on algae at the surface, I could just make out their small emerging legs.

Songbirds were singing everywhere. Wood thrushes serenaded every stretch of the trail. Wood-pewees sang *pee-a-wee* oh so sweetly and the tufted titmice sang *peedle peedle peedle*. Eastern towhees alternated between their *drink your tea* song and their emphatic *wheat* call-note. Red-bellied woodpeckers churred and the pileateds loudly called. The happiest song of all for me was the loud *teacher teacher teacher* of the small ovenbird, whose return I had anxiously awaited. But, this year, I have yet to hear ovenbirds near the Meditation Rock, where I've often heard them in the past. The kingfishers seem less evident at the creek now. Why is that? Are they nesting? We hear, but don't see them. But most of the birds are, thankfully, back at Rock Creek. They are also singing at Sugarloaf.

Two box turtles crossed my path this week, one at Boundary Bridge and one at Sugarloaf. Is this Bill's spirit with his message to Sophie to look, always, where you're walking? Yesterday, a golden retriever named Otis, whom we met on the trail, hid behind Jim for protection and peeked through his legs at the box turtle, who had him a little spooked!

Sunday was Mother's Day, and Jesse came along for our last walk of the weekend in honor of the occasion. He is a teenaged-boy, very much into his teenaged-world. It's hard to get him out on the trail at fifteen going on sixteen, but I know that a love of Nature lives within him. Whenever the season changes, he notices. When the sky wells with clouds, he notices. And I remember how excited he became as a baby every time he saw the moon. "*Moon moon moon!*" he'd exclaim, pointing his baby finger at the sky. He spent his first years of life riding in a snuggly and then a backpack as I hiked on Sugarloaf Mountain and wandered through the Comus countryside. As I researched the two books I wrote about Sugarloaf, illustrated by my friend and artist, Tina Brown, Jesse rode along with me everywhere I went.

Speaking of Comus, I remembered a dramatic dream when I awoke today. We were in our house in Comus with the children and their friends when a stupendous storm came up. I walked out the front door to find a giant icicle hanging from the roof. I yelled to warn everyone to be careful when going in and out of the house and then I walked outside and into an ice storm that was thicker and scarier than any storm I'd ever been in. I looked up to the sky and saw icicles hanging from the clouds. A message from the firmament?

May 21: LOST AND FOUND

THE SUMMER SOLSTICE is a month away, and I wonder, Where am I? What season is it? The woods look and feel like summer, even though it's only May. I feel I don't know Rock Creek Park at all. I've been away from Boundary Bridge for more than a week, and, when I return, a dark-haired man is standing on the bridge smoking a cigarette. The smell of the smoke is not unpleasant (I was once a smoker), but never before have I smelled cigarette smoke at Boundary Bridge.

The day is cool, breezy, and bright, without a cloud in the sky. The brilliance of the sky contrasts with the deeply shadowed forest. The canopy is so thick, from the lower level of spicebush, viburnum, pawpaw, and bladdernut to the highest level at the tops of the blooming tulip trees, that I blink hard to see as I wind my way along the creek's trail.

The lesser celandine has died back further on the forest's floor, and the few remaining Jack-in-the-pulpits are fading fast. Petals of the tulip tree—teardrop-shaped and yellow-green with an orange blush near the base—speckle the trail. Occasionally, a full flower has fallen, and, when I lift it from the ground, it is heavy with yellow stamens and a cone-like cluster of multiple pistils. I note a few botanical details along the trail: The clusters of maple-leaved viburnum flowers are white and vaguely fishy smelling, the leaves soft as down. The wild hydrangea is still in bud, awaiting its summer show, and the blossoms of the mountain laurel are now no longer pink but glow crisp and white against their dark evergreen leaves.

I note those colorful details, but mostly I feel lost in the canopy—its greenness overwhelming, its darkness strange against the vivid blue of the sky. The creek's water runs clear today, but I see no fish, hear no kingfisher, and the only duck in sight is a mallard, purposefully winging its way downstream. I hear birds high in the trees, some familiar and some not, and I assume that many are nesting, busy with activity hidden from view. Once again, because of my intense botanical focus, I have failed to witness the migration of the spring warblers. During the Audubon field trip I led on Saturday at Sugarloaf, two of the participants who had been on one of my Boundary Bridge forays exuberantly reported details of the warblers they'd seen at Rock Creek last week: Black-throated blue, black-throated green, Nashville, Canada, blue-winged, redstarts and blackpolls. I could only give an envious sigh and repeat, as I seem to do every spring, "next year."

Today is cool, but the fullness of the trees overhanging the creek and the sparkling white-gold of the sandy beaches make me think of summer activities—swimming and fishing. That gives me another kind of pang. We humans—Nature's wisest creatures?—won't swim or fish in Rock Creek this summer, because its waters are polluted. Recently, I saw a photograph taken in the 1950s of a full-immersion baptism in Rock Creek. Oh, that we can reach the point of safely immersing ourselves once again in these beckoning waters.

The last few days have been rich and full for me. The University of Virginia Press's Faculty Editorial Board approved publication of the third edition of *City of Trees*, a vote of full confidence, and now only a few weeks of minor revisions and additional photography remain. I led three field trips to Sugarloaf in the last ten days and was rewarded with hand-written and emailed thank yous. *Thank you for opening my eyes; thank you for showing me beauty; thank you for making me feel happy and inspired since the field trip.* I was asked to lead a Sugarloaf trip for Henry (Hank) Paulson, Secretary of the Treasury, and members of the Treasury Department's staff on June 2nd. Apparently, the secretary, a recently appointed cabinet member of the George W. Bush Administration, is a hiker and birder with strong interests in plants and conservation. Who knew?

And, last Thursday, I hosted a family reunion for my paternal grandmother's side of the family—descended from Czech and Hungarian Jews who emigrated to New York City during the nineteenth century. Some were estranged from our family while I was growing up, and I'm just getting to know them as an adult. After dinner, we sat at our dining room table long into the night, eagerly telling and listening to family stories to learn how each of us fits into our ancestral past. Sitting around our table, drinking tea and eating Aunt Marion's apple cake, we laughed and cried as we stitched the family history back together. We made such good progress. Music is a big part of the family's legacy. I learned that one of my grandmother's cousins was a Tin Pan Alley composer who wrote the classic song, "Blueberry Hill." And my grandmother's eldest sister's son is Jerry Wexler, the well-known producer who recorded Aretha Franklin's greatest hits, including "Respect" and many other classics of soul, blues, and rock and roll. He is even credited with coining the term "rhythm and blues" as a music reporter for *Billboard* magazine in the 1940s. Jerry wasn't at this gathering, but I met him a few years ago when my parents gathered the family together in Vermont.

As connected as I've felt to people and places and my own work during the last few days, the feeling of being lost today at Rock Creek takes me by surprise. I climb down to the Meditation Rock, where I find animal footprints in a mud-coated part of the rock. Coons, possums, or the muskrats I sometimes see here? I don't know. But, a half an hour into my walk, I surrender to the sensation of feeling clueless and somewhat lost.

I realize that, during the early spring, I was engaged in a constant game of seeking and finding. Each day brought new botanical surprises, and what I didn't know I would look up in a book or ask a knowledgeable friend. Seek and find. But, now, Nature is a wall of solid green and hides the birds I do not know and cannot see. I can't seek or find. Birds and animals secretly raise their young, and this visitor isn't privy to their private worlds. The exuberant, blooming curve that makes me feel like a purposeful botanist is winding down, and I'm lost in the canopy.

Lost and found—that's how it is with us humans in this remarkable process of life and living over which we have so little control, despite our attempts through science and art and religion. We go from feeling lost to feeling found and vice versa. We lose ourselves and find ourselves through all that we experience. Whether and how we feel lost or found depends on a full array of occurrences and mysteries, big and small, obvious and hidden. As I leave my "wild home," I wonder if I've found my grandmother's family only, perhaps, to lose them again.

TODAY, AFTER DRIVING the carpool and dropping off the kids, I park at the zoo, at the edge of Rock Creek Park, and begin to jog past the animal enclosures. As I bid good morning to a statuesque gray emu, I see that the smoke trees and golden catalpas have begun to bloom, and I make a mental note to come back later with my tripod and macro lens.

As I jog, I listen through my earphones to my favorite prophet—the singer/songwriter Bob Dylan. By the time I traverse the Woodley Park neighborhood and climb the escarpment to the National Cathedral at my crawling jog, I have disappeared through the smoke rings of my mind, ached just like a woman and not thought twice. All along the watchtower and in almost every townhouse garden the roses bloom exuberantly. The sun shines, the breeze shakes the boughs of southern magnolias, and I enter the sacred space of the Bishop's Garden.

On the day my father-in-law died, the bells were ringing as I approached the sculpture of the Prodigal Son, positioned next to the ever-present roses in the medieval garden at the base of the National Cathedral. (The sculpture has since been moved from the rose garden to a nearby weeping Japanese flowering cherry tree.) Today, two women gardeners are digging and weeding. A red calico bag belonging to one of them is positioned next to a boxwood hedge, a water bottle peeking out from the top. I come around the back of the statue, marveling, as I always do, about the father's resemblance to Jim. Not just the bearded face—a near spitting-image—but shoulders, back, hands, legs, the whole body—a replica of Jim's great-grandfather that could be Jim. Most people only have a frayed photo or two of their ancestors. We have a body carved in stone, art as witness to the persistence of DNA. And to something subtler. The old man in the sculpture lovingly holds the son the same way Jim holds our children. And now that Bill is gone, we are left with two ancestors carved in stone, and my whole feeling for the sculpture has changed.

As I smell the roses in the garden—and let me say these are the most fragrant roses in Washington, and fragrance is essential to a rose—I wonder: Is Bill an ancestor now? Is this man who made me laugh and whom I last saw wearing a Boston Red Sox cap, who is immortalized here in stone as a young man, already ancestral?

When Jesse and his cousin, Dan (son of Jim's brother, Dwight) were seven or eight, they were fascinated by a small wooden house no bigger than a bird-house and either Hindu or Buddhist in origin, which sat among a cluster of white birches near the family's summer house in the White Mountains. Bill told his young grandsons that it was a house to honor the ancestors. The little boys seemed to understand, and they brought offerings of flowers and stones to the house each day. I loved looking out from the porch and seeing these ordinarily active little boys—ten weeks apart in age—quietly stand under the white-barked trees in front of the magical little house.

The Bishop's Garden is my "cultivated refuge" in Washington, just as Rock Creek Park is my "wild home," and the sculpture has been a comfort for many years. Shortly after 9/11, a day on which I was distraught at being separated from my children for many hours, I came to the garden and its sculpture to try to convince myself that life in our city would and could go on. Today, with the forest so impossibly deep, green, and impenetrable, I rediscover the need for the cultivated comfort of roses and stone (just as Benedictine monks have been nurtured by the same for centuries). And I come back to the questions, is Bill an ancestor? And what is the role of ancestors in our lives?

As I leave the garden by way of a favorite southern magnolia, I think about how earlier cultures reverently venerated their ancestors. Many throughout the world still do. Why don't we? Suddenly, I'm seized by the perception that we need our ancestors more than ever. We need their love and nourishment, their detached benevolent care emanating from the spirit-world surrounding us. Just as we need fragrance—and not just a pretty-petaled face—in a rose, we need the shining love and wisdom of our ancestors, beaming through our organic world. A green world with a golden halo.

Jogging back to the zoo, I see this vision of the haloed green world embodied in the forest. At the end of Klingle Road, where the Klingle Valley's woodland begins, flowing down toward Rock Creek Park, I cross a stone bridge and look into the dark trees. A single sunbeam breaks through the canopy, spotlighting a tall mountain laurel, lighting up its white blossoms, as if it were an angel.

TODAY IS BOB DYLAN'S BIRTHDAY. Happy birthday, Bob! May you stay "forever young."

In your song, "It's Alright Ma," you opine that "he not busy being born is busy dying." I hope that our Earth is still busily being born. When our family was here for the reunion last week, I stood up before dinner and spontaneously said a blessing for our ancestors and the next seven generations of our family. The youngest generation—Jesse and his third cousins, Claire and Samantha, who are even younger—probably thought I was a nutty old lady, tearing up as I did, stone-cold sober. There are a lot of human follies to tear up about when you think about our children's world, and their children's world, and beyond. War and genocide, poverty and social inequities, environmental degradation and climate change. Are we busy being born or busy dying?

On Earth Day, a cantor and percussionist delivered some African proverbs at All Souls Church Unitarian and, inspired, I jotted them down:

> "Do unto those downstream as you would have those upstream
>   do unto you;"
> "Silence is also speech;" *and my favorite—*
> "Earth was not given to you by your parents. It was lent to you
>   by your children."

How badly we've squandered the loan, the gift of Creation. Tim Ward, a friend and fellow author, once said to me: "Future generations will look back at us and the way we've handled the environment and ask: *What were they thinking?*" Yes, what are we thinking, and can we think again?

Yesterday, I visited Boundary Bridge with Esther Schrader and her two-year-old son, Nathaniel. Our workout plans were scrapped when Nathaniel insisted on climbing out of his baby jogger and jogging himself, which he did on the stony path with great coordination in his small pair of sneakers. Esther apologized profusely, but she was wasting her breath. I can jog any day, but it's been years since I've followed an excited two-year-old up and down the trail.

As we walked, I added some naturalist education to the outing. I showed

Nathaniel how soft and felt-like the maple-leaved viburnum can feel in his small hand and how he can gently lift the top leaf-whorl of the Indian cucumber root plant to find the dangling green flowers with their red pistils underneath the leaves. When he gently touched the small, green flower of this member of the lily family with his little finger, I remembered Jesse at that age and the reverential way he reached out to touch the pouch of a lady's slipper or a Jack-in-the-pulpit's spadix. Looking under the green–and–purple spathe to the chocolate-brown spadix at the age of three, he'd intone: "Jack's home, but his puppets are gone."

I showed Esther and Nathaniel some mountain laurel magic. Esther immediately loved the unopened flower buds, declaring, "They look like mini-meringues!" We looked inside the open flowers of the large clusters to examine their intriguing centers. Purple spots on the corolla lobes mark where the stamens' anthers are inserted into tiny pouches until the moment they break free, springing upward to release pollen. I also shared the pleasures of scratch-and-sniff with a spicebush's twig, as I did with my Audubon group back in January. When we got to Riley Spring Bridge, a phoebe called and we called back.

This is my hope for the future: Generations of Rock Creek phoebes calling, with two-year-old kids and their moms calling back, keeping alive our sense of wonder for the world and rekindling our responsibility toward it as good stewards of our Earth. Let's not squander the loan of life.

May 26: FOCUS

SO MUCH OF WHAT we experience in life depends upon focus; that is, upon what and where we focus our efforts and attention. Unless we are experiencing a physical or emotional crisis, we usually have a choice.

I am in a major juggling mode, because Sophie is home from Spain for a week, Jesse starts final exams next week, and I am facing work deadlines and social obligations galore. Jim and I walk the Boundary Bridge trail while Sophie and Jesse sleep away this Saturday morning. We climb down the Laurel Ledge, where the mountain laurel continues to bloom, to the Meditation Rock. After sitting there for some time, Jim notices a partly submerged bullfrog resting on an adjacent rock. When we startle the frog, it jumps high and far, splashing into the creek. When we get a good look at the mud where it was basking, we see something we've never seen before—three identical imprints of a bullfrog's body, temporarily immortalized in mud. About the size and shape of a small horseshoe, each imprint shows the frog's head, body, and hind legs. The same frog three times or three different frogs? Likely the former, but who knows?

While contemplating this small mystery, our gaze shifts slightly and falls upon a dead baby duckling, lying in the creek. We're instantly saddened, and our frog reverie is interrupted as we embrace another natural occurrence less than a foot from the mud imprints. Later, walking along the creek, we come to a place where a newly fallen tulip tree spans the water. There, we notice a layer of plastic bottles and other trash gathering against the upstream side of the horizontal trunk, a reminder of city life. But the downed tree also interrupts a more felicitous downstream journey: Before us thousands, perhaps millions, of tulip tree petals form a band eight to ten feet wide that stretches from one side of the creek to the other and covers the surface of the water upstream like a swirling, wavy blanket. Given the choice, do we focus on being disgusted by the bottles or enraptured by the petals, or both? Focus on the leaping frog or the dead duckling? I guess Jim and I are "both" kinds of people, but, given the choice, we focus on the wonder of the frog prints and floating petals.

June 7: A NEW FRIEND VISITS THE CREEK

MY LOVE AFFAIR with the Boundary Bridge trail continues, and my affection grows for the bridge itself. I told my friend, Cris Fleming, as we stood side-by-side, leaning on the railing one morning this past week, that this simple bridge is as beautiful to me as the Japanese bridge in Monet's garden, a thought that originally occurred to me when one of our early snows outlined the bridge with white. The bridge is especially enchanting at night when its profile lights up with starlight and moonlight and the creek flows musically below. Cris then observed that the elms, sycamores, and river birches arching over the creek mimic the arc of the bridge, adding to the magical aesthetic. So true.

Today, I meet up with Wendy Paulson, a new friend, for a walk at the bridge. She is married to Hank Paulson. I led a Sugarloaf field trip for Hank and Wendy and several dozen Treasury staffers (as well as several Secret Service agents) last Saturday. Wendy and I quickly recognized the naturalist spirit in each other.

Wendy stands tall and slender with a smile that immediately draws me in and makes me feel comfortable. A consummate birder, she led many walks in Central Park and taught a course called "For the Birds" to students in Harlem when she and Hank lived in New York City. She is just getting to know the larger and wilder Rock Creek Park.

We walk over the bridge, and soon a kingfisher quietly wings its way upstream. I express worry about the recently inconspicuous kingfishers, whose chattering had mysteriously stopped, but Wendy verifies what I'd suspected: They are in a nesting mode and have stopped chattering for now. I intend to take notice of when they begin again.

I've resumed my evening rambles through the park and hear more toads and barred owls. Last evening I saw a handsome black-crowned night heron fishing in the creek. As I share this news with Wendy, she looks up to see a great blue heron flying high above us, so high its distinctive profile is barely visible. The sight of a great blue is always a gift.

Wendy and I spend three hours walking the loop trail, stopping to admire and point out plants and birds to each other. She takes notes on the trees and wildflowers I identify for her, while I lap up her knowledge of birds and her special appreciation of the panic grass and other grasses that flourish along the creek. She has been involved in restoration of native grasses on the Illinois prairie, her home base.

Wendy gives me a great gift: She restores my connection to the canopy. Her eyes and ears are so sharp that she can pinpoint songbirds and their nestlings many tens of feet above in the trees. Blue-gray gnatcatchers, ovenbirds, parula warblers, eastern wood-pewees, wood thrushes, red-eyed vireos, Acadian and great crested flycatchers, and scarlet tanagers are among the small and medium-sized birds she picks out in the dense canopy. Like other good birders, she can recognize a bird from a single call note, which is very different from its distinctive song.

I show her the white blossoms of arrowwood viburnum and the maturing fruit of the blackhaws and bladdernuts. The blackhaw fruit is still green but will become a juicy blue-black in the fall. The bladdernut capsules are green at this time of year, nestled among the leaves, but last year's dry brown lanterns litter the ground below my favorite grove. These brown lanterns rattle when shaken, and one can peel them back to release hard pale brown seeds that look like popcorn kernels. We find a single Venus's looking-glass plant on the bank above the creek, its slender stalk bearing a few pinkish-purple flowers and many heart-shaped "perfoliate" leaves (leaf blades pierced by the plant stalk). Venus and her temperamental mirror, Rock Creek. She will not see her face tomorrow morning when the sediment load following tomorrow's predicted storm will undoubtedly obscure her reflection.

Another delicate woodland plant is in full bloom—the large-leaved houstonia, a small bluet with white-and-pale-pink flowers that exhibit a purplish blush at their centers and small ovate leaves. It is closely related to the summer bluet or houstonia that I know so well from my rambles at Sugarloaf.

Like me, Wendy loves to learn the plants and animals, committing their scientific names and families to memory, but she also likes to stop and witness the serendipitous moments that Nature seems to create for sheer enjoyment. While we are looking at the tiny purple flowers of panic grass through my hand-lens, a pale blue damselfly lands on the terminal flower-cluster, its bulging eyes giving it a sci-fi look at ten-times magnification.

Together we climb down the Laurel Ledge to Rock Creek. I tell her about last year's devastating flood and show her the dead beech tree lying horizontally at the edge of the creek. I explain the loss of the arboreal light show on the undersides of the two touching beech trees that enchanted me before the flood and whose loss causes me much grief. But something fortuitous happens as we stand beside the creek. Looking up at the Laurel Ledge, I notice a subtler but whole new light show—waves of creek-reflected sunlight traveling over the rocks, beech roots, ferns, and hydrangeas. A shift in gaze, direction, and perspective and there it is. While this realization dawns on me, we hear a piercingly sweet birdsong. Wendy identifies it as a Louisiana waterthrush and says it could well be nesting near the ledge.

As we walk back to our hybrid Priuses, I know that the summer canopy will no longer oppress me, because Wendy has helped me pierce its seemingly impenetrable green wall. To look above is to look into a world that I want to know and understand.

June 8: HUMAN NESTING FRENZY

LATE MAY THROUGH EARLY JUNE is a crazy time in the life of any parent with school-aged children. Like the nesting pairs in the treetops, we are all engaged in frantic back-and-forth flight, hoping not to drop the worm!

Today's flight is especially peripatetic. A serious cold front is moving in from the west, and it seems like one that can dump a lot of rain in a short time. I drive to and from Jesse's school twice for music performances—both times in thunderstorms—and to and from a party for graduating seniors. In between the carpooling, I sandwich in some writing time and frantically stake the tomatoes and tall lilies, which are loaded with flower buds, in an attempt to prevent them from toppling in the rain and wind. To add to the mother pressure/time crunch, we have just launched Sophie into her first apartment for her summer research job in Providence.

As I sit at the candlelit dining room table, listening to soothing music, I enjoy a bouquet of pink azaleas freshly cut from the garden before the storms arrived. These late-blooming azaleas are a legacy from the former owners. I haven't seen them elsewhere in any other Washington gardens, so they seem always oddly beautiful and out-of-season in their display.

The deluge has become serious, and the forecast portends this storm to develop much like the one that preceded the big flood of June a year ago. Rock Creek will look like Turkish coffee tomorrow and probably for the following three days. I pray our basement doesn't flood like it did last year. I just checked: So far, so good.

JUST AS I SIT DOWN to write about Jim's and my walk at Boundary Bridge last evening, including—unfortunately—the bulletin about raw sewage posted on the footbridge over Fenwick Branch, I receive an email describing the blocked sewer pipe that caused a serious overflow. Forwarded by FORCE (Friends of Rock Creek's Environment whose name changed to Rock Creek Conservancy in 2012), it contains these words: "STAY OUT OF THE STREAMS! DO NOT TROD ALONG THE STREAM BANKS! . . . Some of the raw sewage has dried up on the stream banks. The guck will remain in the stream and in the park until it is 'flushed' away by several heavy rains."

Jim thinks he saw some raw "clods" when we walked by last evening, and both of us noticed how much clearer the creek was upstream from Fenwick Branch. We heard the low garumph of a bull frog and the banjo twang of a green frog above Fenwick but saw no signs of "our frog" (the one who left those memorable body prints in the mud) downstream from Fenwick at the Meditation Rock. I hope the stream will quickly heal and that few critters died because of this nasty overflow.

This year marks the 100th anniversary of Rachel Carson's birth. To the surprise of many, she lived in nearby Silver Spring, where Fenwick Branch originates. Whenever I smell something less than pristine in that stream (and after storms there's a lot of funky runoff from the neighborhoods even without a leaky sewage pipe), I always think about how far we have to go to finish the work that Rachel Carson began.

The Boundary Bridge area of Rock Creek Park becomes a jungle in mid-June, a dark-green jungle redolent with jungle-like smells and bursting with the jungle calls of birds, frogs, and insects. I am very sensitive to smells. I swoon over the sweet smell of Sugarloaf Mountain the minute I'm out of the car, but Rock Creek doesn't always smell good, especially in summer and especially this week. This bothers me. Today, it has some pleasantly earthy, primal aromas emanating from the vegetation, the critters, and the creek itself.

As soon as I'm over Boundary Bridge and into the braided network of trails that walkers improvised after last June's flood that took out the main trail, I smell the mud and the spicebush. I catch a sudden sense of autumn in the air, rising from the ripening drupes of the spicebush and the many seeds that are already winging from the trees—maple, ash, and tulip tree. Every season contains a hint of the next, and even the one after that. It's not officially summer, and yet I can see and smell the ripening fall!

Wendy Paulson reconnected me with the canopy, and now the wall of green feels less impenetrable, the nesting birds closer and knowable. Last night, as Jim and I rounded the bend near one of Rock Creek's sand-and-gravel beaches, several ebony jewelwings hovered, alighting on the spicebush leaves. Jewelwings are damselflies with wings of blackest midnight and long, thin bodies of iridescent hues that shift from turquoise to emerald in sunlight. The female differs from the male in her slightly duller color and single white spot on each wing.

The setting sun beamed through the forest, highlighting a group of ferns, the trunk of a white oak, a rock in the creek—and creating dazzling patches of red-gold light in the darkening forest. I showed Jim the panic grass lit up on the creek's bank, with its small clusters of flowers made up of pink-purple pistils and blue-purple anthers. I don't know the species, only the genus (*Panicum*), but my heart and mind are beginning to open to grasses and sedges, thanks to Cris Fleming and Wendy.

As Jim and I wound our way down the creek, the wood thrushes serenaded us at every bend. The wild hydrangea looked spectacular in the evening light—its clusters of white flowers brilliantly lit and its leaves somewhere on the continuum between grass-green and forest-green. When we got to the Meditation Rock, we sat peacefully for a long time. One of my favorite aspects of the Meditation Rock is its location just downstream from a large bend in the creek, because I can watch as birds dramatically turn the corner when they come winging past. We were rewarded with a great blue heron flying around the bend, and, as the Louisiana waterthrush sang its piercing song, I decided—as Wendy tentatively surmised—that it might indeed be nesting there!

I'm recording last night's outing at Rock Creek while sitting at our picnic table in the backyard, under a big blue-and-white umbrella with my laptop—my new writing toy. Song sparrows are singing and flowers bloom all around me. This reminiscing is both refreshing and a form of procrastination. I have spent the past few days, and will spend the next few, making revisions to *City of Trees*. Every job has its drudge side. Thank you song sparrows, yarrow flowers, and Rock Creek Park musings for taking the edge off this particular challenge.

June 12: WHEN I CAN'T GO TO BOUNDARY BRIDGE

HERE IS HOW I soothe myself on a beautiful June day when I can't go to Boundary Bridge but must instead tend to my editorial "to do" list: Turn on the sprinkler and watch the water beads collect on the soon-to-bloom red bee-balm, which will send out its bee-balm alert to ruby-throated humming-birds; watch bees dive into the dusky pink coronas of the swamp milkweed; say good morning to the golden mollusk inching across the front walk; fill the bird feeders and listen to the songs of the cardinals, song sparrows, and robins; water the coral hibiscus that Terrie gave us in memory of Bill; collect handfuls of Swiss chard, basil, thyme, rosemary, and tarragon for a breakfast omelet; nibble herbs on the way to the stove; cook an omelet; eat the omelet; resist seduction of the northeast wind and the urge to chuck it all for Bound-ary Bridge; bring laptop with a freshly charged battery to the picnic table; chain bare ankles to the table legs; read and weep over the latest email from sister Ellie: "Hill and I have been running in the evenings. It is that June wildflower scent of strawberry blossom phase; the sound of a hermit thrush sends me into orbit as the light plays through the leaves, and my eyes kiss the birches, ferns, and buttercups." Oh, to be in Rock Creek Park.

June 17: ANOTHER SIGN AT FENWICK BRANCH

THE YELLOW BULLETIN warning about the raw sewage still hangs on a wooden rail of the Fenwick Branch footbridge, but it now has company: A second alert, typed on a plain sheet of white paper with United States Park Police insignia. It says that, on the morning of June 14th (Jesse's birthday), a woman jogger was assaulted on Blackhorse Trail (part of my loop trail) at 9:00 a.m.

and the assailant pulled her shorts down. The assailant is described as a man in his late twenties, 5' 10" tall, 250 pounds, with a "buzz" cut. Sophie (who came home for Jesse's birthday) and I walked that very trail later on the day of the attack, before the bulletin went up. We wondered why ours was the only car in the parking lot on such a delightfully cool summer day.

How do I respond to this news? The Boundary Bridge area of Rock Creek Park is my refuge and inspiration at all hours of the day. In the near term, it is the destination for my third Audubon field trip this coming Saturday. In preparation to lead that trip, I must spend many hours along the trails during the next few days, keying out ferns that are new to me and taking a stab at identifying dragonflies, damselflies, and butterflies. I will plan my teaching based on what is flowering and fruiting and varying from our last trip in April. In the longer term, the place is my sacred font of sanity and connection to our Earth.

I felt a mix of fear and anger after reading the sign. Attacking a jogger at 9 a.m. is a pretty brazen act. The assailant didn't pick a weak person or a less challenging time of day. Was the woman wearing head phones? How did she get away? Of course, I was hungry for details. Will they catch this guy? The physical description was helpful, since I could rule out all the lone men I saw on my route after reading the sign. Another jogger stopped to talk to me after she came up behind me. "I didn't want to scare you," she said, "coming up from behind like that." She said she was "freaked out" by the news and was going to call a friend in the police department to get more information. I told her I was glad to see her and hoped that people wouldn't stop using the trail–otherwise it would indeed become unsafe. She nodded in agreement and jogged on down the trail in her purple shorts and shirt (and head-phones—perhaps a bad idea).

When I first read the bulletin, I thought I'd have to change my behavior. But, by the end of my woodland loop, I was filled with the conviction that life would go on and I would continue to seek refuge in Rock Creek Park, with a bit more caution. I was conscious at the Meditation Rock that my midstream reveries, which are in full view from many hidden spots, might have to be cut short for a while. But I felt completely safe in "Nana's Lap," my earthen seat at the base of a large protective tulip tree, where I am hidden from trail's view as I lean into a comfy crook in the trunk.

Later in the day, over salads on Woodmont Avenue, I asked a friend if she knew of any other primate species in which the males are violent threats to females. She shook her head. I couldn't think of a single species of mammal in which males routinely injure and kill adult females, although the sex act can get rough. I know that male lions have been known to kill the cubs of rival males (territorial paternity behavior is quite universal), but human females are never really safe, and, sadly, most dangers emanate from our own species.

As I sit in my picture-perfect backyard surrounded by leafy trees, blooming plants, chirping birds, and cooling zephyrs, I feel compelled to continue my lament about human affairs on the planet. Often, as I walk along Rock Creek, wishing its waters were pristine, wishing I could bathe in them, nervously scanning the shallows for signs of aquatic life, my thoughts turn to the Ganges River. I think of how the defiled Ganges is still a sacred waterway for millions of people who immerse themselves reverentially, undaunted by the deadly microbes teeming beneath the surface. Sometimes I just want to forget about microbial risk and plunge myself into sparkling but often filthy Rock Creek, to commune with the deities of the stream.

Now I turn to the daily paper, spreading it out on my picnic table, and I am confronted with the latest episode in our ongoing waking nightmare, our dark fairy tale, climate change in the new millennium. "A Sacred River Endangered by Global Warming" reads a headline in today's *Washington Post.* The story with the dateline Varanasi, India, begins:

> With her eyes sealed, Ramedi cupped the murky water of the Ganges River in her hands, lifted them toward the sun, and prayed for her husband, her 15 grandchildren and her bad hip. She, like the rest of India's 800 million Hindus, has absolute faith that the river she calls Ganga Ma can heal . . . .
>
> 'Ganga Ma is everything to Hindus. It's our chance to attain nirvana,' Ramedi said, emerging from the river, her peach-colored sari dripping along the shoreline.
>
> But the prayer rituals carried out at the water's edge may not last forever—or even another generation, according to scientists

and meteorologists. The Himalayan source of Hinduism's holiest river, they say, is drying up.

In this 3,000-year-old city known as the Jerusalem of India for its intense religious devotion, climate change could throw into turmoil something many devout Hindus thought was immutable: their most intimate religious traditions. The Gangotri glacier, which provides up to 70 percent of the water of the Ganges, is shrinking at the rate of 40 yards a year, nearly twice as fast as two decades ago, scientists say.

'This may be the first place on Earth where global warming could hurt our very religion. We are becoming an endangered species of Hindus,' said Veer Bhadra Mishra, an engineer and director of the Varanasi-based Sankat Mochan Foundation, an organization that advocates for the preservation of the Ganges. 'The melting glaciers are a terrible thing. We have to ask ourselves, who are the custodians of our culture if we can't even help our beloved Ganga?'

The story by Emily Wax, of *The Washington Post's* foreign service, continues:

Environmental groups such as Mishra's have long focused on the pollution of the Ganges. More than 100 cities and countless villages are situated along the 1,568-mile river, which stretches from the foothills of the Himalayas to the Bay of Bengal, and few of them have sewage treatment plants.

But recent reports by scientists say the Ganges is under even greater threat from global warming. According to a U.N. climate report, the Himalayan glaciers that are the sources of the Ganges could disappear by 2030 as temperatures rise.

The shrinking glaciers also threaten Asia's supply of fresh water. The World Wildlife Fund in March listed the Ganges among the world's 10 most endangered rivers. In India, the river provides more than 500 million people with water for drinking and farming.

The immediate effect of glacier recession is a short-lived surplus of water. But eventually the supply runs out, and experts predict that the Ganges eventually will become a seasonal river, largely dependent on monsoon rains.

The story points out that India argues that developed countries like the United States should reduce their own greenhouse gas emissions before developing countries have to bear the brunt. The ongoing logic of the United States is: Why should it make sacrifices if India and China won't?

The line in the story that haunts me the most is: "'We have to ask ourselves, who are the custodians of our culture . . . .?'" If there are any cultural custodians in India or the United States, with the will and ability to deliver a wake-up call to the powers that be, would you kindly come forward?

One of Bob Dylan's most haunting lines in his song, "Masters of War," is:

You've thrown the worst fear
That can ever be hurled
Fear to bring children
Into the world.

I felt that fear acutely before I had children, and now I have a new fear: Fear to bring grandchildren into this world. As I write, two of my friends are awaiting the births of grandchildren. When I hear of a birth or an impending birth, I'm filled with hope for the future. I applaud the brave and intelligent young parents who are not afraid to bring children into the world. But I also fear for them, and I know that, if we are going to continue to bring children into the world, we are going to have to bring fewer of them, and we are going to have to turn out the lights above their cradles, light a candle or two . . . and pray . . . our hands cupping whatever sacred waters we can find.

On a happier note, I experienced some moments of rare beauty this past week. I went to the National Arboretum on Wednesday to meet with Joan Feely, the curator of Fern Valley. It started to rain, and, rather than go inside, she and I sat on a stone bench in the midst of Fern Valley, my notes cradled under an umbrella as I conducted a short interview for *City of Trees.*

I had brought along my camera equipment hoping to capture some blooming trees. After the interview, I drove to the magnolia collection, but it was far too wild and windy for picture-taking and frequent, close, cloud-to-ground lightning punctuated the air. Still, I couldn't resist getting out of the car. Being struck by lightning in a magnolia grove would not be a bad way to go. I walked through the trees under my umbrella. All the southern and sweetbay magnolia trees were covered with blossoms, top to bottom. The fragrance of rain-soaked lemon-scented flowers filled the air. And, when I looked to the horizon, silver-gilded white thunderheads were piled thousands of feet into the sky. In the wet seeming-wilderness of the arboretum, I pinched myself yet again. This garden of earthly delights exists smack dab in the middle of northeast Washington, DC. Who, not knowing, would guess?

Perhaps our leaders should get out more so they'll have a clearer idea of what we stand to lose. President John Quincy Adams swam naked in the Potomac River, daily, and other presidents, from Abraham Lincoln to Teddy Roosevelt, gallivanted about Washington's wilderness on horseback. Some of this wilderness is still here, but for how long?

My computer battery is down to twelve percent. Time to sign off and make breakfast for Sophie and Jesse. I only have time to note ever so briefly that a story in yesterday's *Post* was devoted to the sinking Jefferson Memorial. Closest to the Potomac River and built on fill, it will be the first to go as Earth's oceans rise, but the Lincoln Memorial, Washington Monument, and White House will not be far behind, if we don't change our ways and begin to curb the rising sea levels. *Calling all custodians.*

Part III

SUMMER

June 27: WHILE IN BED

SO MANY THINGS are keeping me from full communion with the summer jungle at Rock Creek. First, there was the overflowing Fenwick Branch sewer, making Rock Creek unfit even for the dogs whose swimming we humans enjoy vicariously. Then the jogger in the park was attacked with the shadow of the assailant left behind. (There has been no arrest.) And now the latest: I have contracted Lyme disease, no doubt from a tiny tick who spent time riding on one of the deer in the Boundary Bridge herd and then decided to dine on me.

When I led my third Audubon "Year at Boundary Bridge" field trip last Saturday, before I knew I had Lyme disease, I watched with curious detachment as two women who are Lyme survivors clothed their bodies head to toe, sprayed Deet at vulnerable points of entry, and tied their pant legs around their ankles. One had gotten a pretty bad case a few years ago with neurological impairment in one of her legs, but she suffers no residual effects. The other has the disease chronically and is taking steroids in order to function. We talked about Lyme while awaiting the other field-trip participants, and I had the vague thought that it was remarkable I had so far escaped the disease.

When we lived in the country near Comus, nightly checks for ticks were part of our spring and summer routine, as Jim, Sophie, Jesse, and I checked ourselves and each other over carefully, just like any small band of primates trying to get the upper hand with vermin. The large "dog ticks" were easy prey during these nightly hunts, but the tiny "deer ticks" (vectors of Lyme disease) can be smaller than the head of a pin. When these engorged minibeasts were found too late, in a jar they were put, and off to the doctor they went to be examined under the doctor's microscope. We returned home, almost always clutching a prescription for an antibiotic.

Now that we live in Chevy Chase, we don't do those checks anymore. This seems to be fine for the rest of the family, who aren't in the woods much, but apparently not for me. Why did I feel immune to deer ticks here, where I'm still a woodland wanderer, with little regard for a proper trail when wilder landscapes beckon? How had I failed to think that bounding deer were bound to be carrying small passengers?

I think this is the first time I've written about Boundary Bridge while in bed, with my laptop propped on a flowered pillow. Today, I'm perking up. Yesterday, I did little but sleep, my whole body aching and the rash between my neck and shoulder having blossomed from zero to five inches in diameter the day before. I hope I'm on the mend, but I'll have to be smart to deal with this crafty disease.

The participants on my field trip certainly enjoyed their jungle foray. How much like the forest primeval the Rock Creek woodlands seem in early summer. The trees have escaped the axe for more than a century, and the rich alluvial soil that supports ferns and summer wildflowers again "smells good," in the words of one participant.

As we did in January and April, we gathered on the stone arc of Boundary Bridge and looked up into the trees. The American elm that held tiny new leaves and flat, round, notched samaras during the spring foray was fully leafed, its graceful branches arching over the tea-colored creek. I pointed out how nice it is to admire the profile of an American elm in its native habitat, since we're more accustomed to seeing it as a street-tree. The whole demeanor of this tree in the park was looser and freer than its street-tree siblings, as its trunk gently leaned over the water. Leaves obscured the creamy limbs of the sycamore on the opposite shore, and its ripening fruit was hard to detect in the crown. But, later, we were able to get close to the fruit balls on the fallen sycamore giant, apparently still alive, that lies across the creek near the Skunk Cabbage Swamp. The fresh new fruits look much as they do in the winter but in summer are green, with reddish tints, rather than their winter brown.

On the southwestern side of Boundary Bridge, the tall tulip tree surely held upright clusters of maturing samaras in its leafy branches, but we could only see the tulip-shaped leaves, now less stiffly and uprightly held than when they first emerged in spring. Next to the tulip tree, a much smaller ironwood draped itself with hanging clusters of tiny nutlets attached to toothed, triangular, leafy bracts. (If I were a jeweler, I would design a series of earrings modeled after the fruit and flowers of Rock Creek Park trees.) The long, tall, leaning river birches with their flaky cinnamon bark displayed fully leafed-out crowns, and, on both sides of the bridge, small, gleaming, green spicebush drupes spiced the air.

The walk became a meditation of sorts, a meditation on the green but ripening fruit of woody plants, partially hidden and not usually attracting notice at this stage of development. There were three species of native viburnums (arrowwood, blackhaw, and maple-leaved) with small, firm, clustered green drupes soon to ripen to black or blue-black; a few walnuts had fallen from the tall canopy, encased in round, green husks with the fragrance of butter and lime (dubbed "key lime pie" by Janice Browne, a returning participant); and oak acorns and bitternut, pignut, and mockernut hickories were still small-ish and hard to find, except where they'd fallen prematurely to the ground. Swollen, papery, bladdernut capsules were on the trees, and last year's reddish-brown fruit was on the ground, where they are spilling their small, rattly, popcorn-like seeds. Boxelder samaras hung in long clusters. The samaras from both the green and white species of ash confettied the ground. The small differences in their winged seeds is the best diagnostic for identifying them. Notably, where the terrain was slightly upland from the creek, the samaras were those of the white ash, with short, wide seeds at the top, while in the floodplain most were the slender-seeded samaras of the green ash. ("Wide, white, and lean green" is a helpful mnemonic.) Still-green cherries hung from wild black cherry trees, and we saw green greenbrier berries, another blue-black mature fruit that is green in June. Occasionally, we'd find an entire tulip-shaped cluster of immature samaras from the tulip trees lying in the trail.

Everyone also enjoyed seeing fruit ripening on herbaceous plants, including some we'd seen at the wildflower stage in April such as the mayapple's large single berry, now turning from toxic green to edible gold. But where to draw the line at edibility? This native plant has a noteworthy herbal history, one that includes a recent chapter of very personal meaning for me. One of my botany students from last summer, a sweet and intelligent young man who is an accomplished photographer, was diagnosed with lymphoma. Two rounds of chemotherapy failed to put him in remission, and then he went on an experimental drug derived from the mayapple plant. The herbal drug seems to be working, and he has taken some stunning and appreciative pictures of mayapple plants. Many people's thoughts turn to tropical rain forests when they think of botanical pharmaceuticals, but our temperate woods are filled with medicines known to the native peoples who lived here. This knowledge was often passed on to Colonial settlers and, in some cases—as with the mayapple—is being resurrected and revived by contemporary scientists.

On a more frivolous note, I told my childhood Jack-in-the-pulpit story as we stood next to a cluster of green, soon-to-be-red fruit at the edge of the Skunk Cabbage Swamp. One day when I was in third grade, my teacher started a tale with the warning, "Boys and girls, never try this." That got my attention. I listened carefully as Mrs. Stevens said that she and her husband had hiked over the weekend and found some Jack-in-the-pulpit fruit. She had heard that bears favor the tiny clustered berries and thought she'd try one herself. "Well!" she said, "It was hot!"

The next day or soon thereafter, I corralled my little brother, Mike, who must have been shy of his fifth birthday, and led him out to a Jack-in-the-pulpit patch in a neighboring woodland. There we found the small red-clustered berries. I told him it would probably be hot, "but I'll taste some, if you will."

We both took small, tentative bites but not tentative enough. The oxalic acid crystals in the fruit cut through our tender little tongues. It felt like having my tongue sliced with a knife and set on fire at the same time. We ran home screaming for Mommy. I hope that was the meanest escapade in which I ever engaged my little brother. I also wonder if I paid any more heed to my teacher's admonitions from that day forth, but I suspect her warnings did little to dampen my curiosity.

Although Rock Creek's woodland energies seemed bent on the business of fruiting during this time of the summer solstice, several wildflowers were blooming, and some bore flowers and fruit simultaneously. The latter included two members of the carrot or parsley family, a plant family renowned for its culinary delights—carrots, celery, coriander, dill, fennel, parsley, and parsnips—but also some notoriously poisonous species, including the plant that reputedly killed Socrates: Poison hemlock. Poison hemlock and its toxic cousin, the water hemlock, are plants of the Maryland-Virginia countryside, the former naturalized and the latter native. I have not yet seen either at Boundary Bridge, but a member of the carrot family called honewort is one of the most common June wildflowers near the bridge, blooming both in the floodplain and in the upland woods. Members of this family produce flowers in usually flat, circular, umbrella-like clusters called umbels. Queen Anne's lace is the most common naturalized member of the family in our region, and it's also known as "wild carrot"—of the same species as the garden carrot.

The two species of the carrot family now blooming at Rock Creek have umbels less classically shaped than those of the more familiar Queen Anne's lace. Honewort's small, irregular umbels of tiny white flowers feature incurved petals. Its fruit is a small, narrow, upright "schizocarp," a dry, two-parted fruit typical of the family, and its leaves often arrange themselves in irregularly shaped patterns of threes. A leafy sheath surrounds the lower leaf stalk, typical of the family. A second species, called clustered snakeroot, possesses even less recognizable umbels—small, rounded (not flat-topped), and composed of dainty, greenish-yellow flowers. Its clusters of bristly fruit make more of a visual splash than do the flowers, and its lower leaves are wide and often five-lobed. A third member of the carrot family that just finished blooming in Rock Creek's woods is sweet cicely. By this time of the year, its small, white umbels have been replaced by purple-brown schizocarps. This plant has attractive, softly hairy fern-like leaves and an anise-flavored root.

Another early-summer wildflower we saw along the trails is called enchanter's nightshade. Both its common name and its scientific genus name, *Circaea*—derived from the name of the mythological enchantress, Circe—hint at the role this plant has played in sorcery and witchcraft. I don't know much about its cultural history, but its tiny white flowers, which have two petals that are so deeply cleft they appear to be four, have an "enchanting," fairy-like quality. They grow in small, terminal clusters above opposite pairs of thin, succulent-looking leaves. The flowers are soon replaced by tiny, bristly fruit. We saw plants bearing both flowers and fruit on Saturday. In the White Mountains of New Hampshire, a plant called dwarf or alpine enchanter's nightshade grows in the woods near the summer home of Jim's family, looking very similar but more diminutive.

The common names of wildflowers are often deliciously descriptive and contain clues to the plants' herbal histories. But they are notoriously confusing, which is the reason that even amateur botanists are urged to learn scientific (Latin) nomenclature. Enchanter's nightshade, for example, belongs to the evening primrose family, not the nightshade family. Two plants in bloom at Boundary Bridge on Saturday *do* belong to the nightshade family, and, like the carrot family, that family is a strange mix of important edibles and deadly poisons. It even contains a few plants famous for their narcotic and hallucinogenic properties.

The well-known members of the nightshade family (sometimes called the tomato family) include bell peppers, eggplant, petunias, potatoes, tobacco, tomatoes, and the highly toxic belladonna! Anyone who has grown a vegetable garden is familiar with the small, five-petaled flowers characteristic of tomatoes, eggplants, and bell peppers. One of the native nightshade family wildflowers blooming now at Rock Creek is named horse nettle. (And here's more name confusion—horse nettle is not a true nettle, but at Rock Creek it blooms near members of the true nettle family!) It has flowers very similar to the garden plants. Its fruit resembles a small golden tomato but is better left on the vine, because it's highly toxic. The plant's stalk, lower leaves, and petiole are covered with the sharp prickles that give rise to its common name. A few horse nettle plants grow near the West Beach Drive Bridge. Out in Comus, the farmer who hays our field only gets a single spring cutting because the horse nettle springs up throughout the pasture from mid-summer on, making the hay inedible.

The floral star of Saturday's foray was undoubtedly the jimsonweed, another member of the nightshade family notable for its spectacular trumpet-shaped blossoms and for the story that Janice Browne's husband, Allen, told about it as we gathered on the gravel beach where it grows. Jimsonweed bears large, lavender-white and trumpet-shaped blossoms, like longer but more bodacious versions of its cousin, the petunia. The flower's buds look like spirally folded lavender silk. I knew this tallish coarse plant had a legendary history as an Old World ritual hallucinogenic, but I knew nothing of its fabled reputation in the New World. Apparently, it has been used in sacred rituals from India and Europe to the Americas.

Allen told us that the name "jimsonweed" refers to Jamestown, where some British soldiers got punch-drunk on it for several days and had to be restrained. After the field trip, he forwarded its Wikipedia entry to me, which I read to Jim while he was loading the dishwasher the other night:

> *Datura stramonium* [jimsonweed] is native to either India or Central America [a globally widespread plant of uncertain origin]. It was used as a mystical sacrament in both possible places of origin. The Native Americans have used this plant in sacred ceremonies. In some tribes datura was involved in ceremonies of manhood. The sadhus of Hinduism also used datura as a spiritual tool, smoking it with cannabis in their traditional chillums.
>
> In the United States it is called Jimson weed, Gypsum weed, Angel Trumpet, Hells Bells or more rarely Jamestown Weed; it got this name from the town of Jamestown, Virginia, where British soldiers were secretly or accidentally drugged with it, while attempting to suppress Bacon's Rebellion. They spent several days chasing feathers, making monkey faces, generally acting like lunatics, and indeed failed at their mission.

The Wikipedia article went on to quote from Robert Beverley's *The History and Present State of Virginia* (1705):

> Some of the soldiers sent thither to quell the rebellion of Bacon (1676); and some of them ate plentifully of it, the effect of which was a very pleasant comedy, for they turned natural fools upon it for several days: one would blow a feather in the air; another would dart straws at it with much fury; and another, stark naked, was sitting in a corner like a monkey, grinning and making maws [grimaces] at them; a fourth would fondly kiss and paw his companions, and sneer in their faces with a countenance more antic than any in a Dutch droll.

In this frantic condition they were confined, lest they should,
in their folly, destroy themselves—though it was observed that all
their actions were full of innocence and good nature.

Porky, our pet pig, presided over a jimsonweed garden. No edible plant
escaped his powerful snout in the fenced-in areas around his dwellings at our
Seneca Creek and Comus homes, but he was smarter than a British soldier
when it came to jimsonweed. In fact, Porky assiduously avoided members of
both the nightshade and carrot families, dazzling me with his botanical savvy.
He would leave bell peppers and parsley at the bottom of his feed dish on the
days when I fed him leftover vegetable stews, but he made two exceptions to
his carrot/nightshade rule. He could never resist a juicy tomato. I can still
see the juice dripping down the sides of his bristly jaw as he tipped his head
back and snarfed down a ripe one, grunting with joy. And, although Porky
had turned up his nose at carrots for years, one day he saw me feed carrots
to a horse residing in a pasture next to him. He always became jealous when
I paid attention to this horse, and he would scream his displeasure. After
watching me feed carrots to the horse, he seemed to beg for his own carrot.
So I gave him a nibble to test, and he gulped it down. From that day forward, Porky crossed carrots off the forbidden plant list, having learned from
another animal that they wouldn't kill him, or, perhaps, he was so overcome
with jealousy that he was willing and ready to die to match his rival.

In my Lyme-diseased, antibiotic-hazed state, I've been having vivid
dreams, including a recurring dream about Porky. In the dream, he is living
in a wild place. The terrain is usually hilly and varied, with woods, fields,
fences, stone walls, and small creeks cutting through the steep terrain. Porky
is happy living wild, and he's self-sufficient. But he misses us and journeys
to see us, bringing us back to share his new home. The dreams are a mixture
of peace, wild joy, and a discomforting disconnect between our world and
his. I don't often have recurring dreams, so this is one I want to remember
and understand.

Getting back to the Rock Creek foray of last week, our group stopped at
the Riley Spring foot bridge just before the trail crosses Beach Drive, where
the creek is more of an idle meander than it is at Boundary Bridge. We had
seen no fish in the swiftly flowing water beneath Boundary Bridge, but here

at the Riley Spring Bridge, about a mile and a half into our walk, some small fish swam in the shallows. I asked my friend Cecily if she'd show us how she "conducts" fish.

Cecily wrote a piece in this month's *Audubon Naturalist News* titled "The Joys of June." In it she describes how she learned to "conduct fish." Standing on the bridge over the creek near her home, she noticed that fish reacted to her shadow, swimming away from it, as if she were a great blue heron ready to pounce. She experimented by waving her arms and thus moving her shadow over the creek, and she soon learned how to control the motions of the fish in the creek below her. Her partner, Lou, took a picture of her standing on her bridge "conducting fish" that ran with the story.

Here, the fish responded to her movements but apparently not as dramatically as they do at her own bridge, which is closer to the water. While Cecily was "conducting," a mother wood duck and her babies paddled under the bridge and upstream, undeterred by the fish orchestra. When they got to a big rock in the stream, several babies swam around the rock to the right and several to the left. It sparked a memory for me of last June and the post-ten-inch deluge, when I watched a wood duck family from the same spot on this bridge, log-hopping their way along a debris-strewn creek after the flood. At the time, a giant tree trunk and its twenty-some-foot root-ball was slammed against the stone bridge, probably threatening its integrity, and collecting mountains of trash. I wondered if those baby wood ducks would grow up to be especially adept at log-hopping.

While we were all oohing and awing over the feathered brood and its upstream progress, my binoculared gaze wandered into an uncommon butternut tree next to the bridge, where I discovered bunches of ripening nuts encased in green husks much like those of the walnuts we'd seen earlier, but these were elongated rather than round. When I exclaimed over the botanical find, a few participants shifted their binoculars from wood ducks to butternuts. But only a few. The birders stayed trained on the ducks without flinching, as if I'd never made a peep.

Most people on these field trips have an interest in everything they see: Birds, butterflies, dragonflies, flowers, frogs, or rocks. But there is the birder, and there is the botanist, and each becomes deaf to news from the other when the action starts!

July 8: RECOVERY REVERIE

TRYING TO RECOVER from Lyme disease during the past two weeks has been like an uncomfortable, extended dream, with many hours spent in bed and my few forays into the world shaky, tentative, and short-lived. Coincidentally, the children have been gone, with Sophie working in Providence for the summer and Jesse on a six-week marine biology trip in Florida. What I'd planned as a combination vacation and work-jag (my first extended child-free time in twenty-one years) has become a time of illness and convalescence, where I've ranged from feeling disappointed and demoralized to accepting this disease for what it is, a non-negotiable time of rest and recuperation.

Today, I awake feeling like myself, which gives me such a jolt of joy that I spring from the bed to greet the dawn. Jim has left to play softball on this Sunday morning, and I head out to my favorite retreat.

I feel almost shy as I step onto the familiar stone arc of Boundary Bridge, but my heart sings at the sight of the elms and river birches leaning over the golden-flowing water. I take slow steps into the dark forest, feeling like Gretel without her Hansel or breadcrumbs, enchanted and awed once again by the height and depth of the canopy. A new layer of golden-red soil covers parts of the flood-ravaged trail. The woods smell good, and the rich, springy flood-plain is spiked with scent of spicebush. Filmy sunlight streaks through openings in the canopy, spotlighting botanical wonders of the forest's floor—a cluster of delicate New York ferns, a whorl of four leaves of wild yam, a starry white avens flower, and tiny blossoms of enchanter's nightshade.

The woods are summer-still, an imperceptible shift in the barely detectable breeze signaling a change from northwest to southwest, augmenting a transformation in climate from Mediterranean-dry to New Orleans-steam over the next few days. But I know this secondhand from reading the paper, not from walking through the deep and calming shade, with its dazzling shafts of sunlight.

Beach Drive, running along the western side of Rock Creek, is closed to traffic on Sundays, and the only sounds emanating from it are the crisscrossing whir of bicycle wheels and the calls of cyclists. Dogs splash in the creek, and their owners converse happily by the shore, asking their exuberant canines *please* not to shake the creek's water on them. I walk out onto the wide, gravel beach that has become a garden of jimsonweed and look into the lavender-silk "angel trumpets." My antibiotic requires me to limit exposure to the sun, so I don't linger on the beach but return, through the panic grass and nettle patch, to the forest deep and primeval.

Under the pawpaw trees and past the bladdernut grove I mosey, occasionally touching the massive, grooved trunks of the tulip trees along the trail. A single moth mullein plant leans over the creek's eroded bank, its small, white, cup-shaped flowers with purple, feathery stamens growing up and down its stalk. I pass beneath the West Beach Drive Bridge, from where I see a kingfisher silently winging downstream. The sign announcing the June 14th assault on the jogger is still nailed to the Fenwick Branch footbridge, rust already forming small, orange haloes around the staples that attach it to the wooden railing.

In the Skunk Cabbage Swamp, the orange jewelweed (also called spotted touch-me-not or wild impatiens) blooms profusely. Jewelweed is a time-honored remedy for exposure to poison ivy and nettle stings, and both the toxic vine and wood nettle plants are in evidence nearby. From the swamp, the terrain changes abruptly to rocky upland woods and a whole new plant community: Beech, hickory, oak, witch-hazel, wild hydrangea, and Christmas fern. Here the canopy grows less dense, and the trees, while tall and broad-crowned, grow a little more thinly spaced, so, as I climb the hill into the trees in mid-summer, it feels as if I am leaving the jungle.

As I walk slowly up the switch-backing trail, my heart fills with gratitude, because I feel so much better. My feet are sure stepping along the sandy and rocky trail that, in July, winds through heart-shaped, leaves of white wood aster. My skin revels in the morning warmth. This is the gift of illness: The joy we feel when we can once again do what we most love to do. And what I love to do is simply *be* in the wild world, with no purpose or agenda.

I climb out onto the Laurel Ledge above the Meditation Rock, into a garden of native woody and herbaceous plants—beech, hydrangea, mountain laurel, partridge-berry, pinxter, witch hazel, and rock polypody fern. One invasive plant also grows in this native rock garden—wineberry. My botanist friends tell me I should uproot it wherever I see it, and I know they're right. But I can't do it, especially in July when the jeweled red fruits are ripe and ready to jump from the vine. Yum! I still miss the naturalized wineberries along the country roads of Comus and the way my young children lit into them.

I make my way down the root-woven ledge to the Meditation Rock, now feeling a little tired and shaky. The rock basks in full-sun, so I find shade on an adjacent rock perch and sit there for a long time. The eastern bank of Rock Creek, steep and wooded with tall trees, is shadowed slate-gray to midnight-black, with brilliant patches of sunlit green. White-tailed dragonflies zoom purposefully past me, and delicate damselflies hover over the rocks. Even at a distance I can see small fish dart through the golden-brown shallows, and yellow-and-black tiger swallowtail butterflies glide and dip along the opposite shore.

When I spot a lone female wood duck silently swimming upstream, I wonder why she is alone, but my thought is premature. Her brown-feathered babes are nearby, temporarily hidden by rocks and upturned roots. A little older than the brood we saw on the recent field trip (and probably the very same), they are not in tight formation with mama at the helm but paddling about on their own not far from her.

Familiar birds sing from the canopy: The sweet wood-pewee, the magical wood thrush, the churring red-bellied woodpecker, the red-eyed vireo with its repetitive song, "see me, here I am, see me, here I am," and the eastern towhee articulating clearly and musically "drink your tea." Softly rhythmic crickets and louder cicadas complete the chorus. And then a great blue heron comes winging around the bend in the creek, looking for its next fishing hole.

I sit on the rock and don't give a thought to the raw sewage that may be making its way through the creek, or a lurking human male predator, or the Lyme-disease vectors that fill the woods. The creek simply flows past, and the morning sun touches the dark, wooded ledge, and I rejoice in summer's still-point.

July 13: LADY BIRD

ON THE FRONT PAGE of yesterday's *Washington Post* appeared a picture of Lady Bird Johnson wearing a straw hat with a red band and sitting in a field of red-and-gold Indian blanket flowers in the Texas Hill Country. She died this week at ninety-four. The caption of Joe Holley's tribute—"Champion of Conservation, Loyal Force Behind LBJ"—refers to her great passions and her great loss. She will be most remembered for instigating the drive to beautify America, including the nation's cities, and for anguishing with her husband and worrying about his health during his vigil over Vietnam.

I will remember her as a true nature lover and someone who kindly granted me an interview—conducted by phone from her ranch in Texas— when I was a young, aspiring author struggling to establish myself in the bewildering city of Washington, DC. It was my experience that the people in the highest places were the kindest to me when I was trying to find a professional niche in a seemingly unwelcoming capital. But that is a story for another day.

When I wrote the first edition of *City of Trees*—and interviewing Lady Bird was part of my research—I learned that both Johnsons were passionate conservationists. The "Lyndon Baines Johnson Memorial Grove and Lady Bird Johnson Park" chapter of my book contains this quote from LBJ's writings: "I would have been content to be simply a conservation President...My deepest attitudes and beliefs were shaped by a closeness to the land, and it was only natural for me to think of preserving it." Although Lady Bird is more often identified with conservation than is her husband—who is better known for his "Great Society" programs, the Voting Rights Act of 1965, and the gut-wrenching escalation of the Vietnam War—during the Johnson Administration more than 3,500,000 acres were added to the National Park System, the Wilderness Act of 1964 was signed into law, and important air- and water-quality legislation was passed. The desire to conserve is born of love, and clearly both Johnsons possessed a love of the land, reaching back to their childhoods in Texas.

Lady Bird's legacy commands several pages in today's paper. There are pictures of her looking glamorous in a yellow-and-white gown under a White House chandelier, holding an infant grandchild on the South Lawn, planting pansies along Madison Drive, and standing next to Lyndon and Jackie in her blood-stained suit as he is sworn in as President on Air Force One after JFK's assassination. She looks most relaxed in a shot of her sitting close to Lyndon on a bench at their ranch after the conclusion of his presidency, her hand gently and comfortably on his, a small white dog beside them, and the Pedernales River in the background. Midway into today's tribute are the following paragraphs:

> When Lady Bird was 5, her mother, Minnie Pattillo Taylor, died from a fall. Throughout her life, Mrs. Johnson clung to an image of her mother walking through East Texas woods gathering wildflowers.
>
> Her father summoned a frail maiden aunt from Alabama to take care of his little girl. The beloved aunt permitted her a 'free-ranging sort of childhood,' in which she roamed the pastures and forests near her home and paddled in the dark bayous of Caddo Lake but was taught little about things that traditionally interest girls her age.

I can picture young "Lady Bird"—a nickname attributed to a nursemaid who deemed her "purty as a ladybird"—pondering the mysteries of Caddo Lake and wandering the fields and woodlands of East Texas, remembering her mother.

Little Lady Bird on Caddo Lake was given one of the greatest gifts that Earth has to bestow. Longing for her mother and away from prying eyes and dictates of decorum, she discovered her direct connection to the natural world, a connection that would inspire, strengthen, and guide her throughout her life. Mrs. Johnson, First Lady of a grateful land, wherever you are now, thank you for sharing with us what you learned to cherish and hold dear. And, President Johnson, may you also be remembered for your conservation legacy.

July 15: A TALE OF TWO LILIES

HOW I LOVE my summer-morning rituals. Presiding over a temporarily empty nest is a bittersweet experience, especially when illness is added into the mix. But, even when I was sickest with Lyme disease, I performed the simple rituals of feeding the birds, watering the gardens, and gathering flowers.

The bed, when it gets made, doesn't receive the benefit of hospital corners. The clothes get cleaned but wait awhile for folding and are rarely ironed. I hasten through the indoor chores, my mind lost in thought. This is in direct contrast to the mindfulness with which I engage in my outdoor rounds. This morning, all three feeders, which hang from a single post, are empty. Within two minutes of refill, a red-bellied woodpecker pecks at the suet, and a house finch finds the seeds of thistle. Chickadees and cardinals take turns at the sunflower seeds, and a black squirrel posts himself at the base of the feeders, enjoying the overflow. And since I'm more of a journalist than a poet, I feel compelled to report that, at the moment, all three feeders are overrun with starlings who have bullied away the beautiful songbirds.

As I move the sprinklers around the front and back gardens, my heart fills with beauty. A yellow-and-black tiger swallowtail alights on the spires of the butterfly bush that spreads over the front walk. Bees and small insects dart in and out of the flowers. A song sparrow sings—*Maids maids maids hang up your teakettles teakettles teakettles.* Cicada song rises and falls. Water beads on the basil, mint, oregano, rosemary, licorice-flavored tarragon, and thyme, which are so deliciously tempting that their leaves rarely make it into the house. The cherry plum tomatoes are ripening next to the kitchen door, but not a single one has yet to make it inside or more than a foot from the vine, because into my mouth they go. Even in my own yard I am more of a forager than a gardener.

This morning, as I wander about the garden in my blue-flowered cotton dress and sandals, I am amazed by the budding Joe-Pye-weed, which is now ten feet tall, the spicy purple bergamot, the unfurling black-eyed Susans, and all the wild jumble of annuals and perennials that spill from the soil in our yard. I love the trees in our yard, with their squirrels in residence running up and down the trunks. Our mini-arboretum includes a tall black oak and a tall white oak, a young Southern magnolia (still putting forth its waxy lemon-scented blossoms), a native redbud with its decidedly heart-shaped leaves, and the memory of the American elm that was hit by lightning and had to be taken down two years ago.

But as I reminisce about my daily garden rounds, I am seriously burying the lead, for here's the real news: Our place has been overtaken by lilies. Night or day, the perfume of our many lilies assaults anyone who comes up the walk or even passes by on the street. For the next two weeks or so, anyone who is allergic to strong scents should *stay away!* Roll up your car windows, walk Fido on another block, and jog quickly past, because in mid-July on this property in the Town of Chevy Chase, lilies rule. And the lily plants in our yard are taller than I am! They are stationed in all the gardens facing the street, and their pelican-beak buds, which have been set and ready-looking for weeks, are now opening so fast that it's like skirts being lifted at the Moulin Rouge. Enough of the mixed metaphors, but it's not easy to cut to the chase.

A bumble bee that keeps landing on the flower stalks of the hostas distracts me from what I want and need to write about some cut lilies sitting next to me on my picnic table "desk." They are drinking water in a small blue pottery vase shaped like a cake-style, ice-cream cone. Imaginative young Jesse created several brightly painted pottery "cones" for ice cream in an art class several years ago. More often than ice cream, they find themselves filled with small bouquets of cut flowers from the garden.

And now, of course, they hold pink and white lilies whose sweet fragrance, even in the great outdoors, permeates the air. Underneath my blue-and-white umbrella I am immersed in a lily haze, when only two days ago, or even yesterday, today's blossoms were nothing but upturned bud-beaks that only hinted at the magnificence to come.

A pink lily faces me. A strong white seam runs up the back of each of its six curved-back petals. The petals are dark pink at the center, fading to lighter pink with white edges. Lines of purple speckles dot themselves up and down the pink backdrop. The center of the flower is a greenish-yellow six-pointed star, each star point reaching about a third of the way up its appointed petal. The purple speckles surround and frame the star. The white lily is a bit larger than the pink and contains all the same attributes, minus the pink petals, right down to the tip of its wet stigma, which is also pale pink.

The stamens have stiff, upswept filaments that are three inches long. Their anthers are covered with bright orange-brown pollen that is so potent my right hand and forearm are stained mustard-yellow as I type. This stain remains despite scrubbing with soap and the rough side of a sponge soon after gathering the lilies. But it is the female part, the pistil, that is most incredible. With a style a full inch longer than the surrounding six stamens, its small stigma is shaped like a bulbous heart that is pink and wet. Not only is it wet, but, when you gently touch the liquid beaded on its surface, it forms a strand exactly like the strand formed in a woman's cervical mucous at the time of ovulation. *With exactly the same purpose*—facilitating the journey to the waiting ovary.

Last summer, I cut some of these lilies and placed them in a vase on a table just inside our front door. One night some girls, friends of Jesse's, noticed the lilies when they entered and marveled over them, especially the prominent pistils.

This memory helps me get closer to what I really want to share about lilies. You can clone plants. You can even clone animals. But sexual reproduction is the preferred and most highly evolved means of life-continuance. If you want to see the beautiful truth and get a feel for the mystery that weaves us all together through time, you won't find it in a classroom or even in a church, if the god honored or worshipped is disembodied from the natural world. *Look to the lilies.*

July 22: KINGFISHER CHATTER AND SILKY MORNINGS

I CAN'T SEEM to make it to church this summer. Each Sunday morning offers weather more intoxicating than the last, and my first desire upon awakening is to head for Boundary Bridge. This day is the prize-winner. Air conditioning is off, windows are thrown open, and classical guitar pours forth from the dining room, mingling with the breeze out of the northeast. My laptop is set up on the picnic table, and I'm facing a six-foot stalk crowned with white lilies framed by a ten-foot Joe-Pye-weed plant topped with dusky, pink flower buds. Both plants lean with abandon over our wooden fence. Crickets are singing, dogs and their families pass by, mourning doves coo, and fish crows give their nasal calls on the wing.

With Sophie at home for the weekend, I went to Boundary Bridge before she got up to attend Jim's Sunday-morning softball game. Then we made omelets with our own chard, tomatoes, and herbs and we whipped up fruit smoothies with peaches grown by a family we know: The Allnutts, who have been farming the same land near Seneca Creek in Montgomery County,

Maryland, west of Washington since the 1700s. No one can overstate the organic pleasures of summer. Especially on a day like today, when the skies are blue, the temperature is under eighty, the humidity is low, and puffy white cumulus clouds sail in a southwesterly direction, heralding more cool hours to come.

The black depths of the forest canopy near Boundary Bridge have become my summer fix. This morning, I didn't even take time to make coffee. By 8:00, I was patting a four-month-old golden retriever puppy named BJ as I approached the bridge and the floodplain's forest.

Rock Creek is low. We and significant portions of the South, East, and Southwest are experiencing drought. Parts of Texas, meanwhile, have been getting record deluges. The link to global warming can't be proven (*blah blah blah*), but here we are right on target with all the predictions. As my friend, Jeri Metz (a.k.a. Mother Herb), puts it: "This is the wave of the future, folks—drought and deluge."

The water in the creek flows clear, but it looks sluggish and smells slightly off. Still, this doesn't dampen the giddy spirits of everyone I encounter: Dogs splash joyfully as they retrieve large sticks and then trot with them down the trail, water flying from their fur; cyclists call to each other on Beach Drive; and walkers and joggers of all races and nationalities, in small groups and alone, happily converse or get lost in solo reveries. As I wind down the trail, I can't help thinking that this is as close to a utopian urban scene as one can find. When I drive to and from the creek, the cyclists take over the roadway and cars respectfully wait to be noticed.

Under the tall trees, Rock Creek's mid-summer blooms are emerging. Winged monkey flowers grow around the edges of the vernal swamp pond, which was fenced off for amphibian breeding early in the spring. I never learned the ultimate fate of this year's wood-frog broods. The pond dried up pretty thoroughly in mid-spring, and I hope by then that all young frogs had grown strong enough legs to hop away.

I was thrilled and amazed to discover the swamp's monkey flowers two years ago. Monkey flowers are uncommon in this area, and the winged monkey flowers growing near Rock Creek represent the less prevalent of the two indigenous species. Monkey flowers have traditionally belonged to the snapdragon or figwort family, although genetic research may change their taxonomic status. They got their name because the corolla, with its broad lower lip and narrower upper lip, with a little imagination—resembles a monkey's face. The plants are two-to-three feet tall, although they were taller the year I discovered them and were nearly wiped out by last June's flood. The flowers are pale lavender-pink with a hairy yellow blush at the throat. The common name of the Boundary Bridge species—"winged" monkey flower—refers to the vertical ridges decorating the square plant stalk.

Along the creek's bank near the single moth mullein plant stands a little group of Indian tobacco plants with small pale-blue flowers. This wildflower is a lobelia (related to the cardinal flower and great blue lobelia), and its scientific name, *Lobelia inflata,* refers to the swollen calyx that emerges as the flower dies back.

The jimsonweed is thriving at the gravel beach where dogs can always be found splashing and fetching. (From now on, I'm going to call it "Dog Beach!") The jimsonweed's lavender-silk trumpets are still budding and blooming—purple striped in the center with purple anthers and green stigmas—and a few spiny, egg-shaped capsules have formed, containing the seeds with their famed hallucinogenic properties. Sadly, an invasive vine called Japanese hops and the ever-present and despised Japanese stilt grass have overspread the beach, crowding out native plants, but a native nettle garden is holding its own near the jimsonweed and is now in bloom. Wood nettle (with alternate leaves and stinging hairs) and false nettle (with opposite leaves and no stinging hairs) grow side by side, and both bear tiny, creamy-white flowers in narrow strands. Clearweed, another member of the nettle family with succulent stalk and leaves, grows nearby. (I have yet to see stinging nettle—common along the Potomac River—at Boundary Bridge.) Last week, Jim and I saw a red admiral butterfly visiting one of the nettles. Later, when I looked up the butterfly in my field guide, I learned that nettles are host plants for their larvae.

Lots of smartweed or members of the buckwheat family of the *Polygonum* genus are blooming at the creek. (Plants in this genus have been renamed by some contemporary botanists.) Near the monkey flowers in the swamp are the prickly, sprawling stalks of arrow-leaved tearthumb with its small, greenish-white flowers. Long-bristled smartweed, a rather inconspicuous yet invasive plant with small pink flowers, is common along the trails, and an even more seriously invasive prickly plant called mile-a-minute blooms along the creek. Thankfully, mile-a-minute isn't common in the area around Boundary Bridge. A taller plant called jumpseed or Virginia knotweed (*P. virginianum*, sometimes known as *Tovara virginiana*, and more recently moved to yet another genus by some taxonomists) grows here quite ubiquitously. Jumpseed bears small, greenish-white flowers now in bud. The plant is named for its seeds, which, when mature, "jump" when touched.

Orange jewelweed is blooming in the Skunk Cabbage Swamp, which is encircled by jumpseed. This species of jewelweed bears orange flowers with three petals in front of a sac-like sepal that has a spur at the back. I never learned whether the name refers to the jewel-like flowers or to the seeds or to the way water beads on the succulent leaves. The second name, touch-me-not, refers to the way the pod-like capsules spring open and the seeds disperse when touched, "jumping" in your fingers, much like jumpseed. Sophie and Jesse loved to make jewelweed fruits jump when they were little.

In the upland woods, a plant called naked-flowered tick-trefoil is blooming next to the trail. This plant is in the pea or legume family. Its small, purplish-pink flowers are typical of many in the family, with two fused lower petals (collectively called a keel, because they resemble the keel of a boat), two small side-petals called wings, and a showy upper petal known as a banner or standard. The flowers of this species of tick-trefoil are borne on a leafless ("naked") stalk, and the compound tri-parted leaves are borne on a separate lower stalk. The separateness of the flower stalk helps distinguish this plant from several other confusingly similar native tick-trefoils. The flat, dry, segmented green fruit (a specialized legume called a loment) bears hairs that stick to animal fur and clothing, giving the plant its common names tick-trefoil and beggar lice. Trefoil means three-leaved.

This morning, I wove my way through the woods, stopping to admire the magic of each new blossom and to follow the fickle flight of butterflies and dragonflies. Wood thrushes, eastern wood-pewees, Acadian flycatchers, chickadees, ovenbirds, and Carolina wrens sang from the canopy while robins scratched about in the dry leaf litter. When I got to the Meditation Rock (or, rather, the nearby shadowed rock perch that I have adopted since going on my sun-sensitive antibiotic), I noted how languid the creek looked, with more mud showing than I remembered, almost like a tidal creek. But thoughts of drought soon evaporated as I fell under Rock Creek's spell. The reflected light from the water's surface formed quicksilver patterns on the undersides of the beech leaves above me. A breeze rustled in from the northeast, mimicking the water's flow, a rare summer occurrence. In the early morning light, the silver bark of beech trunks and roots clinging to the rock ledge next to me glowed amidst the breeze-rippled ferns.

I heard once again a favorite sound at Rock Creek, which was interrupted by the spring mating season but now echoes along the rock ledge: The chatter of the kingfisher! As the blue-winged bird dipped into view and then lit on a favorite snag, my question about the kingfisher chatter was answered, for the second time. The Boundary Bridge kingfishers begin chattering again in mid-July, after a month-long silence. At least *this* July. It's wonderful to hear the voice of the guide bird of Rock Creek again after so many weeks of quiet.

The kingfisher helped settle my heart and mind into a deeper place. I watched trails of bubbles from an unknown source arise and dissolve as the creek made its slow way past. I saw fish beneath the surface. I even imagined I saw a small frog hopping across the water's surface. The silver outlines of spider webs glowed gold-rimmed in the steadily rising sun, artfully adorning each limb of beech, both the leafy living and the naked dead (a casualty from last June's deluge). Small pale insects filled the air above the creek in dancing patterns, teasing the watchful spiders.

As I sat on my shadowed rock, a single silken seed (probably thistle or a relation in the daisy family) flew over my head from above and behind my back, then parachuted gracefully to the water. Before my mind could form the question of What is next for the silken seed?, a creature from the water's depths pulled it below the surface. As I watched this small drama, I knew there was no place on Earth where I would rather be.

August 1: LAMMAS MEANDERS

TODAY IS THE EVE of the ancient harvest-holiday Lammas Day or Lughnasadh that falls mid-way between the summer solstice and autumnal equinox. Lammastide marks a seasonal turning point, as do all cross-quarter holidays, which lie at the midpoint on the calendar between solstice and equinox:

Beltane (or May Day), Samhain (or Halloween), and Imbolg (Candlemas or Groundhog's Day). Lammastide, which brings us from the verdant flowering of early summer to the sharp ripening of incipient fall, marked the first harvest-holiday of the Old World.

When the children were little, we celebrated Lammas, which had captivated my imagination years ago while reading a Thomas Hardy novel, by making "corn dollies" from cornhusks, felt, and lamb's wool. One year, when we were in Acadia National Park in Maine, we made the corn dollies under a rising full moon on a pink granite shoulder of Cadillac Mountain. We picked up art supplies in a nearby town and found some lamb's wool at a farm on our way out to Mount Desert Island.

Today's *Washington Post* contains a not-so-felicitous story about corn: "Knee-High Corn in August Dries up Farmers' Hopes." According to the U.S. Department of Agriculture's weekly "Drought Monitor" map: "As of July 24, 69.5 percent of Virginia and 75.4 percent of Maryland were considered to be in moderate, severe or extreme drought." The story says that corn-crop losses in Maryland could range from thirty to seventy percent and as high as eighty percent in Virginia. This news comes juxtaposed with recent flooding from torrential rains in Texas and western Britain as well as drought and freakish changes in temperature in other parts of Europe. I probably can't quote Jeri (Mother Herb) often enough: "This is the future, folks—drought and deluge."

I arrived home from New England at midnight (this is also the summer of record flight delays, it seems) after visiting my family and attending a second memorial service for father-in-law Bill, under a just-beginning-to-wane golden Lammas moon. The service was held in the summer church in Randolph, New Hampshire, near Mount Madison and Mount Adams. We then buried his ashes in a small cemetery next to the ashes of his mother, Kathryn, and his twin sister, Peggy. So many people came to honor Bill that some of them had to stand outside the church amongst the ferns and white birches, fanning themselves with leaves and listening to the reminiscences through open-arched windows. I held the hymnal through an open window, so that two elderly men could sing along. The minister said it was like having angels all around. One of the angels was my friend, Barbie Turnbull, great-granddaughter of Ellen Sewall, the woman Thoreau loved and to whom he proposed marriage when she was seventeen.

I have taken many stunning walks during the last few weeks—along water-falls at the base of Mount Madison, in my sister Ellie's Vermont woodlands and meadows, and along the northern part of the Natchez Trace in Tennessee's limestone country, where Jim and I found a surprising woodland of sugar maples, twinleaf, and other calcareous-soil-favoring plants that we associate with the North. But the sweet-smelling soils of New Hampshire, Vermont, and Tennessee don't send me the way the earth-smells of Rock Creek in summer do.

This morning I approach Boundary Bridge for the first time in more than a week, inhaling the pleasing funk of the summer stream and its alluvial soils as soon as I am out of the parking lot. As I stand on the bridge looking upstream, a red male cardinal flies across the creek and into a sycamore while a yellow-and-black tiger swallowtail flutters in the opposite direction. Rock Creek is low due to the ongoing drought, and the muddy banks and gravel bars are gaining ground, but today the water is as clear as weak tea due to the lack of turbulence. The irony, the irony. Is drought actually more healthful for Rock Creek than storm-water run-off? I sure do see a surprising number of happy-looking fish these days.

As I walk along the creek, noting the foliar dryness of the woody and herbaceous plants next to the trail, I am aware of symptoms linking me to Mother Earth: My still considerable fatigue from Lyme disease, a legacy of one of the creek's creatures after all. I walk slowly, but as a result I see more. I think about the brilliance of the trees, sending their roots deep in the soil, anchoring them in deluge and rendering them drought-proof. I watch a mother deer and her spotted fawn wade through the water, barely making a splashing sound.

I have no energy for a real walk. Usually, I walk along the creek, under the West Beach Drive overpass and across the Fenwick Branch footbridge, switch-back into the upland woods, visit the Laurel Ledge and Meditation Rock, walk across the Riley Spring footbridge and Beach Drive, and then return on a winding trail that crosses Wise Road and loops up and around and down back to Boundary Bridge on part of the Western Ridge Trail. The whole loop is about 2 ½ miles. But, today, I can only mosey, my energy zapped by Lyme and the emotional trip to New England.

When I reach West Beach Drive, I face my physical limitations, and, instead of going under the bridge and continuing my usual hike, I turn left to return via the part of the Valley Trail that I call the swamp trail. The jump-seed plants along the swamp trail offer a cool balm for a hot day. Tallish, with Christmas-green ovate and elliptic leaves, their budding clusters of flowers have multiplied since my last visit. Slender, spiky racemes of small, greenish-white beaked buds flail in every direction, gracefully arching over the forest-green foliage. Walking under the tall trees, I applaud my decision to stay in the dense, cool swamp instead of heading into the more sparsely shaded uplands.

The leaves of the skunk cabbage are dying back to the ground, gold and brown-rimmed at their curled edges. The swamp pond with its amphibian fence is dry, but, along its edges, a sunlit garden of orange jewelweed and lavender-pink monkey flowers framed by flowering nettles advertise the aesthetic sensibilities of the nature gods. As I explore the wild gardens of Rock Creek I often ask myself, "Who can improve on this?"

I notice a deer path headed into the swamp and give in to the impulse to follow it. The path straddles a small creek that winds its way under tall maples, sycamores, and tulip trees. Heart-shaped wild ginger leaves flourish under the trees. Small, yellow agrimony flowers and slightly larger white avens are in bloom. Both are in the rose family with characteristic five-petaled corollas. Brushing up against spicebush branches, I acknowledge that I am my same old bush-whacking self, having been totally unreformed by my brush with Lyme disease. Or perhaps I am following the creative logic of my friend and fellow-Lyme sufferer Terrie who said, "Why worry when you are already on antibiotics?" (I am still taking them.) I plow through the poison ivy (I never get it but have been warned by field-trip participants never to say never), feeling the excitement of exploring new territory.

And then I realize that I am at the center of the small floodplain, in the very spot where I danced to the tunes of toads and barred owls so long ago during a spring evening reverie. I have stumbled on the place from a different direction. And I am in the midst of a giant patch of lizard's-tail plants, sometimes called water dragon plants, which are tall, almost shrub-like, with large, dark-green, heart-shaped leaves and curiously nodding spikes of tiny, fuzzy white blossoms (the lizard's "tail"). I have never seen lizard's-tail at Boundary Bridge, despite the fact that I have passed the spot just a few feet away on a proper trail a thousand times. Thrilled and enraptured, I watch the tiny summer breeze stir the nodding white tails to life. I watch and they dance!

In life, we are comforted by the familiar and often excited by the new. Intimacy with Nature offers both, inextricably and delightfully intertwined: The new and exciting lizard's-tail at the old and familiar Boundary Bridge.

August 2–8: MORE WILD GARDENS

MY ENERGY IS LOWER than Rock Creek during drought. This morning, the 2nd, I move the sprinklers around the yard, fill the bird feeders, and feed myself. Period. I have no energy for anything else but reading and writing. What will I do several days from now when my very healthy and active sixteen-year-old son returns from his marine biology trip and I'm suddenly keeping teenaged hours again? How will I handle the unpredictability of late-night comings and goings and the reverberations of electric guitars? I am bound and determined to get my strength back by then.

As time goes on, our property in Chevy Chase resembles more and more a wild garden. We inherited some very stiff and funny topiary when we rented and then bought this place. I think some of the neighbors were hoping that we'd undo the fanciful tastes of the former owner and tear it all out. But, when it comes to woody plants, I don't have the ruthless gene. Instead, we've allowed the sculpted evergreens and overly cultivated-looking Japanese maples to revert to more natural shapes. Every shrub and small tree needs a haircut that is not going to happen. Jesse, teenaged master of the creative oxymoron, has dubbed the look 'feral topiary.' The former owner—who apparently has engaged in some drive-by behavior—was appalled and couldn't resist sending me a note recommending his topiary barber. But many of the neighbors love the new look and are constantly voicing their encouragement as the place takes on the abandoned-look characteristic of this upscale but "shabby chic" neighborhood.

I have empathy for the former owner, and I understand his note. I have similar desires to encourage the current owners of Strawberry Moon Farm, where my children were raised, to repaint the increasingly badly peeling sign that we left behind.

As native wildflowers thrive and multiply in our yard, butterflies and hummingbirds come flocking. As I look up now, colorful winged insects dip and glide over the gardens in the back yard. The wild blue verbena, which started as five or six plants brought home from a meeting of the Maryland Native Plant Society, has overtaken the yard. I am constantly having to move it and trim it back, and there are probably fifty verbena plants in the yard now, some of them six feet tall. Clumps of black-eyed Susans, Maryland's official state wildflower, are profusely blooming, and the ever-gigantic Joe-Pye-weed is putting forth its fuzzy, dusky-pink blossoms in clusters as large as a bear's head. The swamp milkweed is covered with pod-like follicles bursting with silky seeds, and I've just planted a few young butterfly weeds (another member of the milkweed family). The purple cone-flowers bloom all summer, and the bee-balm is just about done.

All of our flowers, herbs, and vegetables, native and not, spill into each other in orgiastic abandon, which suits me fine. A wild garden is the metaphor I choose for my life. From the moment I was old enough to wander solo in the Vermont woods at age five, I have lived a gypsy-like life. I learned at a young age that one doesn't need to wander far to be a wanderer. I relearned this lesson as a mother watching my toddlers explore the yard, finding daily fascination. I slowly realized the pointlessness of grandiose and expensive family vacations when the kids were young. Yosemite and Glacier national parks were no more compelling to them than a puddle in the driveway. When we remember to think small, as children do, there is always something to see.

And it is as a wild gardener and wanderer of woods that I've connected with the most important people in my life. The kindred spirits I've known share my love of the natural world. Every relationship that has mattered to me has been bathed in sunlight and moonlight and leafy shadows. My sister Ellie and I often felt misplaced on the boys' boarding-school campus where our father taught, coached sports, and later served as headmaster. But there were the endless Vermont woods, where pussy-willows appeared in snowy spring swamps; hepaticas, trilliums, and Dutchman's breeches flowered in April; garter snakes idled on granite outcrops in summer; and sugar maples blazed orange, red, and yellow in October. Our mother taught us a love for violets and mayflowers, and our father taught us and our brother, Mike, to identify common bird songs and to swing birches, just like in the Robert Frost poem. Best of all, the thick, green mosses under the white birch trees made pillows perfect for dreaming during spring and summer afternoons.

I began to fall in love for the first time on an April night when I was sixteen. I was walking with Ellie and some friends during a weekend home from our girls' boarding school near Boston. We wandered beyond the Vermont boys' school campus, as we had done since childhood. As we walked through the upper fields on this chilly night, out of the darkness emerged a curly-haired boy walking barefoot in the wet grass. For me, it wasn't so much love at first sight as it was recognition of a kindred spirit at first sight. Later, when I got my somewhat starved romantic self back to my boarding school, I was convinced I was in love.

Never the shy, retiring type, I wrote a letter to the curly-haired boy, whose name was Ted Tomasi. I'm sure the contents would cause undying embarrassment were I to read them today, but whatever I wrote intrigued him. I soon received a written reply that told me I had indeed identified someone with a kindred love of Nature. His first letter to me is long lost, but I instantly committed the salient line to my everlasting memory: "Raindrops lie on the needle tips of pine. Go there and taste their softness so that I may know you."

It is hard for me to imagine any of the boys who drape themselves over our furniture, play our electric guitars and video games, and inhale pizza by the boxload writing anything like this to a girl. It would lose a certain something as a text message and cause unspeakable shame on Facebook. And when and where would these boys find themselves touching their tongues to rain-soaked pine needles?

And yet Ted was neither a nerd nor a recluse but rather a member of three varsity teams and a good-looking guy. He had discovered the wet pine needles along a trail behind the huge ski jump that he had gamely braved during winter competitions.

We were together for a year and a half, and then he abruptly left me. Our last conversation occurred in a grove of white birch in autumn. I remember the heart-break beauty of that grove, the look of the fall leaves, and the soft moss on the rocks. He went to Colorado and disappeared from my life for thirty-six years.

I met Jim during college at the University of Vermont, which we both attended. The beginnings of our love affair were fully steeped in Nature. I knew he was the one for me when I lay down in the snow under the balsam firs behind his family's White Mountain cottage with the wind howling and the temperature in the single digits. I simply wanted to look up at the sky from that vantage point. Without saying a word, he lay down next to me. We lay there side by side in our winter coats and watched the clouds race across the sky from the northern peaks. In my mind, that was the moment of our wedding as clearly as any ring ceremony.

One evening the following summer, we walked out to a rocky point over-looking Lake Champlain at sunset. The orange glow faded from the sky as it grew dark, but we couldn't bring ourselves to leave the midnight-black lake and the sky now full of pinpoint stars. We were deeply in love and would soon be living together and married the following June. While we sat enraptured on our lakeside ledge, the sky suddenly filled with shooting stars. Neither of us had ever seen anything like this spectacle. It felt like a celestial blessing.

When we finally tore ourselves away from the explosive sky and its reflection in the water, we realized we'd be walking back through an unknown pitch-dark forest. When I easily found the path with my bare feet, unbeknownst to me, I impressed Jim with my intuitive skills. I was just walking through the woods in the dark as I had done numerous times in other woodlands.

Later, we learned that we had witnessed the annual Perseid meteor shower, which I've written down on my current calendar for August 12th, this coming Sunday. Years later, we saw it again in the mountains near Taos, New Mexico, and Sophie was probably conceived under the Perseid meteors in a field near our home at Seneca Creek.

When I became pregnant with Jesse, I knew it right away, because Nature seemed to have intensified its hold on me. Newly pregnant, I left for an October backpacking trip to Dolly Sods in West Virginia with several of my women friends. The red maple leaves falling on evergreen rhododendron and the view of the constellation of Cassiopeia from a rock ledge in the middle of Red Creek held extra sparkles for me. In my tent at night, I dreamed I was giving birth to twin bear cubs. Many twin dreams followed during this pregnancy, so I was surprised when the midwife told me I was carrying only one baby. After Jesse's birth, the reason for the dreams dawned on me: He was a Gemini, sign of the twins!

As soon as I could get out and walk, we took our newborn son to Sugarloaf Mountain, just as we had done with Sophie. I have pictures of her as a three-week-old in her snuggly among the blooming mountain laurel and pictures of Jesse at exactly one week at a summer-solstice celebration on Sugarloaf.

As life goes on, its magic intensifies and linear time collapses. As I write this, I'm not yet fifty-five, but I already understand how elderly people vividly remember moments from childhood, even though what they ate for breakfast escapes them. I remember my personal history as a dream-time, with the most shining moments woven into a tapestry of Nature's beauty. The yesterdays appear as vivid as the moments and hours of today. Times of solitude and communion with others entwine themselves with seasonal threads and tie themselves to beloved places. The dream-like weaving of people, places, and seasons has given my life such richness that I feel I could die at any moment and nothing would be lost. What I currently lack in physical energy while recovering from Lyme disease is more than met by the pulse of intimate knowing and memory of the wild gardens I've explored.

When I look at my children's faces, I see them simultaneously as newborns, as infants and toddlers, and as the young adults they are today. All the moments of their lives reside in their faces, and only occasionally do I long for something from the past—a first word, a small finger excitedly pointed, a child's musical intonations. When I look at Jim's face and body, I don't see just a fifty-six-year-old man, still handsome with silver streaks in his hair, but a person whose essence is familiar and dear to me and who still causes my heart to quicken.

After thirty-six years, my disappearing first love found me again. Last year, out of the blue, I received an email message from him. A few weeks later, he came to visit me. We met in a Greek restaurant not far from our neighborhood, and after lunch we took a walk. His beautiful curly hair was long-gone, and he was almost completely bald. He wore a shirt and tie when I remembered him in a t-shirt and jeans. I probably wouldn't have recognized him in a crowd. But, when I took him to Boundary Bridge and we walked the loop trail side by side, we soon fell into our familiar walking rhythm. He remembered how I shuffle my feet between steps, something I'd never noticed about myself nor has anyone else ever pointed out.

He earned a Ph.D. in natural resource economics. As he gazed at Rock Creek, I wondered if he was sizing up its remedial needs and, perhaps, even assessing the amounts required for its restoration.

As I sat on the Meditation Rock and he stood nearby, I asked him why he had left me. "I just wasn't ready," he said. I replied, "That's exactly what you said to me all those years ago."

As I shared my love of Rock Creek Park's wildflowers blooming along the trail, he remembered what he called my "joy reaction." He had given me the gift of his rain-soaked pine needles many years ago, and I gave him back that image he had long forgotten. His memory is murkier than mine, but I helped him remember touching his tongue to those fragrant needles.

Jim understands the magic of my first love and how it will always be a part of me, and I understand the magic of his former loves. He is a gifted musician and songwriter. My favorite song of his is a love song about a woman he knew when he was nineteen. I must confess, I get a slight pang when I hear the line, "we kissed under the stars." If it were just kissing—without the stars—there would be no pang.

When we love someone, we accept and even embrace their previous loves and each of the tender places we can reach, framed in the larger embrace of Earth itself and its mysterious twin: Time. And, if we are lucky, we have wild gardens to tend and explore. Ellie has named the wildflower garden at her Vermont farmhouse "Nell's Scarf," in honor of a woman who once lived there. Ellie tossed a handful of wildflower seeds near her front door, and she writes, "For some reason, they seeded in the shape of a ribbon."

This morning, the 8th, when I turn on my computer, I open Garrison Keillor's "Writer's Almanac." I discover that today is the birthday of Marjorie Kinnan Rawlings (author of *The Yearling* and *Cross Creek)*, who was born in

1896. And then Garrison offers this extract from *Endymion*, the poem by
John Keats:

> A thing of beauty is a joy for ever:
> Its loveliness increases, it will never
> Pass into nothingness; but still will keep
> A bower quiet for us, and a sleep
> Full of sweet dreams, and health, and quiet breathing.
> Therefore, on every morrow, are we wreathing
> A flowery band to bind us to the earth,
> Spite of despondence, of the inhuman dearth
> Of noble natures, or the gloomy days,
> Of all the unhealthy and o'er—darkened ways
> Made of our searching; yes, in spite of all
> Some shape of beauty moves away the pall
> From our dark spirits. . . .

First, Nell's Scarf and, then, Keats's flowery band, both now linked in
my imagination through the shared magic of Nature. I will now have to
seek Marjorie Kinnan Rawlings's words about how we can live without
every seemingly essential relationship, except for our relationship with
Earth itself.

August 11: SCIENCE BRAIN VS. ART/MYSTIC BRAIN

WEDNESDAY WAS a record-breaking 102, and the weather all week continued
oppressively hot and humid. A cool front, which unfortunately brought no
drought-relieving rain, finally gave us a reprieve from the heat last night.
Today is a Saturday, with the sky blue and the breeze out of the northeast,
and I do what I have longed to do on a weekend morning during the quiet
of a closure of Beach Drive: Fill my pack with binoculars, hand lens, field
guides, food, and water—with a pillow tied to the outside of the pack—and
head out for Boundary Bridge and the Meditation Rock.

I was planning an extended visit to the park despite my continuing saga with Lyme disease. Tests indicate that it's taking a toll on my heart and vascular system—the reason for my ongoing fatigue. I'm now on some additional medications and a slew of supplements, including fish oil. This was a huge decision for me, because I've been a vegetarian for almost fifteen years. But I want to get well and am concerned about suffering chronically, as so many do from Lyme.

When I get to the bridge, several people are leaning over the wooden railing, gazing upstream to watch a canine drama in progress. A determined Chesapeake Bay retriever named Holly is trying to dislodge a fifteen-to-twenty-foot fallen sapling from the water, using every means at her disposal. She paws at the creek's bottom to try to dislodge the tree, then fully submerges her head for several seconds in an attempt to drag it up to the surface. Once she gets it off the bottom, she tries to haul the tree first upstream then downstream, systematically exhausting every option. She repeats this sequence several times. Her human companion, a middle-aged man standing by the bank with a leash in his hands, silently watches her. When she gives up on the tree and splashes through the water to retrieve her floating green tennis ball, he gently says, "Good girl."

After Holly leaves the water, I begin walking along the braided network of improvised trails next to Rock Creek, feeling the smoothness of the packed sandy soil under my feet and reveling in the leafy shadows of the tall, interwoven crowns of the trees. Patches of sky are visible through breaks in the canopy, and the cicadas and katydids sing. Equally as musical are the voices of people calling to each other from their bikes along Beach Drive, and the sounds of splashing dogs. Fallen yellow, gold, and brown leaves from tulip trees grace the trail, far more numerous and layered than last week. I see some curious little three-lobed, mitten-shaped leafy parts of plants lying on the ground, puzzle over them, and then realize they are fruiting bracts that have fallen from the ironwood above.

When I get to Dog Beach, a lone Canada goose sits in the water. As common as Canada geese have become in our area in recent years (considered a nuisance by some), I'd never seen one at Boundary Bridge. The bird is so still, and its vivid reflection is so static in the water that I wonder if it is a wooden decoy that someone has left behind. When I get close, the goose slowly paddles away. Green, brown, and blue damselflies flit along the sand and alight on the vegetation, too swift for identification, so the dragon and damselfly guide in my pack is useless. Yellow-and-black goldfinches fly manically about, and I wonder if they are nesting now that thistledown is plentiful. Tall pink-and-white spider flowers (non-native volunteers from nearby gardens) weave themselves into the patchwork of panic grass and nettles.

Walking downstream, I notice that the single moth mullein plant that bloomed earlier in the summer on an eroded bank is in full bloom once again, its forked upright stalk replete with a second wave of white flowers. (Moth mullein is a plant that can have either white or yellow flowers.) On the opposite side of the trail, a small group of evening-primrose plants boast sunny yellow flowers. I get out my botany book to make sure that the four-petaled blossoms, with their characteristic cross-shaped stigmas, and the small, elongated and erect fruit capsules indicate common evening-primrose (an important woman's herbal now commercially sold) and not a related species such as sundrops.

Further down the trail, near Rock Creek's confluence with Fenwick Branch, pokeweed—a plant I have come to appreciate through the artistic sensibilities of my friend, Tina Thieme Brown—is producing its small white flowers. Tina and I worked on two books about Sugarloaf Mountain over the course of ten years, and I have learned to see plants through her artist's eye. She loves the sturdy magenta stalks of pokeweed and the gleaming clusters of black berries that appear after the flowers in the fall. I always think of her when I see the plant. Wingstem creates warm washes of color next to the creek, its greenish-gold and mop-shaped flower heads growing in terminal clusters on tall, vertically "winged" plant stalks. White asters with small lanceolate leaves are in bud along the creek near the wingstem. Both plants are in the daisy family, which is sometimes called the aster family.

Several milkweed plants have already set their large, pale-green, canoe-shaped follicles. I didn't see their dusky pink flowers when they were blooming at the creek and missed their colorful, striped monarch butterfly larvae, although Jim and I saw the green caterpillars with their bold yellow, white, and black stripes dining on milkweed leaves at our land in Comus earlier in the summer. But, right on cue, an orange-and-black-winged monarch flies past the milkweed plants and on down the creek.

The current blooming "it" plant at Rock Creek is jumpseed. Its small beak-like buds are beginning to open to four tiny, triangular, green-white tepals. Jumpseed thrives in nearly every habitat at the creek, from the floodplain to the dry uplands. Another plant that visually resembles jumpseed, called lopseed, is just past bloom in a few places, its upside-down green "lopseeds" forming.

In the upland woods, the four-parted, felty golden capsules of witch-hazel have matured to full size, and a gall called "witch's hat" (it looks just like a Halloween costume hat) has sprung up on the upper surface of some of its leaf blades. The white wood asters that form their toothed, heart-shaped leaves in early spring are now in bud along the upland trails. So are the blue-stemmed goldenrods. Their slender, arching purple stalks with yellow buds appear obviously drought-stressed, with dry and crinkled leaves.

As I take my slogging, Lyme-diseased naturalist's time walking along the trail, I make botanical notes with a blue pen on a large, green index card. I get to the steep Laurel Ledge overlooking the dramatic bend in the creek below and catch my breath for joy and beauty as I always do. I behold the dramatically curved and angled gray ledge, and admire its garden of native woody plants in full summer leaf: American beech, mountain laurel, pinxter flower, and witch-hazel. The ledge drops steeply into Rock Creek, but I note how its steepness has not stopped wild hydrangea, polypody, New York and Christmas ferns, and even large beech trees from colonizing it.

Making my way down the rocky, root-woven side trail to the Meditation Rock, a change in color attracts my eye. Ashes cover a patch of ground encompassing a network of tree roots and a small colony of viny, round-leaved partridge-berry plants. I quickly scan the trunk of the adjacent beech tree, but see no sign of a lightning strike. This is clearly not the remnant of an illegal campfire. And then I wonder: Did someone strew the ashes of their beloved along this scenic ledge? Ashes are commonly strewn and buried at Sugarloaf, and that's where I've decided I want my final resting place. I can't think of any other explanation, so I say a silent prayer for an unknown someone who might have loved this place as much as I do.

I make my precarious way out to the Meditation Rock, unbalanced by my pack and pillow and lingering weakness. As soon as I arrive, I hear the loud chatter of a scolding kingfisher, and then two wing into view. One flies into the woods above the bend in the creek, and one briefly perches on a dead tree in the middle of the stream. Is this a mated pair or rival males? Or, perhaps, squabbling siblings? In my haste to grab my binoculars out of my pack, I drop my index card, covered on both sides with notes, into the creek, and it swiftly rafts downstream. I must be more exhausted than I think.

The twin worries of lost notes and creek litter fill my mind as the card sets sail. It reaches a place where it stops next to a steep rock. I can see that the blue pen marks are still legible, and I entertain the possibility of recovery. As I climb up from the Meditation Rock to find a long-enough stick, I contemplate what has happened. Did a small northeast breeze lift those notes up and into the creek as a playful message to me? A message to stop being so left-brained and just enjoy the day without having to solve every botanical mystery?

Despite that message, I retrieve the notes from the creek. They are soaked on both sides but are miraculously legible, and I set them to dry in the sun on the Meditation Rock as if they were wet laundry. The cool breeze seduces my Lymey self into a sweet stupor, so I arrange my pillow under my butt and my pack under my head and try to drift off to sleep. I discover it's not easy to sleep on a half-billion-year-old rippled rock angled into the drink. I can't quite lose consciousness, but at least my left brain lets go of its constant inquisitiveness. When I sit up after many minutes in a dream-state, I'm ready to experience the creek on a calmer, deeper level.

I look across to the other shore and notice blue flowers arching over the water. Looking through my binoculars I can see that they have three petals—one white and two a stunning sapphire. They are framed by the green grasses surrounding them. Just below the flowers, a long vine has come loose from the bank and is trailing into the downstream flow, gracefully moving with the slow current. The vine appears bright lime-green in the water, and, as I watch through the glasses, a large and brilliant-blue damselfly flies in and perches on the vine. Blue flowers, blue damsel, undulating lime foliage, and golden brown water. My left brain sneaks in ever so briefly to note that the blue flowers are non-native Asiatic dayflowers, and the vine in the water is the invasive exotic mile-a-minute. But my right brain takes those observations from the other side in stride and fully revels in the artfulness of the moment.

After an hour or two—no linear time keeping—I pack up my stuff and continue along the loop trail back to Boundary Bridge. I walk slowly under the trees, appreciating the tall and ancient oaks and the miraculous appearance of an occasional early acorn on the trail. My botanist brain is still present, noting the shallow cap of the red oak's acorn and the more rounded cap of the black oak, but my art brain prevails. Some of the butternuts at the Riley Spring Bridge have already fallen, and early-autumn leaves fly through the air like birds or butterflies until their travel abruptly slows as they land in the creek. The hop-hornbeam fruits, small nutlets inside hop-like papery sacs, are forming. I walk along the stream near the bridge, and a monarch butterfly flies along beside me, our paces similar as its swifter flight is punctuated by nectar-reconnaissance.

I return to the trail and walk up the fern-lined way toward Wise Road. As I climb the hill past the Beach Drive crossing, it dawns on me that the cranefly orchids could be blooming, because their flowering time corresponds to the Perseid meteor shower (which suburban light pollution and my Lyme-disease fatigue caused me to miss last night). This orchid species produces a single, ovate basal leaf, which is purplish beneath, in the fall. The leaf lasts through the winter and then withers and disappears the following spring, long before the leafless summer flower stalk appears. I remembered that Allen Browne found a cranefly leaf near a loblolly pine on our winter field trip. That leaf is long-gone, probably the victim of deer browsing rather than natural die-back. I check all around the tree without a sign of the orchid.

But then my right brain beckons. *Wander the woods*, it says, and *see what ye shall find*. Off I go in no planned direction, and within a few minutes I find the treasure I so unsystematically seek: Two delicate stalks of purplish cranefly orchids side by side, one in full flower, one in bud, standing in a shaft of sunlight next to a fallen log. The small, purplish-green, insect-like or bird-like flowers display side "wings" and a long spur at the back. I find no others anywhere around. My right brain found the orchids, but my left brain did the botanical footwork in a successful synthesis of science and mysticism, plus a small bit of luck.

JESSE HAS BEEN HOME from his summer studies for almost two weeks. His exuberance about sightings of sharks, manatees, and barracudas observed while snorkeling at a coral reef in the Florida Keys outpaces his enthusiasm for the summer reading assignment he left for the last minute. He's been playing his electric guitar a lot, but, when it gets quiet, I more often find him ensconced in the latest Harry Potter novel rather than the assigned *Oliver Twist* or the biography of Ben Franklin. He is not the only one who has issues with summer reading. I think kids should be able to read whatever captivates them in the summer, even if it's comic books!

Sophie arrived home last night after a ten-hour drive from Providence with her new boyfriend, Doug, a neuroscience major. Before they arrived, I dragged my Lymey self out to shop and clean up around the house, feathering and sprucing up the sagging nest. When they neared Baltimore, I gathered basil by porch-light to make fresh pesto, Sophie's favorite. As we dined by candlelight, Jim returned from a weeklong whirlwind to Memphis, Omaha, and Mobile. Our family's long-distance travel has become routine, and our family is often far-flung. We know that the ease of flight is taking a toll on the planet and I feel guilty partaking of air travel so often since it is a major contributor to greenhouse gases.

Whenever guests are expected, I'm forced to confront my biggest flaw (at least I hope it's my biggest): At best, I'm only an okay day-to-day house-keeper. With Jim's help and Gioconda's once-a-week cleanings, I manage to keep our home fairly orderly and smelling fresh, hoping that my shortcuts are offset by the artistry of my flower arrangements, the paintings on our walls, the lace curtains, and throw pillows. When it comes to REAL housekeeping, however, the kind at which my mother excels, I get an F! Closets, basement, and any flat surface that's at all out of view collect stuff that I don't know what to do with. I keep meaning to tackle these cluttered places, but somehow I never get to it. And then, when people are coming over, I panic, worried they'll immediately pick up on the bad feng shui vibes emanating from the basement, closets, and corners.

This flaw was even more problematic when the kids were little. I'll never forget Sophie's fourth birthday, when I saw my future flash before my eyes.

All those little girls and boys who came to watch her blow out her candles left behind all those little plastic things—Barbies and Barbie paraphernalia, tea sets, trolls, My Little Ponies, doll houses, and garden tools. Then, with Jesse, the situation got way out of hand. From Power Rangers, Mighty Mighty Maxes, and pogs to transformers and Pokemon, we collected the plastic refuse of every craze. He had his own "toy room," and it became a frightening place to enter. Whenever I attempted any sort of purge, I discovered that the toy that had been sitting at the bottom of the blue plastic bin for two years was a sudden favorite. I threw up my hands and gave up. When Beanie Babies came on the scene, they were happily piled on top of everything else by both children, like the most recent era of an archeological dig.

When we made our impromptu "temporary" move to be closer to schools four years ago, I bailed on my responsibilities. Nancy, the same Nancy who is the artist in charge of our gardens, helped me pack and take stuff to the new house in Chevy Chase and to a storage unit in Germantown, where a Choukas-Bradley time-capsule has already accrued a four-year history. No one was willing to let go of favorite items from the past, and so there they sit in boxes that require monthly payments. All the flotsam and jetsam of a pair of packrat American adults and their two children. I always had some or other writing deadline as an excuse to postpone dealing with our archeological layers, plus the knowledge that decisions on kids' stuff can't be made by me alone. And just when would we all be free to paw through boxes?

As I was engaged in frenzied cleanup before Sophie and Doug's arrival, I couldn't help comparing indoor and outdoor realities. As I stuffed one more item into a crammed closet, I remembered the time I shoved a head of cauliflower into a kitchen cabinet before a dinner party, because there was no room in the fridge and guests were imminent. I have absolutely no pride if a door can be closed upon something, but I do have the dignity to be ashamed of all the clutter that can't be hidden.

Luckily, this week there were no cauliflower heads in need of impromptu homes, but there was a great deal to shift around, spruce up, and hide. In the midst of the cleanup frenzy, I went out to gather some cut flowers and do some deadheading in the gardens. As I tossed old arrangements on the ground and dropped dead blossoms next to flowering plants, I was struck by the difference between what happens outdoors versus indoors. I can leave any sort of bouquet or plucked branch lying on the ground, and, although it might be a temporary eyesore, Nature will soon take it to her bosom and transform it into useful nourishing soil, where it can serve as a microbial banquet. No matter how sloppy I am outdoors, I can do no wrong; all is forgotten and forgiven, for detritus nourishes the earth.

If only that could happen indoors with old Barbies and Power Rangers! If only composting could occur in the toy bin! If only all the old toys would sink into oblivion naturally, with no decisions to make and no sense of loss, just a gradual decomposition once something has served its purpose in its season. And would this not be good for the planet as well as good for me and every other overworked parent?

August 22: THE SWEETEST GIFT

I WAS GIVEN the sweetest gift for my birthday—rain. A thunderstorm in the early morning hours awoke me with vivid lightning and gave us a good soaking and then many hours of every other kind of rain—steady downpours, light spritzing, variable rains that lasted through the day and into the next. We turned off the AC, opened the windows, and enjoyed the magic. Jim took the day off, and the four of us crashed in front of movies, dining on home-delivered food and enjoying a respite from life's responsibilities.

Yesterday, Sophie and I drove through Rock Creek Park on our way back from a doctor's visit in Alexandria. The creek was joyfully racing and bubbling over the rocky stretch above Boulder Bridge in places where it had been sad, low, and smelly during the drought. Of course, the water contains all the toxins and oxygen-choking sediments that flood into Rock Creek during and after every storm. But I couldn't help but be thrilled by the sound and sight of rapidly flowing water. We are not out of the woods drought-wise, but everybody got a good drink.

THIS MORNING, as I walk the Boundary Bridge trail, signs of change are everywhere. It rained during the night, and the trail is covered with a thick carpet of wet brown and gold leaves from the tulip trees. Water beads up on the undersides of the little green drupes of spicebush, and, for every hundred or so of the green drupes, a single, shiny red one catches my eye. Incipient autumn and the aftermath of rain are happily entwined at Rock Creek. Amazingly, there isn't much storm-related turbulence in the creek, which is visibly filled with small fish—and a few good-sized ones. A kingfisher flies past in rapid chatter mode, and a great blue heron silently wings its way steadily downstream. A lone eastern wood-pewee sweetly sings, its song reminding me of the many other songbird tunes I probably won't hear again until spring.

I revel in the wildflowers of summer and the emerging fall but regret having too much information about two non-native plants that have sprung into bloom since my last visit. The Japanese knotweed—a *Polygonum*, recently renamed *Reynoutria japonica* by some botanists—bears tiny white flowers in erect and drooping elongated clusters, while the vines of Japanese hops that twist and twine over Dog Beach near the patch of jimsonweed bear slender, erect clusters of small, greenish-white flowers. Sometimes I wish I could wipe the knowledge of invasive plants like these from my brain, so I can quit walking around thinking *bad bad bad invasive* when green, living things are simply grow- ing and reproducing according to Earth's plan.

As I walk under the tall trees, with shafts of light breaking through the thick, wet canopy, I fall under the forest's spell. Two days ago, Jim and I walked side by side along the C & O Canal Towpath near Shepherdstown, West Virginia, a particularly scenic stretch of the Potomac River. "These trees look so small after my Boundary Bridge trees," I said to Jim. "They are about the size of the trees I've known most of my life in the second-growth forests I'm used to. But I've come under the spell of the tall canopy at Rock Creek Park, and these trees don't quite cut it for me any more."

Aware of the park's spell over me, I contemplate the word, for I am especially sensitive to the "spell of place." When I am under such a spell,

I long for the place and feel entranced by it. Spells are powerful, magical, and enduring, whether they are cast by practitioners of ancient arts, by places, by music and dance, or artlessly and unconsciously by loved ones. There are other meanings of the word:

"I am under your spell."
"Come and sit a spell."
"We are having a dry spell,
   or a rainy spell,
   or a spell of bad luck."

A spell is a period of time characterized by a common ingredient, often beyond our control. Even the most prosaic meaning of *spell*—to string letters together—is suffused with powerful magic, if you step back and consider the mystery of stringing complex communications together through small symbols. Spell can be used as a verb with other meanings—something *spells* danger. Let me *spell* you a while. In our computerized world, who does not rely on *spellcheck?*

I love to give myself over to a spell, when it is benign and able to erase niggling and rational thought. Nature casts a spell whenever you let it. There is a butterfly bush—another species that is becoming invasive—that volunteered next to our front door. As a board member of the Maryland Native Plant Society, I knew I should rip it from the ground when it first appeared. But I never got around to it, and now its long, arching clusters of purplish-pink flowers are a nectar banquet for tiger swallowtail and monarch butterflies. I open the door to their magic every sunny summer morning, and my heart fills with joy when I see their fluttering wings. Beauty stops me in my tracks everywhere I go. I am definitely a stop-and-smell-the-roses kind of girl. I live under the spell of the rose, just as I live under the spell of the lily. Is it coincidence that Rose is my middle name, given to me in honor of my godmother, Rose Coronis, when I was christened in the Greek Orthodox Church?

There is even a magic spell-quality to my Lyme disease, it seems, according to my friend, Lisa Lindberg. This evening she sent me an email in which she wrote: "For what this is worth—and hoping you won't take this in any way as insulting: A friend of mine who got Lyme disease several years ago—and who is connected with Native American spiritual people—told me that the Native American view of Lyme is that it is 'deer medicine' for the heart. That being susceptible to contracting this disease reflects the heart's need to slow down and integrate."

I read this email after returning from an evening walk in the neighborhood with Sophie, during which I tell her that I have come to appreciate Lyme's help in prioritizing my life. I have been able to read and write and dream and enjoy Nature, and I have not taken my energy for granted but have devoted the full amount of the depleted energy I do have to things that I love. Everything trivial has seemed not worth it. So, in a way, this *spell* of Lyme disease has been a gift of sorts—"deer medicine." Still, a mosquito is hovering around me in the family room at the moment, and I do not wish to fall under the West Nile spell!

September 1: SEASONAL GOOD-BYES

WHEN JIM AND I get up this Saturday morning, we notice not just a coolness in the air but a strange new light. We can't quite put our fingers on the change. When I go out to pick up the paper from the front lawn, the sky is ablaze in a brilliant blue, with a high, waning corn moon, but something of summer seems to have slipped away during the night. The dewy grass is cold between my bare toes, and there is a distinct autumnal chill to the air. The sun is also decidedly lower in the sky.

Back inside, I share a memory of Sugarloaf with Jim. For many years, a small glass prism hung from the top of a south-facing window in our dining room in Comus. On September 1st of each year, the dining room would fill with rainbows, rainbows that continued to greet us every sunny morning through the fall and winter, dancing on the creamy-white walls as we sipped our morning coffee and fed our children breakfast. These rainbows would disappear again in the spring when the sun climbed too high to reach the prism. I don't remember the date of the disappearance, but the September 1st appearance was an annual event.

When a new season approaches, I feel a primal sense of panic before I'm able to greet it with open arms. In the depths of my heart, this is and always has been almost like cosmic clockwork. I'm reluctant to be thrust out of winter's cocoon, and then I grieve the end of spring. Summer's passing is the scariest of all, and those rainbows at Comus surely helped ease the transition. There is a moment when the dark begins to close in and the lessening of the summer light fills me with fear. It happened this morning.

Sophie leaves for her senior year of college tomorrow morning, Jesse starts school this coming week, I'm in the throes of yet another relapse from Lyme disease, and those realities magnify the impending sense of the loss of summer. So this morning, as Jim and Sophie and I take our last walk of the summer at Boundary Bridge, all is visibly bright and summery, the leaves that fell during last week's rains have dried and are less obvious as casualties, and happy canines splash and fetch. But I am a little off-kilter and turn my left ankle several times. I feel sad when we leave the Meditation Rock, and I ask Jim and Sophie to go on ahead, because I have a reason for lingering behind one of the tall trees. After they are out of earshot, a pair of kingfishers come chattering along the Rock Creek's flyway, gracefully dipping and gliding and interweaving their flight patterns as they fly upstream. When the melancholy of autumn sets in, it tinges everything with its colors. But I remember from years past that, one day, my sadness lifts magically, and then I'm able to give myself fully to the exhilaration of the season.

September 5: THE AMAZING DAISY FAMILY

MY PREDICTABLE PANIC over seasonal change is followed by predictably soothing signs and occurrences. As soon as I fear the impending new season, the current one tells me: *Relax . . . I'm not going anywhere just yet.* Temperatures are back in the high eighties, with summer steam typical for this region cranking up over the next few days, reminding us of the back and forth of the seasons.

I have a whole day to myself for the first time since Jesse returned from his summer trip. Yesterday was a wrenching day, as I watched him ride off to school for orientation with his buddy Joey. As Joey's beat-up Volvo station wagon rounded the bend, many years of buses and carpools flooded my memory. Another letting go. I made chili and cornbread, family nostalgia foods, and grieved.

But today is a new day, and I pack up my field guides, hand lens, and binoculars and head out to Rock Creek Park. As I step out of the car, the humble sight of Boundary Bridge, with its familiar plain-brown railing, cheers me. I inhale quickly the pleasing funk of the creek's bottom and then note how early autumn has punctured holes in the tree canopy, creating a nuanced mix of leafy shadows and sunlight on the sandy trail. There are now two red spicebush drupes for every 100 green ones.

I walk to the center of the bridge and look down into the barely flowing water, clear today and the color of jasmine tea. Golden sycamore leaves break away from their high, cream-colored branches, soothing me with their slow, falling grace. As I scan the creek and its banks, I see a new patch of wildflowers hugging the western shore: Mistflowers, the lavender embodiment of September.

I leave the bridge and bushwhack through the trees and shrubs to the patch of mistflowers, deer ticks be damned. The flowers hug the top of the creek's bank and are flanked by other wildflowers: Indian tobacco, of the *Lobelia* genus, just past bloom, and tick-trefoils, in the pea family, with small, purplish-pink winged and bannered blossoms fading to blue-green. The latter is a different species than the naked-flowered tick-trefoils I'd seen in the uplands earlier in summer, and it's harder to distinguish from several lookalikes. Beggar-ticks or stick-tight are still in bud and, like the mistflowers and so many plants blooming now in our woodlands and fields, are of the amazing daisy (or aster) family. Both plants with "tick" in the name, despite being unrelated, form dry fruits, which stick to fur and clothing, hitching rides to new homes.

I get close to the mistflowers and admire their toothed, heart-shaped or ovate leaves arranged oppositely on upright, reddish stalks. The lavender-hued clusters of dainty flowers spiral me into a September nostalgia. These flowers grow on Sugarloaf and on our land in Comus in a field near a spring-fed creek, where I've admired their "misty" flower clusters on many mist-cloaked autumn mornings.

Turning around, I see yet another representative of the daisy family in full bloom: White wood asters. Their heart-shaped, toothed leaves appeared in early spring in the bottomlands and uplands of Rock Creek, but only now are their flower heads emerging. I get out my hand lens and lean in close to a white wood aster's "flower," getting at the heart of the daisy family's masquerade. Each putative flower has a yellow or lavender center and several creamy-white "petals." But all is not as it seems.

The daisy or aster family has pulled the wool over the eyes of countless generations of pollinators and also human suitors, bouquets historically and hopefully in hand, with a fabulous subterfuge. Each "flower" is actually dozens of flowers, teeming with fertile parts and passing itself off as a single blossom. Through the lens I can see each minute disk flower of the white wood aster, like a five-pointed star, crowded together with its tiny, starry neighbors to form the golden or lavender center. And around the center circle the creamy "petals," actually individual and fertile pistillate flowers called rays.

This arrangement of collective disk flowers surrounded by petal-like ray flowers is one type of the daisy family's masquerade. There are two other common arrangements. The mistflower, historically a member of the *Eupatorium* genus but recently placed in the genus *Conoclinium*, represents a second daisy family pattern: Disk flowers only. Its button-shaped, budding flower-heads open to a starry collection of disk flowers, each of which, through the hand lens, contains a fireworks-like explosion of sexual parts. Then there is a third daisy family pattern, made up of ray flowers only, represented by the familiar and ubiquitous dandelion.

The daisy family, one of the largest and most dynamically evolved plant families, occurs all around the world and includes such familiar plants as sunflowers, ragweed, marigolds, lettuce, goldenrods, endive, daisies, chrysanthemums, chicory, black-eyed Susans, and artichokes. The concentration of so many flowers into a single "apparent" blossom is one of the keys to its evolutionary success, ensuring magnified bang for the buck during every pollinator's visitation.

But the trademark ingenuity of the daisy family doesn't stop with its flowers. Its methods of distributing seeds are equally clever. Think of a child blowing a head of dandelion seeds high into the air. The sepals of this family's flowers, which in most flowering plants are either green and leafy or colored and petal-like, are modified in the daisy family to something called a pappus. They are sometimes light and feathery like dandelion fluff or sometimes hooked and barbed like the beggar-ticks or the infamous burdock, whose pappus bristles and barbed bracts are designed to hitchhike on animal fur or socks and blue jeans.

As someone who has spent way too many hours gazing at plants and marveling over how they make food by photosynthesis according to a recipe of sunlight, air, and water—and not only feed and shelter the animal world, but trick it into helping with the vital business of reproduction—my awe knows no limits. As I walk the Boundary Bridge loop today, after my visual feast with the hand lens, I note all the members of the daisy family with extra respect: The tall wingstem, the even taller Jerusalem artichoke with its blazing yellow ray flowers, the blue-stemmed goldenrod, and even the ragweed. As I look around my backyard at this time of the year, I'm surrounded by the daisy family—the Joe-Pye-weed that nourishes monarchs and tiger swallowtails during its August bloom-time and is now busy feathering its seeds for autumnal flight, the vividly hued zinnias, the small orange-and-yellow marigolds with their pungent petals (um, ray flowers), and the tall, wispy pink and white cosmos. Later, I will make a salad with lettuce and artichoke hearts, all from the amazing daisy family.

My morning botanical reverie at Boundary Bridge morphs into a dragonfly festival when I discover that a smooth log projecting from the creek about a quarter-mile downstream from the bridge serves as a perch for dragonflies. These wonderful creatures take turns alighting on the log and sitting still, double wings outstretched, long enough for me to take a stab at identifying them through my binoculars with the help of my *Beginner's Guide to Dragonflies.* I get a pretty good handle on the common whitetail, but can't figure out whether the dusky, gray-blue-bodied dragonfly is an eastern pondhawk or some other species. No matter. I am entranced by the translucent beauty of its wings and the color of its body and green head, which it wags back and forth. While I am admiring its colors, a larger, gray-blue-bodied creature flies past—my friend, the kingfisher, who today is curiously quiet but as eloquent in its silence as when chattering.

All reveries must come to an end, or at least an interruption, but mine happens prematurely just past the Fenwick Branch Bridge. I hear the loud sounds of machinery whining above the chorus of cicada, katydids, and crickets, and I know in an instant what is happening. As I walk toward the sound, confirming evidence mounts. Orange chainsaws and coils of blue rope lie next to Rock Creek. A backhoe and not one but four trucks and a wood-chipping machine crowd the footpath. The giant fallen sycamore that has lain across the creek since its winter blow-down is about to be hauled out and annihilated. Yellow police-tape surrounds the vehicles, which have seriously chewed up the trail with their tires.

I take one long look at the pale, mottled trunk of the tree, at its still-full crown lying on the ground loaded with seeds, at its many leafy suckers springing up from its fallen body, and then I walk quickly away from the scene. As abrupt and violent as the day would be for this fallen arboreal giant, I still hope that some part of it will live on, through an achene that has bobbed far downstream in a floating fruit ball, from a sucker that has managed to take root and elude the chainsaws and chipper, or, perhaps, from both. Since the winter, Jim and I have stopped many times at this fallen tree, feeling the sadness of its demise but also amazement over all the ways it attempts to carry on. I should have known that, one day, a cleanup crew would come to clear the creek's channel and neaten up the forest.

But, as I climb into the uplands, I develop bigger worries. Over the past few days, I came to realize that the ashes strewn on the ground at the rock ledge above the Meditation Rock probably weren't human ashes. Looking up at a low branch of the beech tree above the ashen spot when I was with Jim and Sophie the other day, I noticed a wriggling mass of fuzzy, white critters totally covering a branch. Sophie was horrified and had to look away, a response I instantly understood, for I've always had a horror for clustered scales of insects and similar infestations. Jim looked up and suggested, "I wonder if those white things and those ashes are connected?"

Well, they are. As I climb into the uplands above the fallen sycamore and beyond the Skunk Cabbage Swamp where the sounds of machinery recede, I find another beech tree with fuzzy, white insects all over a low branch and an ashen spot on the ground below. I now have an email out to my friends in the botany community, and I'm fearful that these fuzzy, white patches of writhing "things" may represent the scale that is spreading Beech Bark Disease, a serious, new disease that threatens trees of the Northeast.

During ten years of botanical research on Sugarloaf Mountain, I watched two of my favorite species of trees nearly disappear from its slopes: Eastern hemlock, infested by another white scaly pest, the woolly adelgid, and flowering dogwood, victim of an anthracnose blight. And, while I walked the trails to conduct research for my two books about the mountain, I saw the suckered remnants of the once magnificent American chestnut, felled by an imported fungal blight that spread from New England to Georgia during the first half of the twentieth century. Four billion eastern North American trees, many of them 100 feet tall and taller, were wiped out in a matter of decades. On Sugarloaf and elsewhere, the suckers continue to spring from the still-healthy roots, but the young trunks soon succumb to the blight.

We know that small shifts in climate, especially warming trends, favor pathogens of many kinds. And, when trees are already stressed by intermittent drought, as our trees are in Rock Creek Park, all bets are off.

Today's *reverie interruptus* resembles so many other recent "walking meditations." When I ponder the genius of life on Earth and witness the glorious display during any woodland stroll, my spirit soars. And then I'm slapped with the obvious results of man's folly and with the fear that what we humans are doing here is *un*doing the natural web, for which so many people have so little true regard. Members of the daisy family, lacking anything resembling a central nervous system, are smart. But the kind of smarts that creates a barb to carry a seed on a deer hide are not the same kind of smarts that drive a chipping machine. All smarts are wanted for survival on Earth. But, when we only admire the chipping machine and never think about the wonder of the barb or the dandelion fluff and their evolution over time, what do we really know, and how can our actions encompass all that we need to know? During the past two or three centuries, people have been moving ever faster, smitten and energized by our human cleverness. Recently, we've begun to see that it might be time to apply the brakes to save our own souls and our planet. If and when we finally slow down, what will there be left to see, and will we have the wisdom to see it? And, if we do, will we be willing to cherish and protect the view?

September 7: MELTING ICE

WHAT A STORY in today's *Washington Post.* It stopped me dead in my tracks. "NOAA Scientists Say Arctic Ice is Melting Faster Than Expected." Lead paragraph: "The Arctic ice cap is melting faster than scientists expected and will shrink 40 percent by 2050 in most regions, with grim consequences for polar bears, walruses and other marine animals, according to government researchers."

Like the kingfisher who quietly flew past me the other day, I'm speechless. Truly speechless, because of the message the melting ice conveys.

Later, words come to me: We need to wake up and pay attention. The facts are the symptoms. And behavior is belief. And the land, air, water, soil, trees, and plants of the world do not lie.

September 18: SEPTEMBER BRILLIANCE

THIS PAST WEEK has been a string of September days, each more brilliant than the last. On Saturday morning, I opened the back door (gingerly, to avoid bruising a sprawling tomato plant) to watch small, feathery cirrus clouds stream across the sky from the northwest. The days since have been jubilantly cool. Nancy, our gardener, planted pansies in the yard in time with the oncoming cool. The tomatoes are still coming, but they're not as fat as August's. All the garden flowers, which were languishing a bit in the late-summer heat, are perking up and putting out new blossoms. The crescent harvest moon adorns the crisp nights, the crickets still sing but a bit more languidly, and the screech-owls are out and about in our neighborhood with their mournful calls.

At Boundary Bridge, Rock Creek now flows low and dark, the color of a strong black tea. Despite rain on Jim's birthday last week (both our birthdays received welcome wet blessings this year), we are still experiencing a drought. I can see the evidence in Rock Creek Park's fall wildflowers. Many are smaller and less vigorous than in past years. We keep awaiting a tropical storm or hurricane to make up the summer's deficit, but none is on the horizon. How well I remember moving into this house four years ago this week, a few hours ahead of Hurricane Isabel, which brought down many of the neighborhood's trees, including one that destroyed a house that is just now being rebuilt.

On this brilliant morning, I am making a rich sauce with our tomatoes, herbs, and chard, and the ripe fragrance fills the house. I'm listening to Loreena McKennitt, the Celtic singer from Canada, who has been adding atmosphere to our family's autumns and winters for many years. My laptop perches on the dining room table in front of overflowing bowls of local apples. I'm surrounded by the sights, sounds, and smells of early autumn, a celebration of Earth's fecundity. And yet my heart feels heavy and my thoughts grow dark. I try to sort through the reasons.

Is my heart heavy because of September 11th, 2001, when the brilliant clarity of an early autumn day was shattered? For us, that day was Jim's fifty-first birthday. Our children were in class at their DC schools, but we were still living in the country at Comus, and we were unable to retrieve them from the city for many hours. I'll never forget the distress on Jesse's ten-year-old face when he finally made it home. He'd thought he might never see us again.

Is my heart heavy because a laughing and joyous and brilliant friend, six months older than I am, is currently in surgery for breast cancer?

Is my heart heavy because of the suffering of so many close friends, whose lives have been altered by cancer and other serious illnesses in their spouses and children?

Is my heart heavy because of the ongoing Iraq war and how helpless we all feel to see a way to a solution?

Is my heart heavy because I'm experiencing a bit of a career lull and feeling disconnected from colleagues?

Is my heart heavy because of the aftermath of an argument I had with Jim after Sunday's church service at All Souls when I wholly applauded our minister's anti-war sermon and Jim did not?

Is my heart heavy over my concern about the infestation of insects on the beech trees at Rock Creek, an infestation I see on more and more trees during each walk?

That's quite a list of questions to start with. Is there a theme underlying my worry? Is the theme *disconnection*, my own disconnection and our collective disconnection from the Earth? Is the theme *dissonance*, between the sunny brilliance of this day and the discontent of my own heart? Or is it that *all is not as it seems*, that there's a cancer at the heart of autumn's verdancy? And is this just *irony*, of life itself, of life as it's always been, or is there a new discomfort, even darkness, more ominous than anything we've seen or envisioned?

Yesterday's *Washington Post* contains more front-page coverage of climate change. Dire news. Not just the theoretical might-bes but the alreadys. In "Climate Change Brings Risk of More Extinctions," David A. Fahrenthold writes:

> By nature's clock, the warming has come in an instant. The mechanisms that helped animals adapt during previous warming spells—evolution or long-range migration—often aren't able to keep up. Scientists say that effects are beginning to show from the Arctic to the Appalachian Mountains. One study, which examined 1,598 plant and animal species, found that nearly 60 percent appeared to have changed in some way.
>
> 'Even when animals don't go extinct, we're affecting them. They're going to be different than they were before,' said David Skelly, a Yale University professor who has tracked frogs' ability to react to increasing warmth. 'The fact that we're doing a giant evolutionary experiment should not be comforting,' he said.

No, not comforting at all.

And so, on this brilliant morning, I send healing energy to my friend in surgery. I water the pansies that Nancy planted. I make comfort-food and listen to comfort-music. And I look for signs of change in myself and the world, real change that can truly mirror the beauty of the September day.

September 19: HEAD FULL OF FIRE

YESTERDAY, MY FRIEND received good news about her lymph nodes after her surgery for breast cancer. Today is yet another sparkling September day, but very autumnal, with a few more clouds, its overall beauty reflected in my friend's happy outcome. The flowers in our neighborhood's gardens are celebrating the cool days with end-of-season splendor. But I wonder, Did the Chinese acupuncturist I just saw for the first time, due to my on-going fatigue from Lyme disease, somehow read what I wrote yesterday? About my funk of unresolved questions?

He looked at my tongue, felt my pulse, checked out my spine, and made the following pronouncements: "You are filled with fire, but your energy is all in your head, and your body is exhausted. You are consumed with worry and cannot shut off your mind. You are dehydrated and don't know what to drink. There are problems with your spine. And, just like a plant, your spine is your core and your root. It needs water and nourishment. Your *chi* is blocked." He then asked me to lie down, and he pushed five needles into my body. I felt warm, radiant energy flow immediately through me, from head to toe. He wants me to come back two to three times a week.

Despite the acupuncturist's disdain for whatever exercise program I'm doing and his certainty that it's only calcifying my spine and refusing to budge my blocked *chi*, I cannot give up my nightly walk in my neighborhood. The human assaulter and the prevalence of deer ticks in the Park have curtailed my nighttime rambles in its woods, which the Park's "closed at dark" signs never managed to do. I can only guess at the nocturnal sounds I've missed in Rock Creek Park this summer. But the rolling contours of our neighborhood provide a delightful venue for evening strolls, and I'm out and about these suburban streets almost every night. I can hug the trees without embarrassment at night and revel in the canopy that our tree ordinance (which I helped draft and continue to help enforce through a citizen appeals board) is designed to protect. Midway on my circle route a giant American beech, with a protective stonewall half encircling it, resides in someone's front yard. Not only does the smooth, silver-barked tree with its carved initials beg to be hugged, but I discovered some months ago that its roots form a perfect cradle. Whenever I can, I tuck myself into the cradle for a short horizontal meditation. Lying on my back and looking at the stars through the tall crown, leafy in summer and bare in winter, rejuvenates me with the skyward view.

Tonight, a perfect harvest quarter-moon hangs in the southeastern sky. A break in the canopy appears at Supreme Court Chief Justice John Roberts's house, and above his roof I can see the great "W" of Cassiopeia. Does he

know it's there? I wish that the stars will bestow some sort of celestial blessing on the Roberts' home that will radiate through the culture. Nighttime
rambles are all about impossible wishes on stars. I am pleased to see the Big
Dipper hanging over our house, pouring its blessing onto our home, when
I return to our front door.

September 20: BELOW THE BOUNDARY

THREE DAYS SHY of the autumnal equinox, I take my sorry self to a part
of Rock Creek Park different from my usual hangout. This is less out of
desire for new experiences and more out of anxiety. Two weeks ago, I accom-
panied Wendy Paulson on a bird walk sponsored by the Nature Conservancy
at the National Arboretum. I wasn't expecting her to haul *City of Trees* out of
her pocket and sing my praises, asking me to contribute my knowledge of the
Arboretum's plants on the walk, but she did. Luckily, I had scanned my chapter about the Arboretum before the outing! On Monday, I'm tagging along on
another of her trips, this one originating at the Rock Creek Nature Center.
Except for my dad, she is the best birding teacher I've ever been with in the
field. Birds will be the focus, and, perhaps, I'll pick up some bird lore. But,
just in case I'm called upon to answer some plant questions once again,
I thought it prudent to familiarize myself with the woody and herbaceous
plants in the slightly more southerly part of Rock Creek Park where the walk
will occur.

This turns out to be excellent therapy for the funk I've been in. There is
something inherently uplifting and empowering about stuffing a pack with
binoculars, field guides, hand lens, power bars, and water bottle and setting
off to discover a new place. I pull into the Nature Center's parking lot just
south of Military Road (downstream from Boundary Bridge) and am instantly
bowled over by the size and beauty of the nearby oak trees.

The chestnut oaks around the center are some of the tallest and fullest I've
seen anywhere. Some less-massive ones grow in the uplands near Boundary
Bridge, and chestnut oak is probably the most common tree growing on Sugarloaf, where it is able to thrive in the mountain's dry, rocky soil. Another

vernacular name for the tree is rock oak. This tree is very good medicine for sad or depressed tree-huggers, because the bark is thick and ridged with a solid, chunky feel. I always urge field-trip participants to touch it, so they can experience its solidity. The chestnut oak is a member of the white oak group, with leaves that have rounded teeth and/or lobes. A chestnut oak's leaves are more shallowly toothed or lobed than most oaks' leaves.

Other magnificent oaks also grow around the Nature Center. The white oak, with its shaggy, ash-gray bark and more deeply lobed leaves, is apparent as are several species in the red (or black) oak group. This group features pointed, bristle-tipped, rather than round-lobed, leaves. I spot red oak, black oak, and, perhaps most prevalent, Southern red or Spanish oak. This tall tree species has an elongated leaf with deeply cut, elegantly pointed lobes—quite an eye-catching and distinctive silhouette.

As I walk among the mighty oaks, I hear a constant and quick knocking sound. Acorns are torpedoing earthward, even though there is no breeze to speak of. Some arrive with caps intact, but many, especially the chestnut oaks', land hatless. I try to solve this small mystery as I walk over ground peppered with green acorns with yellow-haloed tops. Where are their caps? I stand still, staring into the near distance, prepared to be a target. But every time a chestnut oak's acorn lands with a small bounce it is hatless. Is the hat still on the branch? Or lying nearby? I can't tell, I just can't tell. The few acorns of that species that I find intact on the ground are a beautiful chestnut brown, but the hatless wonders are still green and yellow. Ah, so is that it? The youngsters, seduced by gravity, can't wait to mature to the stage where they'd be traveling the distance from branch to ground with head apparel.

I collect a small handful of acorns and have a close look at two from a white oak. One is a lovely olive green, and the other is dark brown, and both have gray-brown caps with thick, bluntly pointed scales. The cap covers about a quarter of the nut. The white oak's acorns fell to the ground with their short, thick stalks attached to their caps. The chestnut oak's elder acorn is a proper chestnut brown, with a cap covering its upper third. Unlike the white oak's cap, the chestnut oak's cap is thin and feels less welded to the nut. It, too, is gray-brown. The impatient and hatless young acorn of the chestnut oak is still green for the most part, with a yellow wash where its hat used to be.

Early this morning, when I went out to water the flowers before my walk, I noticed several small branches in a black oak with still-green leaves and fat acorns tightly attached in various stages of development. I noted that the infants are all capped, with no nut yet showing. The broadly rounded mature acorns have thick, top-shaped, scaly caps covering about half the vaguely striped nut. Leaves of the red and black oak are quite similar in shape, but the acorns are very different. The red oak's acorn has a shallow, saucer-shaped cap.

I'm fascinated by oaks for many reasons. If I were a small, woodland creature, I would make my home in an oak tree. But, since I'm an amateur botanist with a worried head full of fire, I find oaks an especially pleasing genus (*Quercus*) to contemplate. I love the oak theme and the variations thereof. For example, the leaf is usually lobed but sometimes not (as in the willow oak and shingle oak, both denizens of Rock Creek Park, and the live oak of the Deep South), and there are variations in the acorn. In each species, both leaf and acorn have that recognizable "oak look," but they seem to revel in their own unique take on the theme.

After my "acorn festival" at the Nature Center, I walk down toward the creek. The stretch of Rock Creek just south of Military Road is arguably its most scenic. This part of the creek is filled with large, gray rocks that invite rock hopping. Once out in the creek, I find several potholes filled with tea. The music of water flowing over rocks is hypnotic, and many chirping songbirds add to the magic. Among the lowland trees (green ash, ironwood, and sycamore) are Christmas, New York, and broad-beech ferns springing from the ground. I locate a small cluster of slender, purplish-brown beechdrops, a parasitic plant with no chlorophyll, growing near the base of some beech trees, where they take nourishment from the tree's roots.

When I reach Rapids Bridge, a footbridge like the Boundary and Riley Spring bridges, I am in full enchantment mode. The high crescent-arched bridge is prettier than Boundary Bridge (I grudgingly admit), with simple, unpainted wood railings and finials. I walk to the middle of the bridge and park my worry-weary self. Rock Creek stretches in both directions, lined by healthy trees: A green ash loaded with clustered samaras, tall ghostly sycamores arching toward the sun, and alligator-barked tupelos, the first trees to change to autumnal hues in Washington woodlands with their leaves showing tinges of scarlet and peach. The water's music is just what the doctor ordered. And, below me, I can see what I think are catfish probing the creek's bottom.

I breathe deeply, feeling the healing power of Washington's wild, wooded heart, as Rock Creek flows swiftly and surely beneath Rapids Bridge.

Lying back and using my pack as a pillow, I nearly fall asleep. I feel as calm as I did during my acupuncture session two days earlier. I don't hear the man approaching, and when he arrives he towers over me. Weighing two or three times what I weigh, at least six feet tall and adorned with gold jewelry, he doesn't look like a fellow hiker. He is calm and smiling in friendly fashion, but in an abundance of caution (I am thinking about the springtime Boundary Bridge assault) I slowly get up and walk back to the Nature Center along Beach Drive rather than along the trail he was following up the woodland hill.

Just a reminder: Rock Creek Park is an urban park in the real world, not a Buddhist or Benedictine monastery or an acupuncturist's table. It offers refuge to the solitary woman, but she must keep her wits about her. The park is probably not the best setting for a snooze.

PART IV: FALL

TODAY MARKS THE EQUINOX, a day of equal light and dark around the world. For the next three months, the northern hemisphere will lean toward winter, with its shorter and darker days, and the southern hemisphere will tilt toward summer with its longer and brighter ones. On the equinox, especially the autumnal equinox, I feel a palpable sense of balance in the world. Balance is desirable. I welcome it into my personal life.

When Sophie and Jesse were little and we were living in Comus, our cele-brations of the fall equinox on Sugarloaf Mountain were festive events, with the children and their friends painting their faces to resemble their favorite animals, then hiding behind rocks and trees until they were called to our celebration circle by Mother Earth's bell. We scattered seeds for the birds and passed the "wand of the seasons" around the circle, with each person who held the wand sharing his or her favorite aspects of fall. I celebrated the equi-nox today by going to All Souls church with friends, followed by a trip to the farmers' market in DC's Dupont Circle. The day culminated with an evening trip to my favorite trail in Rock Creek Park, where I was greeted at the creek by dipping, gliding, and chattering kingfishers. I sat under a sycamore tree for a long time while a pileated woodpecker hammered away at its decay-ing top. I was quite taken with the rapidity and rhythm of the beak-work, which sent bits of bark flying from the tree. Pieces of the sycamore's bark, curled and hardened like cinnamon sticks, decorated the ground around me. Mourning doves gathered on Dog Beach, with a nearly full moon rising above. As I walked away from the creek back toward the trail, two barred owls called back and forth.

On this equinox, after much trial and error, I discovered the best way to make jumpseeds jump. You place your hand around the lower part of the stem and then move it upwards. As you gently squeeze the plant with an upward motion, the seeds jump high into the air.

Last evening, Jim and I walked on our land at Comus. We arrived as the setting sun was pouring a golden wash over the fields. Due to the continuing drought, the soybean crop had dry foliage, already turning yellow, and our fields held colors more in keeping with the American Southwest. But, despite the not-so-felicitous reason for the golden hues, we basked in the beauty of tall, waving grasses and weathered hay bales. We walked and walked around our fields, through the deepening twilight and into the waxing moonlight, our moon-shadows mingling with the shadows of the large, barrel-shaped bales. Two screech-owls called, sounding like sad, whinnying horses. It is always a thrill to walk in the company of owls.

September 24: MIGRATION

THIS MORNING, on Wendy Paulson's Nature Conservancy bird walk, a wave of fall migrants removed the last traces of my end-of-summer funk. We did a two-hour stint on a high ridge near the Rock Creek Nature Center, where we stood still and watched the fluttering parade. Waves of warblers flitted past, frantically seeking insect-meals to fuel their incredible journeys from the North to the Tropics. Black-throated green, magnolia, bay-breasted, Tennessee and parula warblers darted in and out of the trees, briefly settling just long enough for us to admire their fall colors before they took wing again. We saw a swainson's thrush and a veery. We got good views of a rose-breasted grosbeak and several scarlet tanagers, neither of which I could recognize on my own, their less-colorful fall feathers so different from their spring plumage.

Today's migration, Wendy said, was her first birding experience in Washington to equal the great migrant parade that happens in Central Park, where you simply stand still in awe, watching hundreds of birds of many species fly by. I was only called upon to identify two plants, a chestnut oak and a jimson-weed, so all was well in that department.

Over the weekend, my editor sent me the book cover of the new edition of *City of Trees* and, I must say, it's gorgeous! Two of Susan Roth's images appear on the cover. One is her favorite view of Rock Creek Park, looking down from the Taft Bridge upon the creek and the newly leafed treetops painted in their golden, spring hues. I'm pleased with the way the new cover honors and celebrates both monumental Washington and the city's intimate botanical beauty. Now, I'm gearing up for my final wave of fact-checking, during which I'll look a bit like those warblers, flitting from tree to tree in frantic migration. On top of that, field-trip season looms. I will be one busy bird this fall. But, thanks to lessening effects of Lyme and the benefits of acupuncture, which is also helping my sciatica and my ability to sleep at night, I hope to enjoy the season in waxing health.

I remember a dream from last night: Jim and I were in a theater waiting to see a concert. The rows of seats were made of giant peaches. Looking from the back of the theater toward the stage, we saw row upon row of fleshy pink and gold seats. We sat down, and I showed Jim that, if you touched the seat in front of you, you could peel away the peach skin to get to the juicy golden fruit underneath. You could also create art and write messages by peeling away the skin in patterns. The seats resembled rows of rosy mountain ranges. I won't even attempt to analyze this juicy dream!

September 30: SALLY FORTH

I DOUBT I HAVE EVER used the expression "sally forth" either in conversation or in writing, but this crystal-clear Sunday, the last day of September, simply beckons one to "sally forth." I have already sallied to Boundary Bridge and the bagel shop, I've got a crockpot of split peas simmering, the garden sprinklers are going, and energy is returning after yet another episode with illness, this one "just" a cold but yuck. Sally forth and be gone, cold!

The canopy at Boundary Bridge has thinned a little, letting some autumn light spill through. With cooler days upon us, I've begun to long for flying leaves, liberated branches, and full sun pouring onto the forest's floor. I say to autumn: Bring it on! Today is such a sweet transitional day: Sunny, cool, and still, with no wildness in the wind. The creek is a dark mirror, reflecting the colorful outlines of the sparkling tree canopy and bursts of blue sky, its still pools ruffled only by an occasional drifting leaf of a tulip tree, cottonwood, or sycamore.

My morning walk proved to be a meditation on flower, fruit, and bud. The fall asters still bloom next to the late-flowering boneset, and the dazzling white snakeroot, creating a snowdrift effect along the creek, and goldenrods, mistflowers, Jerusalem artichokes, wingstem, and ragweed—amazing members of the daisy family all—punctuate the drifts with bursts of color. Wouldn't allergy sufferers be surprised to learn that the scientific genus name of ragweed is *Ambrosia?*

Some members of the mint family, which often feature four-sided "square" stems, still flower at the creek. One of my favorites, the native horse-balm *(Collinsonia canadensis),* displays clusters of fringed, yellow, and deliciously lemon-scented blossoms. Horse-balm has been used as a balm for burns and sprains (perhaps for horses as well as humans!) and as a gargle for hoarseness, earning it the moniker "a clergyman's friend." Should it be called "hoarse-balm?" The perilla or beefsteak plant, a non-native fellow member of the mint family, is suddenly tall, and its colorful calyxes are very showy, even though most of the bluish-purple corollas are already gone. Perilla's coarsely toothed pungent leaves will soon fall, but the spiky calyx clusters will endure and persist through the winter in a dried state. Unfortunately, perilla is invasive here, where it is an escapee of gardens, but is prized both as food and medicine in its native Asia.

The drupes of viburnum are at curiously disparate stages of ripeness. The lovely, cobalt-blue drupes of arrowwood have been ripe for some time. I tasted one today and found the flavor a bit insipid. The fruits of maple-leaved viburnum have been blue-black and ripe for a while. The mature fruits of the invasive linden viburnum are attention-grabbing, with their scarlet hues, but the blackhaw fruits remain summer green. They are in abundant, drooping clusters, and I look forward to a sweet nibble when they're ripe and blue-black. I promise the birds awaiting their ripening that I'll only sample one or two!

I think our Boundary Bridge pawpaws, although profuse bloomers during the spring, must be too young to set fall fruit, because I rarely observe any, but I experienced a pawpaw orgy earlier this month at Blockhouse Point, which overlooks the Potomac River north of Great Falls, with my botanist/artist friends Carole Bergmann and Tina Brown. Deer don't usually eat pawpaw (its leaves taste something like gasoline), and Blockhouse Point has become overrun not only with deer, but also with pawpaw trees, even in the uplands where our local pawpaws rarely grow. (My friend, geologist Tony Fleming, tells me that, in Indiana where he lives, the pawpaw is known as "Indiana banana," and pawpaw habitat includes uplands.) The tree belongs to the largely tropical custard-apple family, and it has very large and elongated leaves that make one think of the rainforest. Tina exclaimed over how much the Blockhouse Point woods reminded her of the Costa Rican rainforest where she did field work years ago. Green pawpaws hung from the trees, and purplish-peach/golden fruit decorated the forest floor, ripe for the plucking. The shape, flavor, color, and texture are somewhere between a banana and a mango, a very tropical treat growing on a temperate-zone tree!

The papery, lantern-like capsules of bladdernut exhibit their summery, pale-green hue on Rock Creek's trees today. When I gently shake the little lanterns, their seeds aren't yet rattling. Not ripe. However, last year's lanterns, now deep reddish-brown, still persevere intact on the ground in the small grove of bladdernut near the pawpaw patch. Most of their seeds have already spilled from the handy splits in the capsules' seams, but a few pale brown seeds remain inside as dry as popcorn kernels. I wonder if they are still viable. Clearly, the design of this fruit is genius—a light, flexible, but very durable protective coat, which can float on the water near where bladdernut usually grows, with seams that eventually split, releasing the hard, persistent seeds inside.

Although Japanese knotweed is one of our most aggressive invasives in Rock Creek Park, and it's taking over way too much territory, I can't help admiring the beauty of its small, dry fruit—translucent and papery white with tiny black seeds inside—which I've noticed for the first time this fall. It's shaped like a small, three-chambered heart. My botany manual describes the fruits as "trigonous [three-angled] achenes." I like the poetry of trigonous achenes even more than a three-chambered heart.

One native fruit is most conspicuous in its absence today, reminding me of all the drama I miss at the creek by being a mere visitor. As I search to see how many of the spicebush drupes are now ripe along my route, I look and look but I see only a handful of little red fruits. Have the birds and other critters devoured all the others so quickly? Hoards of starlings are moving through Rock Creek Park—I can hear their raucous calling overhead—and I wonder, Have these non-native and hungry invaders stripped the spicebush fruits or is their teeming presence only a coincidence?

Looking carefully at the branchlets of spicebush, I see something else that makes me smile: Many pairs of small, round, green flower buds line up along the green twigs—next spring's blossoms in embryonic condition. If I were to examine the twigs of all the woody plants of Rock Creek Park during early fall, I would find a similar story. At each axil where a leaf stalk meets a twig, I would find a bud containing next year's flowers and/or leaves tucked away and ready to unfurl at their appointed time, after the long winter. Squirrels bury nuts to get through 'til spring, bears gorge and then hibernate, and woody plants create buds months ahead of opening day.

The buds of one of Rock Creek's woody plant species won't wait in dormancy through the winter until spring. Each round tan flower bud of the witch-hazel will unfurl into four thin, yellow petals later this fall, giving the plant the distinction of being our only native woody plant to bloom during autumn. But the half-moon-shaped leaf bud at the end of each witch-hazel twig *will* have to wait for spring to unfurl.

We are still suffering from drought, as are many other areas of the country and other countries around the world. I am studying Greek for a trip to the Aegean next summer in honor of my father's eightieth birthday. We're planning to visit the island where his father was born and spent his childhood. Greece is one of the spots most vulnerable to drought during climate change, and this summer horrible fires have raged on the Greek mainland, killing many people. And then there are those throughout the world for whom recent weather patterns have brought grief via deluge. Our precious Earth hungers for balance.

The tupelos at Rock Creek should be blazing scarlet by now, but they are merely turning a pale-peach color, because of the dryness. Will our foliage this autumn simply simmer or will it blaze? Droughts sometimes kill autumnal color, but, at other times, the trees rise up at the last minute and put on a show. We shall see. Tomorrow begins the month of fullest autumnal glory in these woods.

As a farewell to summer and September, the pale, waning harvest moon hung in the sky this morning above the upstream side of Rock Creek. I stood in the jimsonweed patch on Dog Beach and said good-bye to the chalky, overturned bowl of a moon that had blazed so brightly on the downstream side just a few days ago.

October 4: CHANNELS

THIS MORNING I SMILED when I went out to feed the birds. A festive pile of acorn caps lay in front of the back door where a squirrel had obviously been picnicking. The squirrels who live in our oak trees are reaping the bounty of their choice of a home site this month!

Still no rain. The weather page of the *Washington Post* features five partly- or mostly-sunny graphics without a single raindrop. No tropical storm has its sights on us, and hurricane season will soon come to a close. Yesterday, I walked along the rocky and botanically diverse Potomac Gorge south of Great Falls with several naturalist friends. One of them said that she'd heard a weather expert say that, for cultural reasons, "global warming" is the wrong description of what is happening to our climate. She said this expert noted that, when it snows in Los Angeles, people are quick to say, "See, this disproves global warming." The language this climatologist recommends is "extreme climate change." So, I'm adding the word *extreme* to my nomenclature.

But, today, I want to focus on the positive, because I have a positive new role model in my life. Wendy Paulson and her husband, Hank, are experts at channeling positive energy. When they want to accomplish a conservation project, they find the channel and don't get side-tracked with dry runs or blocked passageways. They are on their way to visit a barrier island in Georgia, which they saved from development by purchasing three-quarters of the land. The Paulsons use their resources to help preserve sensitive, threatened habitat around the world, and they use their smarts and indomitable spirits to work with other can-do people to accomplish their goals.

Wendy's passion is teaching urban children about Nature, something she's done in Chicago and New York City and recently in Washington, DC. She does a quick-change from her field clothes to her fancy clothes for black-tie dinners and works her magic everywhere. On a smaller scale, this has always been my *modus operandi*, too: Find the common ground, do the good that you can, and don't get sidetracked by negativity, constricting agendas, or operational details. I have never seen this action plan so successfully employed as it is with Wendy.

I have just been given a dream assignment by a magazine editor and publisher whom I serendipitously met at Boundary Bridge. He wants me to follow Rock Creek north from the District of Columbia's line at Boundary Bridge to its source in upper Montgomery County. He said: Travel any way you can—by canoe, car, bicycle, or on foot—and write a travelogue about the creek, its beauty and the ugliness of the threats to its integrity. Before I can wholeheartedly pursue this tempting project, I must finish my revisions and fact-checking for *City of Trees*, a far less compelling and more overwhelming task. But, first things first. I will try to borrow some of that can-do energy from my new friends to do the footwork I need to do before I can hop in a canoe and paddle the new waters that beckon to me.

I've been wandering way beyond my usual boundaries, but I have also been walking at Boundary Bridge, where hallucinogenic jimsonweed seeds are spilling from their open-beaked spiky capsules. I wonder how they affect wildlife. Pigs avoid them like the plague, but I'll have to sit on the beach and see if birds partake.

October 7: WHERE IS AUTUMN?

TODAY, I STILL WANT to focus on the positive, but I can't ignore the reality of the drought and the record-breaking heat-wave that is upon us. Our temperatures have been averaging ten to fifteen degrees above normal, and a record was broken at nearby Dulles Airport three days ago. There's no relief from the heat in sight.

I'm doing my final fact-checking for *City of Trees,* which involves tree hopping through the District's gardens and parks and along the parched city streets. Trees have resources to cope with climate extremes, but urban trees are already challenged by constricted space for roots, impervious surfaces (and thus dry soil due to runoff), and air pollution. When you add prolonged drought and unseasonal heat to the mix, you see the signs everywhere. Young, newly planted trees have not survived, unless they received special watering, which has been a citizen-imperative in some neighborhoods. I'm seeing crowns of mature trees with so much leaf-loss that it looks to be life-threatening. At Boundary Bridge, Rock Creek is low, low, low.

I have a home ritual for the autumnal equinox that I try to perform on the day itself. Two weeks ago this Sunday, I took our friend Scott Brouard's painting of Sugarloaf Mountain down from its perch above the fireplace, where it hangs for nine months of the year, and replaced it with a large autumn collage that Sophie and her friend, Joan, created in a high-school art class. The collage features a grove of autumn trees against a bright-blue sky, brilliant orange, yellow, and red tissue-paper leaves, and real bark for the trees. The girls inscribed poems about autumn in silver, swirling ink all over the collage; my favorite is a quote from John Muir's *Our National Parks*:

> The winds will blow their own freshness into you,
> and the storms their energy, while cares will drop
> away from you like the leaves of autumn.

Where are the winds to blow freshness into us, and where are the storms with their energy? How will cares drop away, if there is no wind and rain to release autumn's leaves? I see the tupelo in Esther and Nick's yard outside my window turning colors, but the colors are muted orange and burnt-bronze rather than their usual scarlet-peach hues. In city and in forest, it's growing drier and dustier by the day.

In church this morning, the children's choir sang a song with an environmental theme entitled "Be Cool" by Bob Chilcott:

Be cool, be green, and get our world clean.
Pollution's mean, not always seen.
Be cool, be kind, get some peace of mind
And leave a better world behind.

Look here, look there,
Let's all be aware,
Listen to the warning, global warming, be cool.

The time is here to change our idea,
And start to clear the atmosphere.
It's good to meet where the air is sweet
Sit back, relax, turn down the heat.

Look here, look there,
Let's all be aware,
Listen to the warning, global warming, be cool.

Be cool and find the channel to change. As Rock Creek found its channel to the Potomac River and the Potomac found its channel to Chesapeake Bay, let us find the channel to healing change. At All Souls church, members each signed green resolutions earlier this year with specific goals for energy-savings at home and in transit. I just reported to our green committee that our family has gotten better, but we're still a work-in-progress.

There's one piece of relatively good news to share. Last week, Cris Fleming and I were showing some young ecologists the Boundary Bridge trail, and I pointed out the feathery, white infestations of insects I've found along the lower branches of several American beeches and the ashy places on the ground below the trees. The young women later returned to the trees with either an entomologist or a plant pathologist, who told them that the insects are native woolly aphids and are not the scary scale that is spreading beech bark disease. What a huge sigh of relief!

October 11: READING THE TEA LEAVES

THE WINDS BLEW their freshness into me this morning! After more record-tying or breaking heat (ninety-four degrees two days ago) and a frustrating thirty-second downpour two nights ago, we got a little soaking rain last night, and today it's in the sixties and *windy,* just as autumn should be!

I park on Beach Drive near Rock Creek and walk past flowering white asters, past sapphire clusters of arrowwood fruit and dangling samaras of boxelder, stepping over fallen acorns of red oak, with their saucer-shaped caps, and onto the sandy, wet bottomland soil. When I come to Boundary Bridge, I lean on the railing and breathe deeply. Looking up, I see a sycamore draped in cream-and-olive bark silhouetted against the sky, its leaves a tapestry of lemon and lime. The leaves of the tulip tree beside the bridge are becoming gold, and its upright tulip-shaped clusters of samaras show through the thinning foliage. The elm leaves remain mostly green, but the trees seem to have a new autumnal grace, with the lower canopy containing a smattering of yellow and gold from spicebush and ironwood.

It is into the creek, however, that my eyes are drawn, for the water is the color of black tea, with bright leaves parachuting into it and drifting on the shining, reflective surface. The leaves flow steadily in the central current beneath the bridge, with swirls and eddies near the shorelines. A dry, brown leaf of a sycamore falls and lands, partly crumpled, and I watch as it touches a flat, neighboring leaf that drifts downstream. The two leaves seem to be communing briefly, and I wonder if reading the autumn "tea" leaves as they travel along tea-colored Rock Creek could be some learned art of divination.

I begin to mosey along the creek's trail. It feels good to walk on at least slightly wet, alluvial soil, kicking through autumn's fallen leaves, some crunchy and brown, some soft and brightly colored gold, yellow, bronze, and—under the silver maples—silver-green. Each fallen leaf boasts its own identifying shape and color. The wind blows out of the north, setting white cumulus clouds a-flying. And the air is pungent with autumn smells, as the wind ripples through the canopy, creating flickering shadows on the forest's floor.

Autumn fruit decorates the path: Black walnuts with their outer green husks decaying to release the hard nutshells within; bitternut hickories, green with "winged" seams on their smooth husks; and paddle-shaped samaras of green and white ashes. The drupes on the blackhaw near the trail are beginning to darken, and so are the lantern-like capsules on the bladdernuts. The spreading clusters of the fruiting wood nettle look quite frilly and decorative, but a close encounter can also bring one into range of the inconspicuous stinging hairs. I confess I rather like the feel of the nettles' sting—and I am also enjoying acupuncture and getting sciatic relief from it as well as an energy boost! Stinging nettles *(Urtica dioica)* have been used to treat arthritis, but I'm unsure about this particular species: *Laportea canadensis.* Next to the patch of nettles grow some waist-high, late-summer-and early-fall-blooming wingstem plants, which have now set seed. I look closely at their small, dry fruits to admire their flat heart-shape with fringed edges and dark centers, which are borne in small, round clusters. I always remind my field-trip participants to look at the fruit. We pay so much attention to the showiness of flowers and so little to the glory and inventiveness of fruit, to which the flowers are merely a prelude!

Some plants seem to insist on having it all at once, and, surprise, surprise, that includes jimsonweed. I have yet to witness a bird actually eating the seeds, which are strong and toxic hallucinogens for humans, but, when I come upon the jimsonweed patch at Dog Beach this morning, I scare up quite a flock of doves, sparrows, and other songbirds. I am sorry I don't have the time to wait for their return, so I can witness any feasting. Lavender-silk, trumpet-shaped flowers still bloom on the jimsonweed, and their capsules are in all stages of development, as if the plants are posing for a formal botanical portrait. Some of the spiny capsules are green, but many have turned brown and have opened, beak up, looking like so many hungry birds.

Gazing out over the beach, I see six mallards in three perfect pair-matches paddling the dark waters, and then my friend, the kingfisher, comes flashing past in all its glory. I rarely get a good look at the bird's breast to determine gender, so fast do they fly. It perches momentarily on a dead tree, chattering away. Such a conversationalist!

The next few weeks will give me little chance to commune with Rock Creek Park, because I'm wandering the city, inspecting parks and streets that I haven't stepped foot in or on for nearly thirty years. When my energy flags, my dear and wise friend, Terrie Daniels, reminds me, "This is not about you. It's about the trees, and you owe it to them to get their facts straight!"

October 12: A PRIZE

THIS DAY FINDS ME wholly engaged with *City of Trees,* in the office and in the field. But I have to share my happiness. Today, Al Gore and the climate change panel of the United Nations were jointly awarded the Nobel Peace Prize for their work to document and contribute to a better understanding of how human activities are altering our Earth's climate. I hope this prize resonates and helps to awaken the world! *An Inconvenient Truth,* the Academy Award-winning documentary about Al Gore's call to action on the climate crisis, is a must-see film for anyone concerned about climate change.

October 15: LATE LEAF CHANGE

A NOTICE FROM the Town of Chevy Chase declares:

Leaf Collection Start Date Postponed.

Unseasonably high temperatures have delayed the start of the leaf season in the Town. As a result, the start of the Town's curbside leaf collection has been postponed one week and will now begin on Monday, October 22."

Despite my exuberance over the cooler weather and the first splashes of color in the canopy at Boundary Bridge, I know this remains a strange autumn. By mid-October, vivid color usually shows up in the sugar maples and many other trees planted in and around Washington and growing wild in the forests. But, where drought has not taken a visible toll, the leaves on most of the trees are still undeniably *green*.

This past weekend I only dreamed of Rock Creek Park, as I tramped the streets and cultivated parks of the city, feeling challenged and frustrated. I go to a place, with the 1987 (second) edition of *City of Trees* and notebook in hand, and try to find the same trees I described back then. In so many cases, magnificent trees have vanished without a trace. I mourn not knowing the time of a particular tree's demise or the reasons for it. I make notes, collect a few botanical samples, and leave a place often with more questions raised than answered.

I'm running against time to complete this task, which would be never-ending if properly and comprehensively done. At each site, I am confronted by my energetic younger self and her ambitious project to document the trees of Washington, DC, and create an accessible guide for viewing and identifying them. My present self thinks she did a pretty amazing job back in the late 1970s and early 80s working with Polly Alexander, her artist-botanist friend, and I don't want to mess up her book!

But, as I wander around town, picking up stray acorns and gazing, stupefied, into the branches of trees I can no longer identify, I have my moments. Friday evening, I was the only person wandering the grounds of the Frederick Douglass home in Anacostia. Born into slavery, Douglass became a forceful writer and lecturer who worked tirelessly for the causes of abolition and women's rights. He is, for me, one of the most inspiring Americans in history. His home, Cedar Hill, has been preserved and renovated by the National Park Service, and I was happy to see that many of the large oaks that I remembered had survived. Cedar Hill crowns a rise in southeast Washington with a stunning *City of Trees* view—across the waters of the Anacostia River to the Capitol, Library of Congress, and Washington Monument and north to the National Arboretum's wooded Mount Hamilton. A sea of green trees blankets the hilly view, punctuated by a few cranes and industrial sites, but it is still extremely pastoral for a modern city, thanks not only to the trees, but to the building-height restrictions so wisely enacted more than a century ago.

Yesterday, I spent more than six hours exploring the trees along the National Mall and in the Lyndon Baines Johnson Memorial Grove and Lady Bird Johnson Park across the Potomac in Virginia. I smiled as I thought of how pleased the Johnsons would be to see the exuberant touch-football game going on next to the LBJ grove of white pine. Several men played, while a small black-and-white dog romped with them right in the middle of the action. I gratefully thought about Lady Bird and her beautification efforts, and, when I found little golden pears growing on one of "her" trees,

I couldn't resist tasting one. It was quite delicious for a wild pear growing next to a highway (the George Washington Memorial Parkway). Eating the pear as I looked out over the blue Potomac to the sparkling white Lincoln and Jefferson memorials on such a beautiful autumn day felt sacramental, like eating the carrots grown during my father-in-law Bill's last summer in the White Mountains.

I had another joyful moment back in the city when I visited Rawlins Park. Many years ago, the park had been planted end-to-end with pink saucer magnolias, and, when I got there, I saw that it is still filled with Asian magnolias that look to be of a goodly age. I could pretty safely say they are the very same saucer magnolias, but, in deference to my younger self, I wanted to be sure. I asked a man strolling past if he remembered the color of the flowers from the spring. He said he was only passing through, but he pointed to three men sitting on the ground at the end of the park near the Rawlins statue. "Ask them," he said. "They live in the park."

When I got near the men, I saw that they were huddled around a radio, and, when I came closer, I realized they were listening to a Redskins game. The "Skins" would later lose the game, but at that point the score was tied, and they looked thrilled. I smiled and apologized for interrupting them, but they all beamed heart-felt smiles back at me and said "no problem" as they turned down their radio. I could see that they had their snacks all set out for the game on the ground in front of them.

I asked if they remembered the flowers on the tree branches above them that would have bloomed during the spring. They nodded yes and smiled again in unison. "Were they pink?" I asked. "Yes, pink", they said. We talked a bit about the beauty of the magnolia flowers and then they said exuberant good-byes and wished me well as I continued on my odyssey and they returned to their game.

Later I realized that a better scientist would have asked "what color were the flowers?" rather than offering the pink prompt. I silently apologized to Younger Self for my sloppy middle-aged ways, but I knew she would probably forgive me. And surely she would have enjoyed the communion with the men in their magnolia park as much as I did.

I SUGGESTED TO MY EDITOR that Susan Austin Roth be hired to create the photography for the piece I'm writing for *Bethesda Magazine* about following Rock Creek northward from the District of Columbia line to the springs on the Laytonsville Golf Course in Maryland, where the main stem of the creek originates. Susan was given the assignment and yesterday I spent the day exploring the creek with her and her camera—and getting to know her as a kindred spirit. We started out in the morning at Boundary Bridge, where she positioned herself among the trees near the end of the bridge, aimed her camera, and snapped away at all the people who were out enjoying the park. It was a cool, partially overcast fall day, and women were jogging across the bridge in their running clothes, friends were strolling together deep in conversation, and men were out walking their dogs. Susan even captured some images of dogs playing in the creek and shaking off the creek's sparkling water.

Later in the morning, we met Steve Dryden, my friend and a founding member of Friends of Rock Creek's Environment (FORCE)—now renamed the Rock Creek Conservancy—who took us to "Clean Drinking Spring" to see a stone replica of a Colonial-era springhouse. He explained that the original springhouse, one of many such eighteenth- and nineteenth-century structures, performed the dual function of protecting the spring and providing primitive refrigeration for perishables such as milk and butter. Then, farther north, the three of us traipsed into the woods along an upcounty road where Steve showed us a quiet and deep creek pool that once upon a time served as a site for baptisms.

I could tell Rock Creek was working its magic on Susan. She was undaunted by every physical challenge, such as wading in the muck of a drought-stricken, frighteningly low Lake Needwood, a reservoir created during the 1960s for controlling sediment and floods by damming Rock Creek. She seemed electrified by her mission of capturing the images of the creek. We had a long list of to-do shots for the day, and time was getting short. I drove while Susan rode with a map on her lap helping me navigate along the small roads that crisscrossed the northern reaches of the creek. We made ten stops in all. Our last was along the North Branch of Rock Creek—its main tributary—where the Intercounty Connector, a controversial highway that will threaten many acres of wetland, was being constructed.

Dusk was descending when we screeched into an illegal parking spot and dashed through the streaming headlights of the rush-hour traffic to the other side of the road. We plunged into the woods with the cumbersome and heavy camera equipment. I lugged the tripod, and Susan toted her camera and lenses in her big backpack. We traversed several tangled, woodland miles with no certain trail to find the creek so Susan could get what will probably be the last photographs of that area pre-highway.

The light was failing when we reached our destination—a rocky creek-bed overhung with yellow fall foliage and a rope swing suspended above a pool in a bend of the creek. Susan expected that she would be able to get her images using her tripod and several seconds of exposure, because the air was blessedly still. When we turned to retrace our steps, darkness descended. Somehow we were able to make it out of the woods by navigating toward the headlights, our hearts simultaneously full of our adventure and heavy with knowing apprehension. Soon there would be headlights aimed directly at the lovely stretch of the Rock Creek tributary that Susan and I may have been the last visitors to see unscathed.

October 24: RAIN, BLESSED RAIN

LATE IN THE DAY, I walk at Boundary Bridge. It is raining, and the dark skies intensify the colors in the leaves. A similar thing happened last week at Sugarloaf when I took a class from Montgomery College to the summit in the midst of a brief deluge. The colors were *intense,* much brighter than on the following day when I led another field trip in the sunshine.

The Boundary Bridge trail is muddy and slippery in the rain, and it is peppered with hickory nuts and acorns topping a carpet of wet fallen leaves. I have to pay attention to keep my ankles from twisting, because my head is lost in the colorful wet canopy. Pink-leaved poison ivy vines, loaded with tasty, berry-like white drupes for the birds, wind their way up the tallest trees. Scarlet-leaved Virginia creeper vines also climb the tree trunks into the high canopy.

The tulip trees glow golden, the sycamores are a brassy brown, and the red maples show off leaves checkered red and yellow. The leaves of the pawpaw trees have passed through the golden yellow stage and now display a translucent flesh color. Sweetest of all are the spicebush, with lemon-yellow leaves and tiny, round, lime-green flower buds. Many trees are still cloaked in chlorophyll green. The shiny black creek courses through the crayon-colored forest, and the wet jimsonweed capsules on Dog Beach fill their thirsty upturned beaks with rain drops. Added to the delicious wet smells of vegetation and the funky odor of the creek, I detect a wisp of fox musk. I can picture the copper-haired beauty slipping away from me between the wet tree trunks.

When I get to the upland woods, a serious downpour falls on the tupelos, their thin, forked, wet-black branches now garbed in the claret tones usually associated with September and early October. But there in the pouring rain my worries about *extreme* climate change lift momentarily, and I smile as rain drips down my nose. For there I see Rock Creek Park's first witch-hazel blossom of the season. Four tiny yellow petals look for all the world like ribbons on a wrapped package, as if they have been curled by a tiny pair of fairy scissors. Perhaps the fairies do this when we're not looking? The golden half-moon leaf buds tipping the witch-hazel twigs would make comfy hammocks for them to rest on after their curling capers. Soon there will be many more petals for them to curl!

A soft rain now falls and the fairies hover over the witch-hazel flowers . . . my sweet imperiled planet. *S'agapo!* That's Greek for *I love you!*

October 25: FIRE AND RAIN

LAST NIGHT I COULDN'T SLEEP, despite the blessing of the autumn rain and a two-hour concert at the National Cathedral in which Jesse and 500 other Washington high schoolers so sweetly sang. Why the insomnia? Southern California is in flames due to Santa Ana winds combined with serious drought and possible arson.

"Just to fill you in . . . Mia was evacuated but is now in her house. Andrea was told to evacuate her home in Escondido, only to be told a little later that the evacuation point was in worse shape than Escondido. The news here in DC says that Escondido is again endangered. I came East on the 20th of September, and I spent a week in Vermont. My California residence is on alert but, as far as I can decipher, has not been evacuated. *We are being sent many messages; are we listening and observing?"* (The emphasis is mine.)

My dad received this email message from Nella Boardman, a family friend from New England who spends part of the year in California near her daughters and part of the year with her son's family in DC. Some of the homes that are burning should never have been built in areas so prone to wildfire. But the Boardman family members whom we have visited in California all live near the Pacific Coast, not inland in the more fire-prone areas.

Earlier in the day, I had received an op-ed clipping from a friend who knows I worry about climate change. It was written by a Danish economist who was basically telling everyone on the planet to chill out and not worry so much. With a warming climate we might even be *better off*, this Danish dude suggested, because not so many people will die of the cold. If we invest in mosquito netting for the potential spread of malaria instead of breaking the bank on this expensive, carbon-capping thing and drain a few wetlands and build some levees, we should be fine. Let's not get all hot and bothered just because both poles are melting. The guy—hopefully tongue-in-cheek, although this is pretty dark humor—went so far as to suggest that signing the Kyoto Climate Treaty (which the U.S. refused to sign) and abiding by it would save only *one polar bear a year.*

I don't know why receiving this clipping bothered me so much. I read stuff like this all the time. But why did this friend, a scientist whom I respect, send it to me? Does he think my worries about climate change are overblown?

I'm sitting at my dining room table with a moss-green candle burning in the center. Arranged around me are three bowls of local apples, a small pile of acorns (for company and identifying), and my botany books and notebooks. Soup made with tomatoes from our garden is simmering on the stove, Brahms's Symphony Number Two is playing on the radio (my all-time send-me-to-the-moon symphony), and it's raining! I should be in full reverie mode, but my heart aches. I am deeply troubled by what is happening here on Earth and by our collective complacency about it.

We are being sent many messages; are we listening and observing?

October 29: COYOTE SERENDIPITY

I MUSTN'T TAKE much time away from work on *City of Trees*, but I have some exciting non-botanical news to share, an item from the mammalian branch of Mother Nature's family. Today Cris Fleming and I attended a ribbon-cutting ceremony for the beautiful new Agricultural Reserve sign that has just been installed at the White's Ferry crossing of the Potomac River in Montgomery County, Maryland. The sign, painted by Tina Thieme Brown, welcomes visitors crossing from the Virginia shore to the 90,000-plus-acre "Ag Reserve," a patchwork of historic farms, open space, and woods that crowns the northwestern part of Montgomery County. A zoning requirement, enacted in 1980 to preserve disappearing farmland, restricts building to no less than twenty-five acres.

We were driving along the rustic, gravel extension of River Road, when we saw a man with a camera standing in the road. He signaled for us to stop and pointed to the field next to the road. We stopped the car, and there before our eyes cavorted a pair of large, healthy, thick-furred coyotes, the first I've seen in Maryland! They were pouncing after mice and rousting about on the ground. These magnificent animals, so unlike the scrawny coyotes I've seen in the West, appeared wolf-like with their black-tipped tails and intelligent, I'm-totally-not-afraid-of-you eyes.

This wild canine pair filled me with hope. The fact that such a large animal can slip through the fields and hedgerows and find a home among us, largely without our notice, well . . . I felt joyous just to see them here on an autumn day.

Coyotes have been reported in Rock Creek Park, and seeing *those particular coyotes* would be a special thrill. I know that coyotes can threaten farm animals and pets, so, perhaps, I should temper my joy a bit.

October 30: OWLS AND SEEDS AND LEAVES, HURRAH!

THIS MORNING, I AWOKE before dawn to the calls of great horned owls, right outside our windows in this suburban neighborhood! While the calls of barred owls and screech-owls can send a chill right through you, the calls of the great horned owls sound deeply soothing. *HoohoohooHOOhoohoo* . . . gentle and vibrant, as if made by a woodwind or stringed instrument, as if chanted by monks or angels. Their quiet sound says the universe is a serene and mysterious place—wake up and pay attention. But don't wake all the way up and lose the thread of your dreams.

I have led so many field trips and researched so many trees during the past few days that my head spins with extraneous facts. I fear it is also spinning because of a relapse from Lyme disease, my first in more than a month. Yesterday I was happily telling friends that I'm finally over Lyme, but, today, that familiar sweep of dizzy fatigue engulfs me despite massive doses of antibiotics. I have acupuncture later this afternoon, and I don't have to be anywhere else until tonight, so I hope I can "rest while I work" and get through this spell without going further downhill.

Three days ago, I led my fourth field trip at Boundary Bridge for the Audubon Naturalist Society, the concluding walk of my "Year at Boundary Bridge" series. A heavy, cold rain was falling as we met under the acorn-clad branches of the shingle oak in the Boundary Bridge parking lot. Only half the group showed up. Had I not been the field-trip leader, I probably would have been among the ones who pulled the covers up under their chins when they saw how hard the rain was coming down. Over three days, we got six inches of rain, and it was a soaking rain! A rain we needed. This will allay some of the severity of the drought, just as a tropical storm would have done, had we gotten one this year.

The coffee-colored creek ran high and wild as we leaned over the railing. Two major currents seemed to be flowing near each bank, and just downstream from the bridge they swirled together in the middle of the creek, creating waves like the wake of a ship. The American elm, still green with a gold-smattering in its crown, the yellow tulip trees and brassy-brown sycamores, and other autumn-hued trees leaned over the rushing water, their leaves sailing into the creek and their branches semi-bare. The rain magnified the cinnamon-colored bark of the river birches and the smooth, muscular texture of the ironwoods. Fall fruits stood out clearly in the thinning canopy—the round dangling clusters of the sycamore's achenes, the candelabras of the tulip tree's clusters of samaras, and the pendant dry fruits of boxelder and ironwood. The river birches bore small, caterpillar-like catkins of male flower buds that will stay on their branchlets all winter, blooming and releasing pollen in the spring. Further along the trail, knocked to the ground by wind and rain, we found green fruits of bitternut hickory with their characteristic ridged husks lying among the wet fallen leaves. Joining them were acorns of several oak species—white, black, red and chestnut—and fragrant walnuts. Still on the branch gathering raindrops were viburnum drupes in wet, hanging clusters and the curiously aesthetic capsules of bladdernut.

Despite the rain, my small group spent hours examining the fruits of these woody plants and also the seeds of some of the herbaceous plants. When we checked out the fruiting clusters of several nettle-family members, I shared two new botanical words from Gleason and Cronquist's *Manual of Vascular Plants of the Northeastern U.S. & Adjacent Canada*: Accrescent: *increasing in size with age, as, for example, a calyx that continues to enlarge after* anthesis, *the period during which a flower is fully expanded and functional, ready to shed or receive pollen*. We had fun examining the accrescent calyxes of the wood nettle and the clearweed up close after anthesis. "Accrescent after anthesis" has great metaphoric potential—for instance, describing life's experiences during middle and old age?

We studied many seeds under our hand lenses, collectively oohing and aahing over the tiny scales, barbs, teeth, and ribs that the naked eye would have missed. Allen Browne, a repeat participant, explained that the name *Bidens* refers to the two little teeth on the flat achenes. The *Bidens frondosa* (beggar-ticks or sticktight) was growing next to another plant with a cleverly descriptive scientific name: *Polygonum*—Latinized from the Greek for "many knees"—referring to the knee-like swellings on the stems of plants in this genus.

The black, shiny seeds of the wet jimsonweed looked like caviar, clustered in their open-beaked, upright, prickly capsules. Again, I missed seeing an actual bird eat an actual jimsonweed seed, but the creekside patch of jimsonweed was alive with songbirds: Sparrows, including an uncommon migrating Lincoln's (which Cecily spotted), cardinals, and a yellowthroat. It sure looked like a throng in the throes of feasting! I thought of hanging a banner on Dog Beach for the birds: Rock Creek caviar in prickled bowls served here!

When we climbed to the uplands, the sun broke out and shone through to the lower depths of the wet canopy, where it was clear that the fairies had been busy curling those ribbon-petals. I hoped they were resting on their leaf-bud hammocks after all that work. After three days of cool rain, the one witch-hazel flower had been joined by thousands. The sun shown on the beribboned wet branches, as the golden, scalloped-toothed leaves of the witch-hazel gently fluttered to the ground, landing amongst the green Christmas ferns.

On the highest ridge of our loop trail, the tupelos were blazing. While gazing into their claret-peach crowns, the group saw something so exciting that I fear it may erase every shared botanical memory of the day—a barred owl. The large bird was perched close by but faced the opposite direction. Soon the owl demonstrated its eerie head-turning skills, as it swung all the way around to stare at us with its penetrating eyes.

And that was only the beginning of our sightings of big birds. It took us so many hours to get to the Laurel Ledge that we all would have been happy simply to eat our sandwiches sitting on the moss-covered rocks under the beech trees high above Rock Creek. But lunch turned into a wild adventure when two red-shouldered hawks landed in a dead tree and posed for a good long time, long enough that we all got to feast our eyes on the beautiful, feathered tapestry of their breasts. A chattering kingfisher flew into view, landing on a snag close to the creek, and then the creek itself filled with at least a dozen wood ducks—drakes, females and young—who flew in and paddled downstream. Appearing unimpressed by the frenzied paddling in the water, a silent great blue heron stood stoically next to the shore. I wondered if it was waiting for the waters to clear in order to reveal some fish. After the rain, that could be a long wait.

Not to be fully overshadowed by the avian world, a member of the reptilian branch of Earth's family tree revealed itself during the walk after lunch. A small, slate-blue, ring-necked snake with its characteristic golden band on its neck bravely confronted us on the trail with its head raised in snake-threatening posture. When we saw that some dogs were approaching it, I attempted to move the small snake by gently grasping it behind the neck at ring-level. But it demonstrated the "now you see me now you don't" magic of snakes, slipping quickly and gracefully through my fingers and away from the too-busy trail to the shelter of the wet leaf litter.

All in all, it turned out to be a perfect field trip but for the knowledge that much of the canopy that was still green shouldn't have been. Allen and Janice remembered the day their son was born, twenty-one years ago, and how all the leaves were turned on that day. It's hard to feel nervous about green leaves, especially when a drought has borne down on you for way too long. But our collective awareness told us that the still-too-green canopy was not unrelated to the too-early-blooming spring beauties that Janice had spotted during our January walk.

After the rain ended, we finally got some real fall weather—cold enough for a jacket! I led a field trip to Sugarloaf for our Unitarian church on Sunday, and one of the participants just emailed a photo of our jacketed group smiling from the quartzite mountaintop under the canopy of wind-sculpted table mountain pines. The rhythms of Nature are a precious gift.

October 31: SAMHAIN, DAY OF THE DEAD

TODAY IS HALLOWEEN, a time of year which is also celebrated as the Day of the Dead, All Saints and All Souls Day, and the Celtic New Year or Samhain. These celebrations have traditionally occurred midway between the autumnal equinox and the winter solstice when, in many cultures, the veil between the spirit and physical worlds is believed to be especially thin and permeable.

I have just hung a skinny, plush black cat on the front door and a green-faced witch from a hook under the eaves above the front porch. The hook remains there all year just for her. I've placed an array of pumpkins of various sizes, shapes, and colors on the porch, all of them grown by my friend David Heisler, a third-generation Sugarloaf-area farmer. He plants more than thirty varieties of pumpkins and gourds each year. His organic farming practices are so effective that this year's drought did little to squelch his colorful harvest. I have displayed orange pumpkins, including a striped one; green, orange and yellow fancifully shaped gourds; and my favorite—a large, pale-blue pumpkin that reminds me of Cinderella's coach. I have candles ready to go outside, and I'll line the walkway with them to light the way for all the little trick-or-treaters of our neighborhood. And then, of course, there's the candy, not in short supply here. I made a lame attempt to counteract the peanut butter cups and Baby Ruths with a few boxes of raisins. We'll see how popular they turn out to be.

I'm not a big costume person or candy-eater and had little interest in Halloween as a young adult. But, when I had children and visited the Jack-o-lanterned, cobweb-draped porches of historic, rural Barnesville with my eager little ones, my own happy memories of trick-or-treating as a child in Vermont came flooding back.

As I gained a deeper understanding of the day through my research of Old World "pagan" traditions (pagan simply meaning "country dweller"), I started to love the holiday. On All Souls Night, the living extend hospitality toward the dead, inviting them to return and commune with us. The carved Jack-o-lantern with a candle inside becomes a perfect symbol of the occasion. The round, earthy pumpkin, which fattens and grows orange while lying on the ground, is gutted, a face is carved in it, and a living light is placed inside. The ephemeral magic of Jack-o-lanterns on this one night of the year is something that all the commercial excess in the world cannot undo or overshadow.

Disguising oneself in a costume hides the ordinary self and gives life to a bolder more expressive self. Whether the costume is lovingly hand-sewn or store-bought, it doesn't matter. What's important is that one's face is hidden and one's body cloaked in something too outrageous for everyday existence.

My own little trick-or-treaters are pretty grown up, but they will wear their costumes tonight. Last night, Jesse finished his chemistry lab homework, pulled a picture of a silver mask worn by a particular rapper up on the Web, found a cardboard box, some tin-foil, scissors, tape and glue, and, before I could say "boo," he'd created his Halloween mask. I just spoke with Sophie, who has pulled together a wacky costume with white go-go boots, oversized sunglasses, and a wildly colored coat. Both kids are thinking about going trick-or-treating with their friends, and I hope they do.

I will fill our house with candlelight and Loreena McKennitt's music, and in the spaces between trick-or-treaters I will commune with my grandparents, my friends who have passed to the other side, and my father-in-law, Bill. They will all be welcome in our home on All Souls Night.

November 1: DREAMS

LAST NIGHT I had several intertwining dreams about being lost in the woods along tributaries of Rock Creek. I wish I could remember the details, but they involved trying to find my way through thick undergrowth, using the stream's channels as guides. Then I dreamed that a tall, gray funnel-cloud came roaring down the National Mall in Washington, carrying some sort of stone-and-glass tower on top. Sophie and I were standing near the Air and Space Museum, and some of the debris rained down upon us as we ran for cover. The pieces of debris were shiny and jade-colored. And on that mysteriously dire note I'm off to the Mall and Capitol grounds to do some final fact-checking for *City of Trees*.

November 6: GRIEVING FOR NATURE

SEVERAL YEARS AGO, I drove alone through the outer reaches of Virginia's Great Dismal Swamp National Wildlife Refuge. I was en route from the Outer Banks to the Blue Ridge to pick Jesse up at camp, and I didn't have time to walk through the watery depths of this mythic, tupelo-cypress terrain. Instead, I fantasized about the allure of the Great Dismal Swamp as I drove under the trees around its perimeter. I had planned my driving route to include a brush with its dark mysteries. I love the spooky yet beckoning atmospheres of the big Southern swamps: Great Dismal, Francis Beidler, Okefenokee, Everglades.

I was listening to National Public Radio, as I often do while driving, and the popular show called Car Talk was on the air. Tom and Ray Magliozzi, aka Click and Clack, the celebrity brothers who host the show, often end up talking with callers about subjects only tangentially related to cars, and, on this day, as I skirted the swamp, a young woman called to ask them to recommend a car for her to use in the field, somewhere in the West, where she worked as a research biologist. She was doing an inventory of plants and wildlife and said that she and other research biologists informally call this work "documenting the decline." A conversation with the Magliozzi brothers ensued about how sad and depressing her work was. Ray and Tom tried to cheer her up with a recommendation for a spectacular four-wheel drive vehicle she'd really enjoy. This young woman's words stayed with me, entwined as they were with the memory of my meander in the Great Dismal Swamp. *Documenting the decline.*

Last evening, after riding the DC Metro home from my Greek language class, I emerged from the underground to find the streets shiny with an unexpected rain, and speckled with brown, gold, and orange fallen leaves. This simple occurrence, an autumn shower bringing down leaves and a wet street glowing under street lamps, filled my heart with joy and, then, almost immediately, concurrent grief. Autumn's rain, something we can no longer take for granted. Where was this evening shower in September or early October when the parched ground was desperate for it?

Poets and nature writers of the past have eloquently expressed their grief in the presence of Nature. They have lamented ephemeral summers and unforgiving winters, the blossom that too briefly blooms, the fruit too soon plucked from the vine. In Greek mythology, the goddess Demeter mourns her daughter, Persephone, when she is abducted to the Underworld, and she punishes Earth with several months of winter. But, in the bargain that is struck with Hades, Demeter's beloved daughter is allowed to return to her each spring for half the year, awakening joy—and new life—on Earth.

Within this annual mythic cycle, writers and artists find rich moments of unexpected grief and joy. Wasn't it T. S. Eliot who dubbed April "the cruellest month"? No matter how closely we stay tuned, Nature is constantly surprising us, and we surprise ourselves with our responses to its ever-changing theater. We might feel exhilarated during winter's first cold wind and inexplicably saddened by the blossoms of spring. But, whatever gets stirred up in us and however unpredictable that might be, we have been able to count on Nature's cycles—our summers and winters, our dry and rainy seasons, our familiar. Droughts come and go, epic floods occur, one winter might be violently cold and a summer unbearably hot, but, however severe things get, we've known somewhere deep inside that a pendulum swings across a balanced center.

And now that center may not hold. As I rode the Metro, before emerging from the underground to find unexpectedly wet streets and fallen leaves, I had the words of an apocalyptic Leonard Cohen song called *The Future* in my head, especially the line "things are gonna slide, slide in all directions . . . won't be nothing, nothing you can measure anymore." I'm not entirely sure what the song is about, but I love Leonard Cohen for going straight to my heart with his music while making a cryptic meander around my brain. I love the richness of his words and haunting melodies. I find poets who express the darkness of our souls uplifting. But, in all their grappling with the earthly and metaphorical dark, the promise of light returning provides a hopeful note. And now?

I know I can be too sensitive, and I sometimes wonder if my worries about global warming are really just my own troubled thoughts projected onto a planetary stage. I have noticed that the people who seem most deeply troubled about climate change tend to be women and overly sensitive people. A junior-high science teacher whom I met at Boundary Bridge while walking this summer said that her female students were all worried about climate change, because they could empathize with wildlife. Just mention the plight of polar bears, and the girls are concerned, she said. But boys often need statistics and extra "proof" of warming.

I will stay tuned to Nature in an intimate way, because I know no other way to live. I will cleave to the hope that Demeter will go on grieving for only half the year and that we can continue to expect Persephone's descent to the Underworld in the fall and her return each spring. I will not drive when I can walk, I will remember to turn out the light when I leave the room, and I will pray that the Great Dismal Swamp gets to continue being its mythical, dark self while, to its north, Rock Creek goes on flowing under Boundary Bridge. And, when I sit down to write about plants and animals, I hope I will not be documenting their decline, wittingly or unwittingly. But the facts are hard to overlook.

November 9: BENEATH THE LEAF WE ARE ALL BONE

TODAY, IT IS RAINING again but with a twist. After an October that felt like August, I am so happy to say, "It's cold outside."

I've been working with my copyeditor for *City of Trees* 24/7 on last-minute revisions to the manuscript so I've had very little time lately for Rock Creek Park. But, yesterday, before my evening's acupuncture appointment, I stole away some time from work. As I drove toward the Boundary Bridge parking lot, the white upper limbs of the sycamores along the creek stood out in new relief among their colorful, brassy-gold crowns.

I bounded out of the car, crossed the bridge, and entered the bottomland's forest, filling my lungs with the fresh, cold air. The thinning canopy held every slightly muted hue of the late-autumn palette—soft yellow and gold, pinkish-red, and burnt-orange—and an artistic array of leaves with their varying shapes and colors, lined the path. On display were the sycamore's large, leather-brown leaves with pointed lobes, the ovate green boxelder leaflets, the lacy silver maple's leaves with butter-yellow upper blades and paler undersides, and the red and sugar maples' palmately cut leaves in every hue of yellow, orange, gold, and red. The leaves blanketed the ground in a tapestry that looked so artistically designed I laughed in admiring disbelief. How I wish I could walk the trail each and every day, because I'm missing so many world-class works of Nature's art.

The jimsonweed along Dog Beach was nearly leafless, but its spiny capsules still held their hallucinogenic caviar. Several male cardinals, garbed in red, perched among them, while doves, sparrows, wrens, and other birds fluttered up from the creekside and into the trees.

My veins filled with the exhilaration of late autumn—and not just this late autumn but of autumns past. Childhood memories of Vermont flooded my thoughts: Of collecting maple leaves and bringing them home to iron between sheets of waxed paper, of jumping over burning leaf piles, of roasting pumpkin seeds, and, most of all, the simple thrill of seeing anew the architecture of bare, leafless trees. I have always felt keenly the connection between the trees and myself, and I always come alive in the company of trees.

My acupuncturist has made me aware of how critical my spine is to my overall health, calling the spine the body's "root." As I walked with my new-found extended posture—after weeks of lying on his roller bed with needles sticking out of my forehead, ears, and legs—I inwardly celebrated the upright growth of Boundary Bridge's tallest trees: The soaring tulip trees with their massive arms, the ashes with their pitchfork branches, the mighty oaks and hickories and walnuts with their distinctive shapes. But, most of all, I enjoyed the bone-white sycamores, now emerging from a cloak of foliage as if to say, *Beneath the leaf we are bone*, a sentiment that seemed oddly uplifting as I walked along the creek.

As I left the lowlands and began to ascend to the upland woods, a chipmunk scurried across my path, running up the slope through the Christmas ferns and twisted roots of beech to rest upon a fallen log. From that perch, it turned to assess me. The picture was almost too adorable to be real: Chipmunk, fallen log, Christmas ferns, silvery roots of beech, and—to put it totally over the top—the branches of witch-hazel above, lit up with their fairy-curled, yellow flowers.

I had started the day reading a favorite piece of writing, Cecily Nabors's "The Joys of a Beechen Wood." Cecily published this story about her neighborhood's woodland in the *Audubon Naturalist News* years before I knew her. I loved it at first sight. Once I got to know her, I asked her to send it to me, and I enjoyed the second reading even more than the first after she became my friend. In the story, she wrote:

> In homage to British naturalist Gilbert White, I call this my
> 'beechen wood.' (It's only mine out of proximity and love.)
> Many of the beeches here are tall old trees, with canopy too dense
> and roots too greedy to allow much undergrowth. Where several
> beeches are close, they create a splendid open look of dappled
> glades and thick silvery trunks; spaces are pillared and vaulted
> like cathedral cloisters. Great gray rivulets of roots cascade down
> the slope, merging with the earth as if the trees were melting into
> the hill. Mossy root-laced paths thread through the woods.

As I walked into the upland heart of my own beechen wood ("mine out of proximity and love"), I said the delicious words *beechen wood* to myself. My walking stride felt effortless, as if fueled by the essence of November. When I got to the Laurel Ledge, beechen boughs were dressed with golden leaves and entwined with the limbs of white oak, tupelo, and other trees. I looked across the creek from the Meditation Rock beneath the ledge to admire the hillside above the creek, which was cloaked in scarves of color. The creek itself was a still, copper mirror with the golden crowns of the hillside's trees casting reflections on the water that created a mirage of branches reaching down into the depths. Fallen leaves languidly floated down the mirror's surface. Unlike Demeter, I celebrated Persephone's descent, while I also fondly and vividly remembered how the hillside looked from my favorite rock during her most recent springtime return.

November 16: TALKING LEAVES AND AN APPLE CAKE

SOMETHING MYSTICAL began happening last fall, and it's happening again. A little over a year ago, I was washing freshly plucked basil leaves in our porcelain-white kitchen sink. The intoxicating smell of wet basil never fails to awaken my senses and arouse my imagination. I shook the colander with extra vigor to release the aromas into the air. As I was lifting the colander from the sink, I noticed that a single leaf had fallen out and was lying against the sink's bottom. And this is where the mysticism creeps in. *It seemed to me that the leaf was talking to me, not with a human voice but with a clear and prescient leaf voice.*

Now, I may be considered by some to be on the lunatic's fringe of Nature worship, but I had never before been the recipient of a message from a talking leaf. Here's what the basil leaf seemed to be saying: *I am a leaf, and I hold the key to life on Earth. This thing that I do, photosynthesis, is the scientific magic on which your existence depends.* And then I sensed that the leaf was distressed about alterations to our climate and was warning me to pay attention to its message.

This was September. Later, when leaves began falling from the trees, the mystical thread continued. I'd be walking along, and suddenly a single leaf would stand out from the fallen carpet on the ground. I'd get the sense that a sugar maple's orange leaf or a ginkgo's yellow fan was talking to me, delivering the same message as did the basil leaf.

In November, Sophie and I took a trip to Martha's Vineyard, where we stayed in a bed-and-breakfast inn. On our first morning, I went out for an early run while she slept. As I headed out to the Edgartown lighthouse, a brilliant red leaf from a Japanese maple, lying on the white porch steps of the inn, repeated the message. When I returned from the run, a man with a broom was sweeping the leaves from the steps, but his broom missed the talking leaf! As I bounded up the steps past the man, who was sweeping in what seemed like a trancelike state, the leaf that escaped his broom seemed to be shouting its message.

Yesterday, almost a year to the day later, my Prius was parked in the rain under our redbud tree. I ran out without a coat or umbrella, because I was late to visit my Aunt Marion, who was going to teach me how to make her apple cake. I hopped in the car and pushed the start button (the Prius needs no ignition key), and I began driving in the rain to the retirement community called Leisure World. Halfway to Aunt Marion's, I noticed that a redbud's small, heart-shaped leaf was stuck to my car's side mirror. The pale, yellow- green leaf was about a third the size of the large, heart-shaped leaves that had been falling from our redbud all week.

When I arrived at Aunt Marion's, she was already wearing her apron, the apples and apple peelers were lying on the kitchen table, the cinnamon and sugar were mixed together, and the oil and flour were pre-measured. We sat down and began peeling apples. Soon, we were layering cinnamon-coated apples into the batter and sliding our lovely apple cake into the hot oven. Marion then washed every baking dish and spoon, and the two of us dried them. "Now," Marion said, as she grabbed two umbrellas and a bulging bag of fruit and vegetable peelings: "Let's go bury all this compost!"

Aunt Marion could hardly contain her excitement about showing me her plot in her retirement home's community garden. She plucked a pitchfork from the neatly arrayed row of tools hanging in the tool shed. In the pouring rain, we splashed over the puddled ground with the pitchfork and compost, through the neatly fenced plots. Most were bare, since it was late fall, but one plot still held bouquets of hot red peppers, and one was filled with fresh, blooming pea plants.

I wasn't surprised that Marion's plot was as tidy as her apartment, all put to bed for the winter and covered with a protective layer of leaf-mulch. Marion tossed off her umbrella (decorated with a motif of Monet's water garden that included the Japanese bridge), raked away the mulch, and energetically pierced the ground with the pitchfork. Gleefully, even joyfully, she spilled the contents of her compost bag into the center of her garden, where she had made a hole with the pitchfork, and then covered it over with soil and mulch. The whole scene was very Peter Rabbit/Beatrix Potterish, and I was so happy to be far from my laptop and the writing deadlines arching over it.

The aroma of apple cake filled the kitchen and living room when we returned to the apartment. If only I had an alter ego who could bake cakes so that I could smell their wafting aromas while I write! The act of writing seemed so prosaic compared to the magic of baking a cake. The cake came out of the oven—*perfect!* While we and her sister, Dora, who lives in a nearby apartment, devoured it, they taught me some juicy Yiddish phrases from their childhood, including the earthy curse: *May you be planted upside down like an onion with your head in the ground and your feet in the air.*

After lunch, it was time to return to the reality of the laptop. The rain had stopped, and a dazzling afternoon sun poured through the wet leaves and black branches as I drove home.

The *Washington Post* ran a story by Kristen Mack in the Metro section this week titled "Dry and Warm, Nature Is in No Mood to Paint," about how the drought and heat had messed with the process of autumn's color. Well, clearly nature's mood had changed. Never have I seen such vivid color south of Vermont. As I turned onto Thornapple Street and into our neighborhood, the brilliantly backlit canopy dazzled me with its color. Then I noticed something that gave me a happy chill. My redbud heart still clung to my rain-spattered mirror, after hours of rain and an hour of driving. There was a new message coming from this leaf: *I am love.*

As I sit here writing, red-and-yellow-speckled leaves land on the skylight, and each leaf speaks to me. If I crane my neck, I can see my neighbor's tall, red maple tree that is the source of these fluttering, flying, talking wet leaves: *We hold the key to life on Earth. We are love.*

November 26: THE CREEK WELCOMES ME HOME

WE HAVE JUST RETURNED from celebrating Thanksgiving in New England with our extended family. The beloved hills of Vermont and New Hampshire flanking the Connecticut River valley where I grew up held deciduous,

gray-trunked trees bare of leaf, punctuating white birches, and deep, dark-
-evergreen pines, firs, hemlocks, and spruces. Back home yesterday morning, Sunday, I got up early and hopped on my new bicycle to explore the
Rock Creek Trail, a paved trail that runs along the creek from the District
of Columbia line to Lake Needwood. It proved to be an excellent welcome
home to our Maryland woods and Rock Creek, so much humbler than
the Connecticut River but no less beautiful and even more cherished for
its present familiarity.

I rode about thirty miles round trip to Lake Needwood, crossing and
recrossing the creek many times. My bike rolled like butter over some of the
wooden bridges, with their cross-hatched, metal railings, and trip-trapped
over the ones with loose slats. I pedaled in and out of the late-autumn
woods, through flocks of robins and hammering woodpeckers, conducting
impromptu interviews with visitors to Rock Creek along the way for my
Bethesda Magazine article.

Just south of Lake Needwood, I sat on the creek's mossy bank next to
a beaver dam and ate my lunch in a patch of mountain laurel. The water
flowed musically over the dam, a red-shouldered hawk wheeled above me,
and the oaks and hickories mothered me as oaks and hickories will do.

Today, my friend, Carole Bergmann, who is Forest Ecologist and Botanist for Montgomery County, Maryland, Parks, took me on a tour of many
parts of Rock Creek's Stream Valley Park in Maryland, pointing out the
dangerously destructive, non-native woody vines of several species that are
choking the park's lowland trees. Carole described the valiant efforts that she
and her staff make on a shoestring budget, waging war against invasive vines
with machetes and carefully targeted applications of herbicide. Carole has
trained an army of volunteers to combat the ongoing threat of invasive plants,
and she is the one who coined the phrase "weed warrior." Seeing the park
through her concerned and caring eyes opened mine.

I've scheduled visits with other experts later this week as I research my
story. I'm going back and forth between fact-checking for *City of Trees* and writing the magazine article, and I'm under intense deadline pressure for both.
My editor at the magazine wants me to cover Rock Creek in Maryland only
(the magazine is aimed toward residents of Bethesda, Maryland), and I miss
spreading the word about my wild DC refuge!

The creek is the creek, however, whether I enjoy it in Maryland, where it originates, or in DC, where it flows through the city's heart and into the Potomac River. Later this week I'm going to visit the creek's origins in the springs near Laytonsville with a park manager. It's thrilling to explore new territory that is so familiar—because it's Rock Creek—and to think about the trickling waters of springs north of here that will eventually flow under Boundary Bridge and continue on to the Potomac River, Chesapeake Bay, and into the Atlantic ocean. What a journey! It is also a joy and privilege to spend time with people who are working so tirelessly to maintain Rock Creek's integrity in the face of enormous threats.

November 27: NORTH BY NORTHWEST FROM BOUNDARY BRIDGE

MY FRIEND, Steve Dryden, and I dip our canoe paddles deep in silt. We are trying to paddle up Rock Creek north of Boundary Bridge as part of my research for the article I am writing about Rock Creek. The celestial Mormon temple, with its white façade and gold, needle-sharp steeples, glows on the horizon. Rock Creek is a dark mirror reflecting the now-leafless branches overhead. Up ahead, the Beltway (I–495) looms. Our difficult silt-paddling pays off, and we enjoy a few moments of clear sailing while our paddles dip only water until we reach the next rocky stretch, where we drag the heavy canoe up the viney bank and portage through the mugwort and stilt grass to the Beltway's underpass.

"This must be a first," I say to Steve, as we gingerly climb down a rock wall to put in directly under the multi-laned Beltway. The constant hum of traffic above us and a loud trip-trapping that sounds like a frightening contemporary version of Billy Goats Gruff disturbs the peace and prevents further conversation. But, once our canoe is in the water again, we enter a strange land of enchantment even as the Beltway continues to hum over our left shoulders:

Trash hangs from the trees like plastic Spanish moss, marking the last high-water mark, beer and soda cans are strewn across the beaches, and submerged tires seem almost strategically placed in the creek's bottom, providing extra leverage for our silt-paddling.

A flock of wood ducks swims upstream, fleeing away from us, and I concentrate on watching them instead of listening to the traffic.

Bottomland trees lean over Rock Creek in all their late-autumn semi-naked beauty: Bone-white sycamores still hold a few rusty leaves, boxelders show off their wheat-colored chains of samaras, ironwoods are dressed in elephant-gray bark, and river birches add to the display with their peeling cinnamon-colored bark.

Leaves from the red and silver maples float downstream, twirling in the current.

Amidst the Dr. Pepper cans, raccoon prints are stamped into the muddy shore, and a mother deer and her fawn climb down the bank and stand in the creek drinking.

From my place in the bow, I'm amazed by the contrast of wild beauty and suburban degradation. Just as the trees seem most enchanting in the gathering twilight, the large green Connecticut Avenue sign next to the Beltway springs into ghostly view above us, its arrows pointing to Kensington and Chevy Chase. I feel like I am viewing my daytime reality from the deep, dark realm of dreams.

Steve and I could go on paddling forever, but darkness is gathering, and rain is beginning to spritz, so we reluctantly turn the canoe around and head downstream. Between the silt paddling and frequent portaging, we have gotten quite a workout, but I am not tired and feel exhilarated and rejuvenated. We drag the canoe out of the creek for the last time under a partially cloud-obscured gibbous moon and walk over a wooden footbridge back to the parking lot. A middle-aged man is also crossing the bridge with two black Labradors.

"Did you put that canoe in here?" he asks, incredulous.

When we say yes, he replies, "I'm impressed."

I ask him if he's ever seen anyone else canoe here. He shakes his head and says, "Not in ten years of coming here."

We did it for the sake of journalism and environmentalism, but it was just what I needed for the current state of my soul. I've been run ragged by the pressure of deadlines and worries about friends and family who are going through troubled times, so this small, urban-wild drama provided a measure of salvation. Earlier in the day, in the midst of a much more conventional paddle around the relatively pristine and navigable Lake Needwood, Steve had startled me from the back of the canoe.

"May I ask you a personal question?"

"Okay," I said warily.

"Did you grow up in a dysfunctional family?"

"Why do you ask?" I responded, guessing that my worries must somehow be showing.

"Because you have such a love of Nature, I figured you must have been running from something."

Well, I didn't grow up in a dysfunctional family. Both my parents have always been very nurturing. But my mother had given birth to three children by the age of twenty-five, an exhausting reality I could never imagine for myself. As the eldest child with two younger siblings close in age, I learned to escape to the woods as often as possible for quiet and calm. I still seek nurturance directly from Nature. Tree hugging has served me well, but occasionally it strikes me as a sad state of affairs that I sometimes feel closer to trees than to people. And once, when I was seven- or eight-months pregnant with Jesse, I felt nearly paralyzed thinking about this facet of my personality.

I was walking with our two dogs, Emily and Honeysuckle, on Sugarloaf Mountain, and, as I climbed a steep slope of the mountain's White Trail, I was suddenly seized by grief. It struck me as tragically sad that here I was wandering a mountainside alone in search of solace. I hugged an oak tree, and its trunk felt cold and alien. It started to rain, and I lay down on a log and let the cold drops of water fall on me while I cried. When my dogs returned from a deer-chase, they were clearly alarmed at my behavior. In deference to them and to get away from their loving tongues, which were all over me, I got up from the log and kept walking up the mountainside. The mountain walk proved healing, as mountain walks will do.

I soon returned to my joyful self but the memory of lying on the log stayed with me. Perhaps all modern-day lovers of Nature experience this sort of sadness and alienation on occasion. But was it always so? I wonder.

EVER SINCE THANKSGIVING I've been longing for some solo time at Boundary Bridge. This morning I was supposed to conduct an interview for my story at Meadowbrook Stables, just upstream from Boundary Bridge. I don't receive the interviewee's message of postponement until I am already at the stables, so I immediately head toward my favorite refuge with delight in my heart.

Instead of crossing Boundary Bridge and setting off downstream through the floodplain as I usually do, I start my loop trail on the other side of Beach Drive in the upland woods. The morning sun shines through the late-autumn trees of the rocky forest, reflecting off every surface. If only I could polish my holiday silver to look like those smooth, silvery beech trees, all lit up on their eastern sides! The tulip trees hold their gold-white candelabras of samaras against the blue sky, an early winter salutation. The branches, bark, and roots of each woodland tree stand out in newly liberated eloquence, and the wheat-brown floor of the forest plays a symphony of reflected sunlight. The white oaks hold onto a few wine-red leaves, while the crowns of the red oaks are still clad in bronze and gold. Pinkish-orange-beige leaves make the beeches marcescently resplendent; these leaves will cling to their branchlets throughout winter, gradually bleaching to pale apricot and adding brightness to the forest throughout the coldest months. Some of the ironwood trees will also keep their dried and bleached leaves through winter, decorating the shores of Rock Creek.

The cold, clear air, the newly revealed branches, and the sunlit carpet of fallen leaves invite me to give thanks to the pale gold sun as it splinters through the canopy. I feel a deep peace wash over and through me, as I walk along the hilly, winding trail. The evergreen leaves of two late-spring/early-summer wildflowers—partridge-berry and striped wintergreen—peek out from the leaf litter. I sit for a long time in the crook of Nana's Lap.

At the Riley Spring Bridge, I look down into the creek, which is shiny-clear with deep reflections of dark trees and wispy white clouds. By altering my gaze, I can see Rock Creek either as an infinite mirror of sky and canopy or as a shallow and muddy-bottomed stream with slowly floating leaves.

A single bird appears at the Laurel Ledge—a white-breasted nuthatch, who climbs down, first the trunk of an oak and then the trunk of a beech before flying away over the creek with its petulant two-note call. The pinxter azaleas are loaded with tiny, tulip-shaped, woody capsules clustered at the tips of twigs near their fat flower buds. An acorn lying on the ground already bears a scarlet sprout. I climb down to the Meditation Rock and sit there for as long as my work-driven conscience allows. Christmas ferns and mountain laurel, both evergreen against the reddish leaf litter, festively adorn the steeply sloped banks. The creek is finally full again, after autumn's rains.

The demands embodied in my laptop seem far away and inconsequential as I watch the compelling drama of a white oak leaf break away from a clump of floating leaves, get blown upstream, and then settle into the middle-of-the creek's downstream current. The pink leaf's rounded lobes are turned upward like beseeching fingers. It sails past the fallen beech tree on the opposite shore that came down in last year's June deluge. A white trash bag hangs from its roots like a flag gently waving in the slight breeze as if saying: "I surrender." I could sit here all day watching autumn leaves—flat, upturned, smooth, and crumpled—float, join, break apart, and float again in their ever-fascinating journey downstream.

I meditate on what is going on in front of me—the flowing water, the trees reaching for the sky, the falling, floating leaves. What can possibly be more beautiful or compelling than this, Earth's life-giving art, shot through with autumn sunlight? I think about how we've made our biggest environmental missteps simply by turning away and refusing to see and honor this beauty. And then I realize that all my underpaid, overly laborious work— all the books, articles, and field trips—can be boiled down to a one-word message, one of the first words I learned to read in a Dick, Jane, and Sally book: *Look!*

December 2: UPPER ROCK CREEK AGAIN

YESTERDAY, JIM AND I bundled up on a cold morning and headed to the north side of Lake Needwood to explore new territory along the wild, northern shores of Rock Creek. We had no idea what we'd find—easy walking or brambles, trash or pristine beauty, a sense of wholeness and calm or environmental degradation.

We brought sandwiches and spread a picnic out on a fallen log near a wetland north of the lake, where we found a beaver dam and a large, noisy flock of mallards. While we ate, we surveyed our surroundings—healthy populations of ironwood, sycamore, and river birch lined a clear-watered stream, and oaks and mockernut hickories grew in the uplands near the stream. Thick mockernut shells, emptied of nutmeats by squirrels and other creatures, carpeted the ground, and a few mockernuts still clung to the leafless branches of the trees above us. We were picnicking near the confluence of Mill Creek and Rock Creek, which held a thin sheen of ice in places. Jim noticed that autumn leaves skated across the ice when the wind blew.

Soon another couple moseyed toward us, the woman in a hooded blue winter coat, the man with binoculars around his neck. I hurriedly finished my sandwich and took my notebook out of my backpack. I've gotten used to conducting impromptu interviews along Rock Creek for my article. This one was as rich as the others have been. The couple, Bob and Marian Schwenk, live near Mill Creek and frequently walk along both creeks. They told stories of spring migrants and barred owls, fox cubs peeking out of dens, beavers climbing to the high ground during floods, sightings of mink, spring wildflowers, and the magic of the wood thrush's song. Their love for Rock Creek, Mill Creek, and their inhabitants was palpable. When I asked how they felt about the highway about to be built across the creek just north of where we were standing, the "intercounty connector" or ICC, you could feel their hearts sinking. Marian said she calls the Sierra Club every time she spots something rare or unusual (like the mink she once saw) in a desperate attempt to try to stop construction of the road.

After talking with Bob and Marian for some time and exchanging contact information, Jim and I bushwhacked up the eastern side of the creek for many miles. The area looked pristine. The water looked clear (although we saw no fish), and there was very little trash. We saw pairs of pileated and downy woodpeckers, chickadees, nuthatches, and a great blue heron circling in to roost in a tree at twilight. Skunk cabbage sprouted through the moist soil. The creek meandered wildly through the floodplain, creating a few near-oxbows. Giant sycamores and tulip trees stood out in the low angles of the afternoon and early evening light.

When we got to the loveliest stretch of northern Rock Creek, *our* hearts sank. The creek babbled over rows of rocks that formed a mini-fall line near Muncaster Mill Road. Steep banks rose from both shores. Tall oaks of several species reached toward the autumn sky. A wide swath of these trees, however, was festively adorned with colored ribbons—blue, red, orange, yellow, and pink. The decorative appearance of the ribbons belied their murderous intent. These trees, we realized, would be sacrificed for the road, the road that many, many residents of Montgomery County do not want and don't believe will relieve traffic congestion, as its proponents claim. For Bob and Marian and for the wild plant and animal inhabitants of Rock Creek Park, this couldn't seem like a worse idea. To Jim and me, standing there in beauty on the first day of December, it seemed like a violation of the creek itself. Where the afternoon sun now danced on the waters as they musically riffled over the rocks, next year there would be a dark shadow cast by the looming specter of a multi-lane highway bridge and its traffic. This may be the last autumn sun these rocks will ever see. The shadow of the highway looms over Rock Creek's two main tributaries.

December 4: FIRST SNOW

I WOKE UP to snow flurries! The season's first snowflakes seem to come from nowhere. The air fills with flying, white crystal flakes, and the heart dances. And then, just as quickly and unexpectedly, the flurry is gone. By the time I go out to feed the birds, the flurry is past, but I try to hold its ephemeral magic in my heart all day.

December 5: MEASURABLE SNOW

IT SNOWS ALL DAY, and the world is white. What a difference a day makes: Yesterday my heart danced with the unexpected flurry, and, today, I've just felt heavy, heavy, heavy with work, work, work on *City of Trees* and my article for *Bethesda Magazine*.

One cool thing happened that I've been too heavy hearted to appreciate. Dean Norton, the longtime director of horticulture at Mount Vernon, has chosen to share with me some big news: Recent core samples have authenticated the ages of several of the trees purported to have been planted by George Washington or under his direction. In addition, core sampling has verified that a chestnut oak in the Mt. Vernon woodlands dates back to "no later than 1673," according to Norton.

I've spent the last two days integrating new material into *City of Trees.* I've long felt close to George Washington and Thomas Jefferson through their love of trees and gardening. Last month, I was quoted in *The Washington Post* talking about how much it pained Jefferson to see the capital's trees unnecessarily felled during his presidency, calling it a "crime little short of murder." (I found the quote many years ago while researching the first edition of *City of Trees*, in a 1906 book by Margaret Bayard Smith called *The First Forty Years of Washington Society*.)

For now, I just want to feel the magic of the whitened world. Oh, how lovely Rock Creek must be today under its light cover of white.

December 6: SKIING AT THE CREEK

I RATIONALIZE that I need to do it for my writing projects and for exercise, but really I need to do it for my soul! So this morning I ski across Boundary Bridge, where four inches of snow blanket the railings, swishing through the many human and animal tracks already traversing the bridge. The scene is one of stark contrasts: Black and white. The ice-free waters of the creek below shine obsidian-dark against snowy banks. Snow coats the tree trunks on their northeastern sides and outlines the gnarled tree roots reaching down over the eroded banks. The air is cold and still as I glide on my skis down the winding trail, gingerly stepping over fallen trees. Looking up to the crowns of the tulip trees I smile when I see their golden cups of samaras holding clumps of snow against the deep-blue sky like celestial ice cream cones. Everything glistens in the bright, morning sun reflecting off the forest's snowy floor.

I don't hear a sound, not even a chickadee, until a kingfisher comes chattering down the snow-draped flyway. A few mallards silently glide under the whitened, overhanging canopy. The spiny jimsonweed capsules, now nearly free of seeds, hold rosebuds of snow.

I ski under the West Beach Drive Bridge and on to where the uplands begin. My heart sings, and I regret that yesterday I let myself shut down during the magic of the falling snow because of pressure from work. When I get home, I write an email to the editor of *Bethesda Magazine* with some new story ideas and tell him I'd been skiing at Boundary Bridge. He quickly writes back: "You're breaking my heart! I wanted to go skiing last night, but I didn't think there was enough snow."

Christmas is coming, and our doorstep is still decorated with pumpkins. But they look festive frosted with snow. I have usually gathered greenery to "deck my halls" by this time, but this year I've been too weary and work-stressed. After taking a nap, I awake to the sound of a child's voice singing Christmas carols outside. *Hark! The Herald Angels Sing* and *Silent Night*. What pure delight to be awakened by that one small voice.

December 22: WINTER SOLSTICE

FOR ME, THE WINTER SOLSTICE is the most mystical day of the year. On the day of the longest night, the light of the new year is born.

On this solstice morning, I receive an email from my friend, Lisa Lindberg, telling me about some ancient sites in Ireland that are older than Stonehenge and the pyramids. On the morning of the solstice, light pours through narrow crevasses of the temples, filling specially designed rooms with glowing sunlight. For fifteen years, Lisa and I celebrated the winter solstice with our families and large gatherings of friends on Sugarloaf Mountain. I enjoy hearing from Lisa on the solstice and being reminded of the ancient roots of our celebrations.

This year on the solstice, I am working on a writing assignment, and, when not working, am decorating and shopping. But, in the evening, under a partially cloud-obscured waxing Yule moon, Sophie, her friend, Katherine, Jim, and I head out to Comus for an old-time solstice celebration of music in the Langstaffs' shed next to our land. The Langstaffs are the family that brought the Christmas Revels to America by adapting Old World traditions. This year, friends of theirs from all over the nation are converging inside their shed for hot wassail and ancient carols. When Cyndie Langstaff sings *Oh Holy Night*, I feel the presence of Christmas angels filling the shed, which had recently sheltered cattle.

After the caroling we walk over the winter wheat fields in the adjacent land we still own. Under the solstice's moonlight, we walk around our hayfield, dining on wild persimmons plucked from the hedgerows. Katherine had never eaten a persimmon, and Jim tells her: "You probably wouldn't eat them if you could see what they look like by the light of day!" True. They are quite blackened and shriveled this time of year, but they taste so cold and brown-sugar sweet in the dark!

When we lived in the country, my connection to the day and night was so strong that the loss of the light in the fall and its return in early winter deeply affected me. I was always tuned to the phases of the moon and the positions of the constellations in the country, where the skies were big and there were few street lights. When we moved to Chevy Chase, I could not adequately explain to others how difficult it was for me to live among street lamps and lose my connection to the sky and the light cycles of Earth. I bemoaned being unable to find the Big Dipper to my sister, Ellie, and she said: "Don't worry, Mel. The Big Dipper isn't going anywhere." Still, it is disconcerting to have to search for it and guess which way its handle is pointing.

December 26: CHRISTMAS IN ROCK CREEK PARK

I CAN'T REMEMBER a Christmas Day when Jim, the kids, and I ever left our cozy house. But this year, as a gift to me, we all walked at Boundary Bridge together, dressed in Santa Claus hats and sweatshirts with college logos that Sophie had put under the potted Norfolk Island pine that serves as our Christmas tree. The day was warm for late December, and people were joyfully out and about on the trail. The costumes helped us connect with new and familiar friends along the trail, who greeted us with old-fashioned Christmas cheer. A golden retriever rolled over on her back in the middle of the trail, begging us crazy-looking strangers for a belly rub. She reminded us of Christmases past, when our own golden retriever, Honeysuckle, did the same thing in a living room strewn with toys, ribbons, and wrappings.

The female kingfisher came chattering past and landed on a snag so close to us that we could admire the rusty band on her belly. She represents one of the few species of birds in which the female is more colorful than the male. We saw wood ducks that had not yet headed south paddling in Rock Creek below the Laurel Ledge, and we admired the samaras of the tulip trees against the sky. I think the greatest gift of the day, for me, was the gift of my family rejoicing with me in my most beloved spot on this good Earth.

Tonight, I'm honoring the season by bundling up in bed with a novel and peppermint tea and trying to recover from my recent work jags, which ran up until Christmas and then morphed into a frenzy of shopping and decorating. I'm uncertain how I feel as the year ends and the secret pendulum begins its swing toward spring. Will this winter be cold enough to invite many hibernating evenings with mugs of hot tea? Will it be cold enough to ensure that the seasonal pendulum continues to swing across a balanced center?

People are waking up to the staggering problem of climate change, but we're doing so little about it. War and violence remain the game on the world stage, as they have been too often during recorded time. Poverty and starvation are all that billions of people know.

But just as the kingfisher can't live without its chatter, I can't live without hope. As long as tea-colored Rock Creek flows under Boundary Bridge, I will continue to believe that it's possible for us to return to a more intimate relationship with the woods and waters. And I hope I will remember, every day, to connect with the mysteries that give lift to the elements in the dance of life. This I know: Enjoying natural beauty is our birthright. In honoring our own birthright, may we remember Nature's birthright and the interwoven miracle of all living things.

Epilogue
EARTH DAY 2014

SEVEN YEARS HAVE PASSED since my year of recorded observations in Rock Creek Park. During that time, our children, Sophie and Jesse, have completed college and grown into thriving young adults. My husband, Jim, and I made the adjustment to empty-nest status, a painful process at first but one that eventually offered an invitation to a new and unexpectedly joyful phase of life. I recovered fully from Lyme disease; as it turned out, I had a co-infection with another bacteria carried by ticks.

I continue to visit Rock Creek Park at every opportunity and to marvel over its restorative powers. When Jim's youngest brother, Dr. Paul Bradley, died earlier this April, nearly seven years after their father's death, the beauty of the Rock Creek stream valley provided much-needed comfort for Jim and me. On the last day of Paul's life, Jim read to him from a book about the White Mountain trails of New Hampshire they had hiked many times as boys and young men and for which Paul had lovingly carved and painted signs that still direct hikers up and down the high peaks of the Presidential Range. Paul, an ordained minister, requested the White Mountain readings alongside passages from *The Holy Bible*. Shortly after he died, Jim and I heard the healing sound of four barred owls calling back and forth across Rock Creek as we walked together and reminisced about Paul.

I have led a nature walk in the Boundary Bridge area of Rock Creek Park in each season for the Audubon Naturalist Society, and in seven years I've cancelled only one walk—and that was due to a relentless and cold autumn rain. I have made many new friends during these and other walks, both idle rambles and planned botanical forays. Susan and I often visit the park together, and she never seems to lose her enthusiasm for Rock Creek Park's photogenic self, especially when the skunk cabbage blooms!

The environmental problems plaguing Rock Creek Park remain, including the spread of invasive plants, damage from stormwater run-off, and contamination from sewage, but countless individuals and numerous organizations and governmental bodies are tackling them with renewed energy in their efforts to maintain the integrity of the wild, wooded heart of Washington, DC. The Rock Creek Conservancy, for example, has become even more active in protecting and promoting the park, and it seems that the number of friends and fans of Rock Creek Park has grown by leaps and bounds. Susan, who recently became a Virginia Master Naturalist, is among many volunteers both here in Rock Creek Park and in other national and regional parks who combat invasive plants.

Steve Dryden is another who is making a difference. A friend of Susan's and mine, he received funding to involve school children in the protection of this precious parkland through a new initiative aimed at planting native trees and protecting the habitats of migrating songbirds. Steve has opened my eyes to the reality that dogs off-leash can potentially threaten nesting birds, one of the complex problems facing an urban park. I understand his concern and take it to heart, but I can't remove canine exuberance from my year of record in Rock Creek Park, as it was such a joyful and integral part of the experience. The universally friendly dogs of Boundary Bridge are an important part of the culture.

During the past seven years, extreme weather events have become a staple of local, national, and international newscasts. This book's year of record, 2007, is sandwiched in time between historic storms that destroyed large sections of two major American cities, New Orleans (Hurricane Katrina, in 2005) and New York (Hurricane Sandy, in 2012). As I write, searchers are still looking for bodies trapped by a massive mudslide that occured on March 22 following torrential rains in a community four miles east of Oso, Washington. The poles and glaciers are melting faster than scientists' predictions of even several years ago, and record droughts and deluges of rain regularly occur around the world. On a personal note, in August 2011, I watched on television the mid-nineteenth century covered bridge in Rockingham, Vermont, get swept away during the 100-year flood caused by Hurricane Irene. The historic bridge was located five miles from where I grew up. It has since been reconstructed. Here, in Washington, our winters have varied from an almost perpetual spring to the very cold and snowy winter of 2014 that lingered beyond the spring equinox. The only variable that seems predictable about weather patterns here and around the world is that we can expect the unexpected.

Susan and I continue to believe that the answer to healing ourselves and our planet lies in reawakening our connection to the natural world. Doctors in Washington, DC, and elsewhere have begun using their prescription pads to prescribe "Nature"; here in Washington, one doctor has seen great benefits when he prescribes visits to specific parks based on a patient's address and needs. Even the National Park Service is supporting such efforts. Many parents now talk sentimentally about their own relatively feral childhoods, lamenting the overscheduling of a generation of children with no time simply to play in the woods. Increasingly, educators are acknowledging that children of all ages benefit from a close connection with the natural world.

Here in the nation's capital, as more and more people, including policymakers, gravitate toward the wild, wooded heart of the city, I believe that nothing but good can come from it. The conservation ethic is born in a love of place and wildness. The public servants who protected Rock Creek Park in 1890 gave a gift to the city of Washington with the power to resonate far beyond the borders of the capital. May it continue to do so for generations to come.

A Photographic Journey in
Rock Creek Park

BY SUSAN AUSTIN ROTH

About the Craft

Although I am a professional photographer, I am mostly self-taught. My photographs improved dramatically when I learned, years ago, to step back from the love of my subjects and to study the images I create with an objective eye.

Since I focus on the natural world, whether in Rock Creek Park or in a garden, I strive to compose a beautiful picture and not merely a picture of something beautiful, which can be a difficult lesson to learn when photographing nature. In creating the images for this book, I struggled with how to avoid the trite and obvious images of nature and how best to capture the subtle intricacies of the trees, wildflowers, and scenery of Rock Creek Park that I so love. The images are intended to share the delight and reverence that both Melanie and I experience when the arms of the natural world embrace us.

All the camera equipment in the world will not help anyone achieve a great photographic image. The emotion and beauty in an image derive not from the camera but from the photographer's "eye." In my work, I've cycled through a number of Nikon 35mm-film cameras and digital cameras over the years. And I use high-quality Nikon or Sigma lenses, rather than the most expensive, slow, prime lenses.

As a garden photographer, I often tote forty or more pounds of camera bodies, lenses, filters, film, batteries, and reflectors as well as a tripod from location to location. During the course of photographing for this book, I needed to lighten my pack as I hiked my gear through Rock Creek Park's forests and swamps and up its steep inclines. This approach often led me to discard the tripod and to rely on vibration-reduction lenses. I also began to use zoom lenses to reduce the number of lenses I needed to carry.

One multi-purpose zoom lens created many of my favorite images—those with a sharp focus on an unfurling leaf, for instance, with a landscape blurred in the background. Sheer practicality gave birth to this new style, which was borne from my not wanting to change my lens to the close-up lens stored deep in my backpack or not having carried it with me in the first place. Early on, when I downloaded these images onto the computer, I was delighted with what I saw. Thereafter, I often purposefully attempted to achieve that style.

The serendipitous discovery of the artistic possibilities of that particular lens and the spontaneity of no longer being tethered awkwardly to the tripod freed me creatively in ways I never imagined. With this freedom, I can quickly bend and twist, crouch down low, stand on tip-toe, and tilt my head to aim the camera at whatever catches my eye and preserve that vision as a photo-graph to share. I constantly discover new wonders in the seemingly ordinary, and I hope the images in this book open the readers' eyes to a fresh way of seeing and loving the natural world.

THE FOUR SEASONS

PLATE 1

PLATE 2

PLATE 3

PLATE 4

PLATE 5

PLATE 6

PLATE 7

PLATE 8

PLATE 9

PLATE 10

PLATE 11

PLATE 12

PLATE 13

PLATE 14

PLATE 15

PLATE 16

PLATE 17

PLATE 18

PLATE 19

PLATE 20

PLATE 21

PLATE 22

PLATE 23

PLATE 24

PLATE 25

PLATE 26

PLATE 27

PLATE 28

PLATE 29

PLATE 30

PLATE 31

PLATE 32

LIST OF PLATES

FRONTISPIECE: River birch and boxelder frame Boundary Bridge and Rock Creek.

WINTER

SPRING

A Glossary of Botanical Terms, Plants, and Wildlife

Achene: A dry, one-seeded fruit that does not split open.

Calyx: The outer part of a flower, consisting of leafy or, rarely, petal-like parts called sepals.

Capsule: A dry fruit containing two or more seeds. A capsule splits open and is formed from a compound ovary.

Catkin: A long, thin cluster of apetalous, unisexual flowers.

Corolla: All the petals of a flower, either fused or separate.

Dioecious: Bearing male and female flowers on separate individual plants of the same species. (Monoecious plants bear separate male and female flowers on the same plant.)

Drupe: A fleshy fruit with a bony center, usually containing a single seed.

Follicle: A dry fruit that splits along one suture.

Legume: A dry fruit of the pea or legume family that usually splits along two sutures.

Pistil: The female part of the flower, including the stigma (receptive tip), style, and ovary.

Samara: A dry, single-seeded winged fruit that doesn't split open. Maples produce samaras in pairs.

Spadix: A spike or head bearing small flowers on a fleshy axis (as in Jack-in-the-pulpit and skunk cabbage).

Spathe: A large bract enclosing or partially enclosing a flower cluster (as in Jack-in-the-pulpit and skunk cabbage).

Stamen: The male part of the flower, including the pollen-bearing anther and the supporting stalk called the filament.

Tepal: A word used to describe a petal or sepal when they look alike.

PLANTS IN ROCK CREEK PARK MENTIONED IN THE TEXT

Due largely to genetic research, the scientific classification and naming of plants is in a state of flux. In this glossary, newer plant names published in the *Flora of Virginia* by Alan S. Weakley et al. (2012) that differ from the USDA (U.S. Department of Agriculture) Database of Plants (July 1, 2014) are given within brackets. The names of individual species that appear in parentheses are long-standing traditional plant names that have undergone recent change. The USDA Database of Plants lists synonymous scientific names, both traditional and new, and it is an excellent resource when confusion about names ensues. Within each listing appear the common name of the species, the scientific name of the species (in italics), and the common and scientific family names. An asterisk (*) indicates a non-native plant to eastern North America.

Ferns

Broad Beech Fern; *Phegopteris hexagonoptera;* Marsh Fern (Thelypteridaceae).

Christmas Fern; *Polystichum acrostichoides;* Wood Fern (Dryopteridaceae).

New York Fern; *Thelypteris noveboracensis* [*Parathelypteris noveboracensis*]; Marsh Fern (Thelypteridaceae).

Polypody Fern; *Polypodium virginianum;* Polypody (Polypodiaceae).

Herbaceous Flowering Plants

Aster, White Wood; *Eurybia divaricata* (*Aster divaricatus*); Daisy or Aster (Asteraceae).

Aster species *Symphyotrichum* (*Aster*); Daisy or Aster (Asteraceae).

Avens, White; *Geum canadense*; Rose (Rosaceae).

Beechdrops; *Epifagus virginiana*; Broom-Rape (Orobanchaceae).

Beggar-Ticks; *Bidens frondosa*; Daisy or Aster (Asteraceae).

Bloodroot; *Sanguinaria canadensis*; Poppy (Papaveraceae).

Burdock, Common*; *Arctium minus*; Daisy or Aster (Asteraceae).

Buttercup, Bulbous*; *Ranunculus bulbosus*; Buttercup (Ranunculaceae).

Celandine, Lesser*; *Ranunculus ficaria* [*Ficaria verna*]; Buttercup (Ranunculaceae).

Celandine Poppy; *Stylophorum diphyllum*; Poppy (Papaveraceae).

Chickweed, Star; *Stellaria pubera*; Pink (Caryophyllaceae).

Clearweed; *Pilea pumila*; Nettle (Urticaceae).

Dayflower, Asiatic*; *Commelina communis*; Spiderwort (Commelinaceae).

Enchanter's Nightshade; *Circaea lutetiana* [*Circaea canadensis*]; Evening
  Primrose (Onagraceae).

Evening-Primrose, Common; *Oenothera biennis*; Evening
  Primrose (Onagraceae).

Geranium, Wild; *Geranium maculatum*; Geranium (Geraniaceae).

Ginger, Wild; *Asarum canadense*; Birthwort (Aristolochiaceae).

Goldenrod, Blue-Stemmed; *Solidago caesia*; Daisy or Aster (Asteraceae).

Goldenrod species; *Solidago*; Daisy or Aster (Asteraceae).

Honewort; *Cryptotaenia canadensis*; Carrot or Parsley (Apiaceae).

Horse-Balm; *Collinsonia canadensis*; Mint (Lamiaceae).

Horse Nettle; *Solanum carolinense*; Nightshade or Tomato (Solanaceae).

Houstonia, Large-Leaved; *Houstonia purpurea*; Madder (Rubiaceae).

Indian Cucumber Root; *Medeola virginiana*; Lily (Liliaceae).

Indian Tobacco; *Lobelia inflata*; Bellflower (Campanulaceae).

Jack-in-the-Pulpit; *Arisaema triphyllum*; Arum (Araceae).

Japanese Knotweed*; *Polygonum cuspidatum* [*Reynoutria japonica*];
  Smartweed (Polygonaceae).

Japanese Stilt Grass*; *Microstegium vimineum*; Grass (Poaceae).

Jerusalem Artichoke; *Helianthus tuberosus*; Daisy or Aster (Asteraceae).

Jewelweed, Orange or Spotted Touch-Me-Not; *Impatiens capensis*; Touch-Me-Not (Balsaminaceae).

Jimsonweed [origin unknown]; *Datura stramonium*; Nightshade or Tomato (Solanaceae).

Jumpseed; *Polygonum virginianum* (*Tovara virginiana*) [*Persicaria virginiana*]; Smartweed (Polygonaceae).

Lizard's-Tail; *Saururus cernuus*; Lizard's-Tail (Saururaceae).

Lopseed; *Phryma leptostachya*; Vervain (Verbenaceae) Lopseed [Phrymaceae].

Mayapple; *Podophyllum peltatum*; Barberry (Berberidaceae).

Milkweed, Common; *Asclepias syriaca*; Milkweed (Asclepiadaceae) Dogbane [Apocynaceae].

Mistflower; *Conoclinium coelestinum* (*Eupatorium coelestinum*); Daisy or Aster (Asteraceae).

Monkey Flower, Winged; *Mimulus alatus*; Snapdragon (Scrophulariaceae) Lopseed [Phrymaceae].

Moth Mullein*; *Verbascum blattaria*; Snapdragon (Scrophulariaceae).

Mugwort*; *Artemisia vulgaris*; Daisy or Aster (Asteraceae).

Nettle, False; *Boehmeria cylindrica*; Nettle (Urticaceae).

Nettle, Wood; *Laportea canadensis*; Nettle (Urticaceae).

Orchid, Cranefly; *Tipularia discolor*; Orchid (Orchidaceae).

Panic Grass; *Panicum* spp.; Grass (Poaceae).

Perilla (Beefsteak Plant)*; *Perilla frutescens*; Mint (Lamiaceae).

Phlox, Wild Blue; *Phlox divaricata*; Phlox (Polemoniaceae).

Pokeweed; *Phytolacca americana*; Pokeweed (Phytolaccaceae).

Ragweed, Common; *Ambrosia artemisiifolia*; Daisy or Aster (Asteraceae).

Rue Anemone; *Thalictrum thalictroides* (*Anemonella thalictroides*); Buttercup (Ranunculaceae).

Saxifrage, Early; *Saxifraga virginiensis* [*Micranthes virginiensis*];
  Saxifrage (Saxifragaceae).

Skunk Cabbage; *Symplocarpus foetidus*; Arum (Araceae).

Snakeroot, Clustered; *Sanicula gregaria* [*Sanicula odorata*]; Carrot or
  Parsley (Apiaceae).

Snakeroot, White; *Ageratina altissima* (*Eupatorium rugosum*); Daisy or
  Aster Asteraceae).

Solomon's Seal, False or Plumed; *Maianthemum racemosum* (*Smilacina racemosa*);
  Lily (Liliaceae) Ruscus [Ruscaceae].

Solomon's Seal, Smooth; *Polygonatum biflorum*; Lily (Liliaceae)
  Ruscus [Ruscaceae].

Smartweed, Long-Bristled*; *Polygonum cespitosum* [*Persicaria longiseta*];
  Smartweed (Polygonaceae).

Spring Beauty; *Claytonia virginica*; Purslane (Portulacaceae) Montia [Montiaceae].

Sweet Cicely; *Osmorhiza claytonii*; Carrot or Parsley (Apiaceae).

Tearthumb, Arrow-Leaved; *Polygonum sagittatum* [*Persicaria sagitatta*];
  Smartweed (Polygonaceae).

Tick-Trefoil, Naked-Flowered; *Desmodium nudiflorum* [*Hylodesmum nudiflorum*];
  Pea or Legume (Fabaceae).

Tick-Trefoils; *Desmodium* spp.; Pea or Legume (Fabaceae).

Toothwort, Cut-Leaved; *Cardamine concatenata* (*Dentaria laciniata*);
  Mustard (Brassicaceae).

Trillium, Yellow; *Trillium luteum*; Lily (Liliaceae) Trillium [Trilliaceae].

Trout Lily; *Erythronium americanum*; Lily (Liliaceae).

Venus's Looking-Glass; *Triodanis perfoliata*; Bellflower (Campanulaceae).

Violet, Common Blue (or Purple); *Viola sororia*; Violet (Violaceae).

Violet, Smooth Yellow; *Viola pubescens* [*Viola pensylvanica*]; Violet (Violaceae).

Virginia Bluebells; *Mertensia virginica*; Borage (Boraginaceae).

Wingstem; *Verbesina alternifolia*; Daisy or Aster (Asteraceae).

Woody and Herbaceous Vines

Asiatic Bittersweet*; *Celastrus orbiculatus*; Staff-Tree (Celastraceae).

English Ivy*; *Hedera helix*; Ginseng (Araliaceae).

Grape, Wild; *Vitis* spp.; Grape (Vitaceae).

Greenbrier, Common; *Smilax rotundifolia*; Greenbrier (Smilacaceae).

Japanese Honeysuckle*; *Lonicera japonica*; Honeysuckle; (Caprifoliaceae).

Japanese Hops*; *Humulus japonicus*; Hemp (Cannabaceae).

Kudzu*; *Pueraria lobata* [*Pueraria montana*]; Pea or Legume (Fabaceae).

Mile-a-Minute*; *Polygonum perfoliatum* [*Persicaria perfoliata*];
  Smartweed (Polygonaceae).

Poison Ivy; *Toxicodendron radicans*; Cashew (Anacardiaceae).

Porcelain Berry*; *Ampelopsis brevipedunculata*; Grape (Vitaceae).

Virginia Creeper; *Parthenocissus quinquefolia*; Grape (Vitaceae).

Winter Creeper*; *Euonymus fortunei*; Staff-Tree (Celastraceae).

Yam, Chinese*; *Dioscorea oppositifolia* [*Dioscorea polystachya*]; Yam (Dioscoreaceae).

Yam, Wild; *Dioscorea quaternata* [*Dioscorea villosa*]; Yam (Dioscoreaceae).

Shrubs/Small Trees

Bladdernut; *Staphylea trifolia*; Bladdernut (Staphyleaceae).

Fringe-Tree; *Chionanthus virginicus*; Olive (Oleaceae).

Jetbead*; *Rhodotypos scandens*; Rose (Rosaceae).

Hydrangea, Wild; *Hydrangea arborescens*; Hydrangea (Hydrangeaceae).

Mountain Laurel; *Kalmia latifolia*; Heath (Ericaceae).

Partridge-Berry; *Mitchella repens* (sub-shrub); Madder (Rubiaceae).

Pawpaw; *Asimina triloba*; Custard-Apple (Annonaceae).

Pinxter (Pink Azalea); *Rhododendron periclymenoides*; Heath (Ericaceae).

Rose, Multiflora*; *Rosa multiflora*; Rose (Rosaceae).

Spicebush; *Lindera benzoin*; Laurel (Lauraceae).

Viburnum, Linden*; *Viburnum dilatatum*; Honeysuckle (Caprifoliaceae) Moschatel or Muskroot [Adoxaceae].

Viburnum, Maple-Leaved; *Viburnum acerifolium*; Honeysuckle (Caprifoliaceae) Moschatel or Muskroot [Adoxaceae].

Viburnum, Arrowwood; *Viburnum dentatum*; Honeysuckle (Caprifoliaceae) Moschatel or Muskroot [Adoxaceae].

Viburnum, Blackhaw; *Viburnum prunifolium*; Honeysuckle (Caprifoliaceae) Moschatel or Muskroot [Adoxaceae].

Viburnum, Doublefile*; *Viburnum plicatum* var. *tomentosum*; Honeysuckle (Caprifoliaceae) Moschatel or Muskroot [Adoxaceae].

Wineberry*; *Rubus phoenicolasius*; Rose (Rosaceae).

Wintergreen, Striped or Spotted (sub-shrub); *Chimaphila maculata*; Pyrola or Shinleaf (Pyrolaceae) Heath [Ericaceae].

Witch-Hazel, Common; *Hamamelis virginiana*; Witch-Hazel (Hamamelidaceae).

Trees

Ash, Green; *Fraxinus pennsylvanica*; Olive (Oleaceae).

Ash, White; *Fraxinus americana*; Olive (Oleaceae).

Beech, American; *Fagus grandifolia*; Beech (Fagaceae).

Birch, River; *Betula nigra*; Birch (Betulaceae).

Boxelder; *Acer negundo*; Maple (Aceraceae) Soapberry [Sapindaceae].

Butternut; *Juglans cinerea*; Walnut (Juglandaceae).

Cherry, Black; *Prunus serotina*; Rose (Rosaceae).

Crabapple, Flowering*; *Malus* sp.; Rose (Rosaceae).

Dogwood, Flowering; *Cornus florida*; Dogwood (Cornaceae).

Elm, American; *Ulmus americana*; Elm (Ulmaceae).

Hickory, Bitternut; *Carya cordiformis*; Walnut (Juglandaceae).

Hickory, Mockernut; *Carya tomentosa*; Walnut (Juglandaceae).

Hickory, Pignut; *Carya glabra*; Walnut (Juglandaceae).

Hop-Hornbeam (Ironwood); *Ostrya virginiana*; Birch (Betulaceae).

Ironwood, Musclewood or Hornbeam; *Carpinus caroliniana*; Birch (Betulaceae).

Maple, Red; *Acer rubrum*; Maple (Aceraceae) Soapberry [Sapindaceae].

Maple, Silver; *Acer saccharinum*; Maple (Aceraceae) Soapberry [Sapindaceae].

Maple, Sugar; *Acer saccharum*; Maple (Aceraceae) Soapberry [Sapindaceae].

Oak, Black; *Quercus velutina*; Beech (Fagaceae).

Oak, Chestnut; *Quercus montana*; *(Q. prinus)* Beech (Fagaceae).

Oak, Red; *Quercus rubra*; Beech (Fagaceae).

Oak, Scarlet; *Quercus coccinea*; Beech (Fagaceae).

Oak, Shingle; *Quercus imbricaria*; Beech (Fagaceae).

Oak, Southern Red (or Spanish Oak); *Quercus falcata*; Beech (Fagaceae).

Oak, White; *Quercus alba*; Beech (Fagaceae).

Oak, Willow; *Quercus phellos*; Beech (Fagaceae).

Persimmon, Common; *Diospyros virginiana*; Ebony (Ebenaceae).

Pine, Loblolly; *Pinus taeda*; Pine (Pinaceae).

Pine, Virginia (Scrub Pine); *Pinus virginiana*; Pine (Pinaceae).

Redbud; *Cercis canadensis*; Pea or Legume (Fabaceae).

Sassafras; *Sassafras albidum*; Laurel (Lauraceae).

Shadbush (Serviceberry); *Amelanchier arborea*; Rose (Rosaceae).

Sycamore, American; *Platanus occidentalis*; Plane Tree Family (Platanaceae).

Tulip Tree; *Liriodendron tulipifera*; Magnolia Family (Magnoliaceae).

Tupelo (Black Gum); *Nyssa sylvatica*; Tupelo Family (Nyssaceae).

Walnut, Black; *Juglans nigra*; Walnut (Juglandaceae).

The scientific classification of some species of amphibians currently varies among different sources. Alternative names for these species appear below in parentheses. The scientific names of the birds come from the first edition of *The Sibley Field Guide to Birds of Eastern North America* (2003). The Cornell Lab of Ornithology (founded in 1915) uses different scientific names for some of the species listed below. The names used by the Cornell Lab are listed in parentheses after Sibley's names and are derived from its Website (www.birds. cornell.edu/onlineguide) as of July 1, 2014. Within each listing appear the common name and (in italics) the scientific name of the species.

Amphibians

Bullfrog; *Rana catesbeiana* (*Lithobates catesbeianus*).

Frog, Green; *Rana clamitans* (*Lithobates clamitans*).

Frog, Wood; *Rana sylvatica* (*Lithobates sylvaticus*).

Spring Peeper; *Pseudacris crucifer*.

Toad, American; *Bufo americanus* (*Anaxyrus americanus*).

Birds

Bluebird, Eastern; *Sialia sialis*.

Cardinal, Northern; *Cardinalis cardinalis*.

Chickadee, Carolina; *Poecile carolinensis*.

Dove, Mourning; *Zenaida macroura*.

Duck, Mallard; *Anas platyrhynchos*.

Duck, Wood; *Aix sponsa*.

Flycatcher, Acadian; *Empidonax virescens*.

Flycatcher, Great Crested; *Myiarchus crinitus*.

Gnatcatcher, Blue-Gray; *Polioptila caerulea*.

Goldfinch, American; *Carduelis tristis* (*Spinus tristis*).

Goose, Canada; *Branta canadensis.*

Grosbeak, Rose-Breasted; *Pheucticus ludovicianus.*

Hawk, Red-Shouldered; *Buteo lineatus.*

Heron, Great Blue; *Ardea herodias.*

Kingfisher, Belted; *Ceryle alcyon* (*Megaceryle alcyon*).

Kinglet, Golden-Crowned; *Regulus satrapa.*

Night-Heron, Black-Crowned; *Nycticorax nycticorax.*

Nuthatch, White-Breasted; *Sitta carolinensis.*

Ovenbird; *Seiurus aurocapillus* (*Seiurus aurocapilla*).

Owl, Barred; *Strix varia.*

Owl, Great Horned; *Bubo virginianus.*

Phoebe, Eastern; *Sayornis phoebe.*

Redstart, American; *Setophaga ruticilla.*

Robin, American; *Turdus migratorius.*

Screech-Owl, Eastern; *Otus asio* (*Megascops asio*).

Sparrow, Lincoln's; *Melospiza lincolnii.*

Sparrow, Song; *Melospiza melodia.*

Sparrow, White-Throated; *Zonotrichia albicollis.*

Tanager, Scarlet; *Piranga olivacea.*

Thrush, Hermit; *Catharus guttatus.*

Thrush, Swainson's; *Catharus ustulatus.*

Thrush, Wood; *Hylocichla mustelina.*

Titmouse, Tufted; *Baeolophus bicolor.*

Towhee, Eastern; *Pipilo erythrophthalmus.*

Veery; *Catharus fuscescens.*

Vireo, Red-Eyed; *Vireo olivaceus.*

Warbler, Bay-Breasted; *Dendroica castanea* (*Setophaga castanea*).

Warbler, Blackpoll; *Dendroica striata* (*Setophaga striata*).

Warbler, Black-Throated Blue; *Dendroica caerulescens* (*Setophaga caerulescens*).

Warbler, Black-Throated Green; *Dendroica virens* (*Setophaga virens*).

Warbler, Blue-Winged; *Vermivora pinus* (*Vermivora cyanoptera*).

Warbler, Canada; *Wilsonia canadensis* (*Cardellina canadensis*).

Warbler, Magnolia; *Dendroica magnolia* (*Setophaga magnolia*).

Warbler, Nashville; *Vermivora ruficapilla* (*Oreothlypis ruficapilla*).

Warbler, Northern Parula; *Parula americana* (*Setophaga americana*).

Warbler, Tennessee; *Vermivora peregrina* (*Oreothlypis peregrina*).

Waterthrush, Louisiana; *Seiurus motacilla* (*Parkesia motacilla*).

Woodcock, American; *Scolopax minor*.

Woodpecker, Downy; *Picoides pubescens*.

Woodpecker, Pileated; *Dryocopus pileatus*.

Woodpecker, Red-Bellied; *Melanerpes carolinus*.

Wood-Pewee, Eastern; *Contopus virens*.

Wren, Carolina; *Thryothorus ludovicianus*.

Yellowthroat, Common; *Geothlypis trichas*.

Fish

Alewife; *Alosa pseudoharengus*.

Blueback Herring; *Alosa aestivalis*.

Shad, Hickory; *Alosa mediocris*.

Shad, Gizzard; *Dorosoma cepedianum*.

Insects

Butterfly, Monarch; *Danaus plexippus*.

Butterfly, Eastern Tiger Swallowtail; *Papilio glaucus*.

Butterfly, Red Admiral; *Vanessa atalanta*.

Butterfly, Zebra Swallowtail; *Eurytides marcellus.*

Cicada Species (Order Hemiptera).

Cricket Species (Order Orthoptera).

Damselfly Species, including Ebony Jewelwing (Order Odonata).

Dragonfly, White-Tailed & other species.

Katydid Species (Order Orthoptera).

Stoneflies (Order Plecoptera).

Tick, Deer; *Ixodes scapularis.*

Mammals

Beaver; *Castor canadensis.*

Chipmunk, Eastern; *Tamias striatus.*

Coyote; *Canis latrans.*

Deer, White-Tailed; *Odocoileus virginianus.*

Fox, Red; *Vulpes vulpes.*

Opossum, Virginia; *Didelphis virginiana.*

Muskrat; *Ondatra zibethicus.*

Raccoon; *Procyon lotor.*

Squirrel, Eastern Gray; *Sciurus carolinensis.*

Reptiles

Box Turtle, Eastern; *Terrapene carolina.*

Ring-Necked Snake; *Diadophis punctatus.*

Works Cited and
Additional Readings

Works Cited

Adams, John Quincy, as quoted in Shirley Briggs, ed., *Washington—City in the Woods* (Washington, DC: Audubon Society of the District of Columbia, 1954), 7.

Alexander, Russell George, ed., *A Plain Plantain* (Ditchling, Sussex, UK: St. Dominic's Press, 1922).

Beverly, Robert, *The History and Present State of Virginia* (London, UK: R. Parker, 1705).

Chilcott, Bob, "Be Cool," from *Green Songs: Four Songs on Environmental Themes* (Oxford, UK: Oxford University Press, 1998).

Choukas, Nita, with illustrations by Gillian Tyler, *Bayberry & Beau* (White River Junction, VT: Chelsea Green Publishing, 2006).

Choukas-Bradley, Melanie, with photographs by Susan A. Roth, "A Creek Runs through It," *Bethesda Magazine* (September–October 2008): 154–65.

———, with illustrations by Polly Alexander, *City of Trees: The Complete Field Guide to the Trees of Washington, D.C.*, Third Edition (Charlottesville: University of Virginia Press, in association with the Center for American Places, 2008).

———, "Lessons along Rock Creek," an op-ed in *The Washington Post*, Outlook Section, Close to Home: "After the Deluge" (July 2, 2006): B8.

Choukas-Bradley, Melanie, "Where Water Goes," *Audubon Naturalist News*, "Arts and Literature Issue," Vol. 33, No. 2 (February/March 2007): 1.

Cornell Lab of Ornithology, Online Bird Guide; available at www.birds.cornell.edu/onlineguide.

Eliot, T. S., *The Wasteland* (New York: Horace Liveright, 1922).

Estés, Clarissa Pinkola, *Women Who Run with the Wolves: Myths and Stories of the Wild Woman Archetype* (New York: Ballantine, 1992).

Fahrenthold, David A., "Rock Creek Fish Head Home Again—With Obstacles Removed, Herring Return to Spawning Area," *The Washington Post* (March 31, 2007): A1.

———, "Climate Change Brings Risk of More Extinctions," *The Washington Post* (September 17, 2007).

Frost, Robert, "Nothing Gold Can Stay," in *New Hampshire* (New York: Henry Holt and Co., 1923).

Gleason, Henry, and Arthur Cronquist, *Manual of Vascular Plants of Northeastern United States and Adjacent Canada*, 2nd ed. (New York: The New York Botanical Garden Press, 1991).

Gore, Al, *An Inconvenient Truth*, a documentary film directed by Davis Guggenheim that premiered at the Sundance Film Festival (January 19–29, 2006) and then opened in Los Angeles and New York City on May 24, 2006.

Gleason, Henry, and Arthur Cronquist, *Manual of Vascular Plants of Northeastern United States and Adjacent Canada*, 2nd ed. (New York: The New York Botanical Garden Press, 1991).

Grieve, Maud, *A Modern Herbal* (San Diego, CA: Harcourt Brace & Company, 1931).

Holley, Joe, "Champion of Conservation, Loyal Force Behind LBJ," *The Washington Post* (July 12, 2007): A1.

Keats, John, *Endymion: A Poetic Romance* (London, UK: Taylor and Hessey, 1818).

Mack, Kristen, "Will Drab Fall Turn Over a Brilliant New Leaf?" *The Washington Post* (November 13, 2007): B1.

Muir, John, *Our National Parks* (Boston, MA: Houghton, Mifflin and Company, 1901).

Nabors, Cecily, "The Joys of a Beechen Wood," *Audubon Naturalist News*, Vol. 30, No. 2 (March 2004): 10.

Nikula, Blair, Jackie Sones, Donald Stokes, and Lillian Stokes, *Beginner's Guide to Dragonflies* (New York: Little, Brown and Company, 2002).

Rawlings, Marjorie Kinnan, *Cross Creek* (New York: Charles Scribner's Sons, 1942).

Sibley, David Allen, *The Sibley Field Guide to Birds of Eastern North America* (New York: Alfred A. Knopf, 2003).

Smith, Margaret Bayard, *The First Forty Years of Washington Society* (New York: Charles Scribner's Sons, 1906).

Thoreau, Henry David, *Walden; or, Life in the Woods* (Boston, MA: Ticknor and Fields, 1854).

Wax, Emily, "A Sacred River Endangered by Global Warming," *The Washington Post* (June 17, 2007): A14.

Weakley, Alan S., J. Christopher Ludwig, and John F. Townsend, *Flora of Virginia* (Fort Worth, TX: Botanical Research Institute of Texas Press and the Foundation of the Flora of Virginia Project, Inc., 2012).

White, Gilbert, *The Natural History and Antiquities of Selborne* (London, UK: Benjamin White, 1789).

ADDITIONAL READINGS

Brown, Russell G. and Melvin L. Brown, *Woody Plants of Maryland* (Baltimore, MD: Port City Press, 1992).

Carson, Rachel, *The Sense of Wonder* (New York: Harper Collins, 1965).

Choukas-Bradley, Melanie, with illustrations by Tina Thieme Brown, *An Illustrated Guide to Eastern Woodland Wildflowers and Trees: 350 Plants Observed at Sugarloaf Mountain, Maryland* (Charlottesville: University of Virginia Press, in association with the Center for American Places, 2008).

Dryden, Steve, *Peirce Mill: Two Hundred Years in the Nation's Capital* (Washington, DC, and Berkeley, CA: Bergamot, 2009).

Fleming, Cristol, Marian Blois Lobstein, and Barbara Tufty, *Finding Wildflowers in the Washington–Baltimore Area.* (Baltimore, MD: The Johns Hopkins University Press, in association with the Center for American Places, 1995).

Garland, Mark S., *Watching Nature: A Mid-Atlantic Natural History* (Washington, DC: Smithsonian Institution Press, 1997).

Halle, Louis J., *Spring in Washington* (New York: William Sloane, 1947).

Horton, Tom, *Bay Country* (Baltimore, MD: The Johns Hopkins University Press, 1987).

Hugo, Nancy Ross, with photographs by Robert Llewellyn, *Seeing Trees: Discover the Extraordinary Secrets of Everyday Trees* (Portland, OR: Timber Press, 2011).

Hunt, Nancy Nye, *Aldo Leopold's Shack: Nina's Story* (Chicago, IL: Center for American Places at Columbia College Chicago, 2011).

Leopold, Aldo, *A Sand County Almanac and Sketches Here and There* (New York and Oxford, UK: Oxford University Press, 1949).

Maloof, Joan, *Among the Ancients: Adventures in the Eastern Old-Growth Forests* (Washington, DC: Ruka Press, 2011).

———, *Teaching the Trees: Lessons from the Forest* (Athens: University of Georgia Press, 2007).

Mathews, F. Schuyler, *Field Book of American Wild Flowers* (New York: G. P. Putnam's Sons, 1902).

McKibben, Bill, ed., *GWR: The Global Warming Reader* (New York: OR Books, 2011).

The National Climate Assessment Report (http://nca2014.globalchange.gov).

Newcomb, Lawrence, *Newcomb's Wildflower Guide,* (Boston, MA, and New York: Little, Brown and Company, 1977).

Rutledge, Archibald, *Life's Extras* (New York: Fleming H. Revell, 1928).

Sibley, David Allen, *The Sibley Guide to Trees* (New York: Alfred A. Knopf, 2009).

Spilsbury, Gail, *Rock Creek Park,* (Baltimore, MD: The Johns Hopkins University Press, 2002).

Wilson, Edward O., *Naturalist* (Washington, DC: Island Press, 1994).

Youth, Howard, with illustrations by Mark A. Klingler and photographs by Robert E. Mumford, Jr., *Field Guide to the Natural World of Washington, DC* (Baltimore, MD: The Johns Hopkins University Press, 2014).

ACKNOWLEDGMENTS

MELANIE CHOUKAS-BRADLEY

MY FIRST ACKNOWLEDGMENT IS TO SUSAN AUSTIN ROTH, who has demonstrated that a photographer whose pictures have graced the covers of *Better Homes and Gardens* and numerous national gardening magazines and books can also work wonders when photographing skunk cabbage. Thank you, Susan, for your artistically sensitive photographic tribute to Rock Creek Park and Boundary Bridge.

My heartfelt thanks go to George F. Thompson, my publisher and editor whose hundreds of books about the cultural and natural landscapes of North America and the world comprise a body of work that has quietly yet profoundly transformed our awareness of place and the preservation of landscape over many decades. I am grateful that he has had a hand in all of my published books as editor, packager, and now publisher. Thank you to editorial advisor and fellow natural history author Nancy Nye Hunt, editorial and research assistant Mikki Soroczak, copyeditor Purna Makaram, book designer and art director David Skolkin, and everyone else at George F. Thompson Publishing who had a hand in creating this book. Thank you, also, to the staff at the University of Virginia Press, with special thanks to director Mark Saunders and sales and publicity director Emily Grandstaff.

Many of the people who inspired me are recognized within the pages of this book, and I hope my readers enjoy their company as much as I do. Since I completed this year of record, I have shared the joys of Rock Creek Park with many other people, and you all know who you are! Thank you one and all.

It is my great joy and privilege to be part of a community of naturalists in the Washington, DC, area, who are generous with their knowledge and steeped in the love of Nature. I wish to thank, in particular, the dedicated people at the National Park Service, Maryland-National Capital Park and Planning Commission, Rock Creek Conservancy, Audubon Naturalist Society, Casey Trees, United States Botanic Garden, United States National Arboretum, Maryland Native Plant Society, Virginia Native Plant Society, Potomac Appalachian Trail Club, and Friends of Peirce Mill, for all they do to teach people about the green spaces of Washington and the region and to protect the integrity of our regional ecology and the Rock Creek watershed. Special thanks go to Bill Yeaman, the natural resource manager for Rock Creek National Park, Neal Fitzpatrick, former Executive Director of the Audubon Naturalist Society, Lisa Alexander, current Director of the Audubon Naturalist Society, and Stephanie Mason, Senior Naturalist at the Audubon Naturalist Society. Thank you to birders Cecily Nabors, Anne Sturm, Wendy Paulson, and my dad, Michael Choukas, Jr. Many thanks to Polly Alexander, for sharing her knowledge of birds and plants over many years, and to Elizabeth Rives, for sharing her extensive knowledge of woody plants in winter. Thank you to Dr. Anne Osgood Pfeffer and Barbara Koopman Turnbull, for sharing information about Ellen Sewall, their great-grandmother.

Thank you to my wise readers, for guiding me to a much better book, beginning with Sophie Choukas-Bradley, who, among her many other talents, is a gifted editor. Ellie Choukas Anderson and Hill Anderson, Carole Bergmann, Tina Thieme Brown, Michael and Nita Choukas, Jim and Jesse Choukas-Bradley, Terrie Daniels, Cris Fleming, Kate Maynor, and Susan Austin Roth—to all of you, I extend my deepest thanks, for your essential and creative editorial advice! And thank you to everyone in the Bradley and Choukas families, for sharing your knowledge and love of Nature with me through the years, with a special thanks to geologist Dr. Dwight Bradley. Thanks, also, to Gail Ross, who has given me excellent counsel for more than thirty years.

SUSAN AUSTIN ROTH

MY UTMOST GRATITUDE GOES TO MELANIE, for her friendship, understanding, and generosity and for introducing me to the wonderful wild joys of Rock Creek Park. The first time she took me there, I had been living in DC for two years and longed for the quiet beauty of the forest, not realizing it was only blocks away. These days, the park nourishes me with its bird song, wind song, and creek song. I am also grateful for her belief in my photography and for offering me the opportunity to commune with Nature and stretch my artistic skills in creating the photographs for this book.

I thank Kate Maynor, for her friendship, insightful assistance in helping select the images for this book from a plethora of photographs, for sharing her special piece of Rock Creek Park, the Melvin Hazen Trail.

I thank Elizabeth Rives, an inspiring instructor, for teaching me to identify trees and shrubs in winter by their bark and buds and for indirectly introducing me to my own little piece of Rock Creek Park, the area surrounding the Normanstone Trail near my DC home.

I thank Maria Terol, my amazing exercise therapist (who introduced herself to me in Rock Creek Park), for helping me regain my strength and then making me stronger than ever, so I can tote the camera equipment into the woods.

And I thank JEH, for guiding and accompanying me back to the serenity of the forest that I once knew and for offering all the exciting new possibilities that are unfurling before me like leaf buds bursting in spring.

Susan Austin Roth (left) and Melanie Choukas-Bradley (right) in Rock Creek Park.
Photograph © 2014 Judy Licht.

About the Author and the Photographer

Melanie Choukas-Bradley is a writer, naturalist, and teacher and the author of three critically acclaimed books: *City of Trees: The Complete Field Guide to the Trees of Washington, D.C.*, illustrated by Polly Alexander, whose third edition was published in 2008 by the University of Virginia Press; *Sugarloaf: The Mountain's History, Geology, and Natural Lore*, illustrated by Tina Thieme Brown (University of Virginia Press, in association with the Center for American Places, 2003); and *An Illustrated Guide to Eastern Woodland Wildflowers and Trees*, illustrated by Tina Thieme Brown (University of Virginia Press, in association with the Center for American Places, 2004). In 2014, she was awarded one of four inaugural "Canopy Awards" by Casey Trees for her efforts to educate people about the trees of Washington, DC, and she has been a long-time contributor to *The Washington Post* and other publications. She also teaches courses about woody plants and wildflowers through the Natural History Field Studies Program sponsored by the Audubon Naturalist Society and the Graduate School USA, lectures widely, and regularly leads field trips and tree tours for the Audubon Naturalist Society, Casey Trees, Maryland Native Plant Society, Nature Conservancy, and United States Botanic Garden. She has appeared as a guest author and expert on *All Things Considered*, *The Diane Rehm Show*, and *The Kojo Nnamdi Show*, and she served as the director of programs and education for the 25th anniversary celebration of Montgomery County, Maryland's nationally acclaimed Agricultural Reserve. As a staff member of the House Commerce Subcommittee on Oversight and Investigations, she played a major role in the first post-Love Canal Congressional hearing on hazardous waste disposal chaired by Al Gore, then a member of Congress. Melanie is a former news director for a New Hampshire radio station and currently serves as a member of the Maryland Native Plant Society's Board of Directors, the Chevy Chase Tree Ordinance Board, and the Montgomery Countryside Alliance Advisory Committee. Born in North Carolina and raised in the Vermont village of Saxtons River, she attended Pierce College in Athens, Greece, and earned her B. A. in English at the University of Vermont. She lives in Chevy Chase, Maryland, with her husband, Jim, an attorney. They have two adult children.

Susan Austin Roth, a writer and photographer who specializes in gardening, landscape design, and nature, is the author and photographer of ten best-selling gardening books (published by Rodale Press, Timber Press, Houghton Mifflin, Home Planners, and Better Homes and Gardens). For seven years she worked as a field editor and assignment photographer for *Better Homes and Gardens* magazine, and her photographs appear regularly in books, national magazines, and calendars. The Garden Writers Association has honored her work with three awards. Susan is also a playwright whose plays have been produced to critical acclaim in New York City and Washington, DC. Recently, she became a Virginia Master Naturalist and devotes her volunteer work to battling invasive plants in local and national parks. She attended Mount Holyoke College, where she studied theater arts and botany, and she earned her B.S. and M.S. degrees in ornamental horticulture from Cornell University. Born in West Virginia, she grew up there, in Los Angeles, and in West Hartford, Connecticut. She recently moved from Washington, DC, to Alexandria, Virginia, and to a 156-acre farm near Shenandoah National Park.

About the Book

A Year in Rock Creek Park: The Wild, Wooded Heart of Washington, DC, was originally brought to publication in October 2014 in two editions: A softcover edition with flaps, issued in 1,800 copies and featuring a forty-page gallery of thirty-three color photographs by Susan Austin Roth, and a limited hardcover edition, issued in 350 copies, of which 330 are slipcased and signed, and featuring an eighty-page gallery of eighty-nine color photographs by Ms. Roth. A second printing of 1,500 softcover copies was issued in June 2015. The text was set in MrsEaves, the paper for the text is 120 gsm weight and for the galleries of photographs is 150 gsm weight, and the book was professionally printed and bound in China by PChan & Edwards. The photographs by Susan Austin Roth that appear on pages 11, 49, 107, and 165 are, respectively, details of the frontispiece on page 218 and of Plates 15, 21, and 29. The originals are in color. The original photograph of the author and photographer by Judy Licht is in color and is used by permission of the photographer.

Special Acknowledgment: Many thanks to Mark Saunders, Director of the University of Virginia Press, for his advice, counsel, and support throughout the publishing process.

Publisher and Editor: George F. Thompson
Editorial Advisors: Nancy Nye Hunt and Warren Hofstra
Editorial and Research Assistant: Mikki Soroczak
Copyeditor: Purna Makaram
Book Design and Production: David Skolkin

George F. Thompson Publishing, L.L.C.
217 Oak Ridge Circle
Staunton, VA 24401-3511, USA
www.gftbooks.com

22 21 20 19 18 17 16 15   2 3 4 5

The Library of Congress Preassigned Control Number is 2014942130.
ISBN: 978–1–938086–26–7 (limited edition hardcover, slipcased)
ISBN: 978–1–938086–24–3 (softcover, with flaps)